SHIFTING BOUNDARIES

TIM SCHOULS

SHIFTING BOUNDARIES

Aboriginal Identity, Pluralist Theory, and the Politics of Self-Government

UBCPress · Vancouver · Toronto

09 08 07 06 05 04 03   5 4 3 2 1

Printed in Canada on acid-free paper

National Library of Canada Cataloguing in Publication Data

Schouls, Timothy A.
   Shifting boundaries : aboriginal identity, pluralist theory, and the politics of self-government / Tim Schouls.

   Includes bibliographical references and index.
   ISBN 0-7748-1046-7 (bound); ISBN 0-7748-1047-5 (pbk.)

   1. Native people – Canada – Politics and government.★ 2. Native peoples – Canada – Legal status, laws, etc.★ 3. Native peoples – Canada – Government relations.★ 4. Pluralism (Social sciences) I. Title.
   E92.S43 2003   323.1'197071'01   C2003-911132-6

Canadä

UBC Press gratefully acknowledges the financial support for our publishing program of the Government of Canada through the Book Publishing Industry Development Program (BPIDP), and of the Canada Council for the Arts, and the British Columbia Arts Council.

This book has been published with the help of a grant from the Canadian Federation for the Humanities and Social Sciences, through the Aid to Scholarly Publications Programme, using funds provided by the Social Sciences and Humanities Research Council of Canada, and with the help of the K.D. Srivastava Fund.

Set in Bembo by Carol Aitken
Printed and bound in Canada by Friesens
Copy editor: Dallas Harrison
Proofreader: Jeannie Scarfe
Indexer: Annette Lorek

UBC Press
The University of British Columbia
2029 West Mall
Vancouver, BC V6T 1Z2
(604) 822-5959 / Fax: (604) 822-6083
E-mail: info@ubcpress.ca
www.ubcpress.ca

CONTENTS

ACKNOWLEDGMENTS

This work would not have been completed had it not been for the faithful companionship of a number of people. I am most grateful to those who read earlier versions of this book and who lent their affirmation to it by means of incisive questioning and comments. In particular, I would like to thank Avigail Eisenberg, Don Blake, Alan Cairns, Samuel LaSelva, Bruce Miller, Peter Meekison, and UBC Press's two anonymous assessors. I extend a special thanks to Paul Tennant, an ever-present source of support and reassurance as this book moved from infancy through to maturity. Thank you for your generosity of spirit and for teaching me so much about the nature of scholarship.

Others supported and sustained me as well. For my colleagues at Capilano College, in particular Paul Mier, David Winchester, and Cam Sylvester, I am most grateful. Thank you for the opportunity to teach and for sharing your wisdom. To UBC Press, especially Jean Wilson, Peter Milroy, and Darcy Cullen, thank you for guiding me through the publishing process with the greatest of civility, good humour, and care. To my friends Hamish Telford, Peter Sinnema, Jan Wesselius, William and Lois Cooke, Tony Sayers, David and Roseanne Sovka, Brian and Kaycie Burtchett, Lionel and Lynn LaCroix, Harry Kits, and Lorraine Land, thank you for your many words of encouragement along the way. Most of all, I thank the members of my family who uphold me in so many ways: Lynn and Marc, Michelle and Tim, Cliff and Claude, Bob and Chris, Teresa and Wes, Simon and Henny, and especially my remarkable parents, Peter and Jeanette.

Finally, my greatest debt of all is owed to my children, Emma, Darren, and Adrian, and to my spouse, Rita. To Emma, Darren, and Adrian, thank you for the indescribable joy you bring to my daily existence. And to Rita, thank you for your constancy and love, which fill my heart with gratitude. It is to you that I dedicate this work.

INTRODUCTION

Canada is a plural nation with a variety of ethnic, cultural, religious, and national identities. Some societies possess more diversity than others; Canada is among the most multi-ethnic. While Canadian history contains instances of intolerance and oppression, it also contains measures that have tried to accommodate Canada's multi-ethnic population. For this reason, Canada is often called a pluralist state.

Taken together, the concepts of group power and equality can be seen as forming the core of pluralist thinking. There are, however, no sustained studies in which Aboriginal self-government is discussed specifically in terms of the set of concepts that characterize the analytical tradition of pluralist thought. These concepts, in turn, are closely related to the political ideas of participation and self-definition at individual and community levels.

While the idea of Aboriginal self-government now receives broad support within Aboriginal communities and from Canadian governments,[1] it nevertheless remains controversial. The Aboriginal claim to self-government challenges non-Aboriginal Canadians to adopt new ways of thinking about the relationship between themselves and Aboriginal peoples. Ultimately, the claim rests on the idea that Aboriginal peoples should be able to choose their own destiny within Canada, free of external compulsion. Put this way, the claim seems to be straightforward enough, yet it compels all Canadians to confront the most fundamental of moral and political questions. My purpose in this book is to answer some of those questions.

Aboriginal self-government is usually discussed as an issue of cultural preservation or national self-determination. The most commonly held assumption shared by both approaches is that self-government arises from the Aboriginal desire to safeguard a list of cultural and national traits of community identity. Put most simply, identity is understood to refer to those traits of culture and nationhood unique to an Aboriginal community. Community survival is then understood to depend on the preservation of those traits, and self-government is seen as the principal means by which this is to be accomplished.

The theoretical perspective presented here arises from consideration of the following question: is the understanding of the motivation for Aboriginal self-government promoted by the cultural preservation and national self-determination approaches accurate? Or do these approaches trace a truncated picture, yielding an incomplete understanding of the complex phenomenon that Aboriginal self-government represents? For example, culture-based approaches tend to start from the assumption that Aboriginal cultural affiliations are at root primordial and fixed. But does this assumption not neglect the possibility that the Aboriginal struggle for self-government may be about Aboriginal individuals engaging in conflict with one another over what expressions of Aboriginal culture really mean? Nation-based approaches, meanwhile, tend to start from the assumption that Aboriginal nations are the primary source of all Aboriginal political identity and relations. But is this assumption not also challenged by the fact that many Aboriginal individuals today possess complex, layered, and overlapping political identities in which national affiliation may be but one element?

In my view, these questions and others have created the need for a perspective on Aboriginal self-government that does not accept unequivocally the arguments of either the cultural preservation or the national self-determination approach. I attempt here to offer such a perspective, one that takes its point of departure from the analytical tradition of pluralism. The political tradition of pluralism, while aiding in an understanding of Aboriginal self-government, also has the internal coherence and practical flexibility to reflect light back on questions surrounding the self-government debate that have not been dealt with elsewhere in a succinct fashion. A pluralist approach compels us to think again about the phenomena that we call Aboriginal culture and nationhood, their components and characteristics, and the relation that each has to the Aboriginal individual. It also leads us to think again about a perennial political problem, the question of identity. Which characteristics distinguish Aboriginal communities from non-Aboriginal ones and members from nonmembers? And what is the nature of the relationship between Aboriginal communities and non-Aboriginal governments that the Aboriginal right to self-government is intended to protect? It is my view that dealing with these questions through concepts central to pluralist thought allows for an analysis that reaches into the very centre of the Aboriginal self-government debate.

At the same time, it is important to make distinctions within the tradition of pluralism, for not all instances of pluralist theory are alike. Pluralism is often viewed as a public arrangement in which distinct groups live side by side in conditions of mutual recognition and affirmation, but what precisely this "recognition" and "affirmation" consist of depends on the pluralist perspective that one adopts. I perceive three contemporary faces of pluralism, which may be distinguished by the labels "communitarian," "individualist," and "relational." Within this triad of pluralisms, the communitarian and individualist faces provide normative assessments of Aboriginal self-government that rely on understandings that equate the source of Aboriginal identity with specific cultural and national traits. I am convinced, however, that this is an undersophisticated response to the complex reality that Aboriginal identity represents.

Clearly, the topic of Aboriginal self-government is complex. What follows, then, is a conceptual and normative analysis of this complexity, an attempt to establish a framework in which the relation between Aboriginal identity, pluralist theory, and Aboriginal self-government can be appreciated. The major hypothesis suggests that Aboriginal self-government issues and their resolution are better understood if we adopt an "identification" perspective on Aboriginal identity as opposed to a "cultural" or "national" one and if we link that to a relational theory of pluralism as opposed to a communitarian or individualist theory. Essentially, I examine how an identification approach leads to a discussion of Aboriginal identity not in terms of possessing cultural or political attributes but in terms of identification with, and political commitment to, an Aboriginal community and the way of life promoted by that community. In addition, I examine how framing Aboriginal self-government issues within the context of relational pluralism leads to a discussion of Aboriginal politics in terms of a problem of power differences within Aboriginal communities and between Aboriginal communities and the Canadian state. Framed in this way, Aboriginal politics involves demands to equalize current imbalances of power so that Aboriginal communities and the individuals within them can construct Aboriginal identities according to their own designs. Less conspicuous in this approach is the idea that Aboriginal self-government should be seen as a tool to preserve cultural and national differences on the purported premise that these are goods in and of themselves. I believe that finding morally defensible and politically viable answers to questions raised by the Aboriginal assertion to power is a more accurate way of framing one of the greatest political challenges facing Canada today.

In what follows, I am concerned less with technical problems of detailed political models than with addressing some fundamental moral and political questions associated with the Aboriginal right to self-government. Specifically, three sets of questions motivate my analysis. The first set concerns the basic question of identity. What currently constitutes Aboriginal identity? Is it primarily cultural? Is it primarily nation-based? Or is it broader than its cultural and national expressions? And, if broader, should this make a difference to how one should think about the Aboriginal right to self-government?

The second set concerns questions of justification and intent. What justifies self-government? Is it the Aboriginal desire to protect culture? Is self-government justified because it flows from historical nationhood? Are culture- and nation-based justifications comprehensive enough? Or should self-government be justified in more comprehensive terms, perhaps with respect to criteria that relate the right to self-definition?

The third and final set confronts the question of limitations on Aboriginal political power. On what grounds should the right to self-government be constrained? Is individual freedom of choice the criterion to be used here? Or does this liberal criterion diminish the capacity of Aboriginal communities to preserve their cultural distinctiveness? Should non-Aboriginal Canadians revise their conceptions of individual freedoms and collective rights so that questions of political restraint are framed in a different way?

In August 1991, in the aftermath of the 1990 Oka crisis, the Canadian government set up the Royal Commission on Aboriginal Peoples (RCAP). From April 1992 to December 1993, the commission toured the country garnering opinions from Aboriginal and non-Aboriginal organizations and individuals to define problems and propose solutions in all aspects of Aboriginal life. It is the official transcripts of the commission's public hearings that form the basis of this book. These hearings constitute the most extensive gathering of public opinion ever undertaken on Aboriginal life in Canada. It became apparent in my examination of these transcripts that questions about Aboriginal identity and the nature and extent of Aboriginal political power were of central concern. I will emphasize those aspects of the hearings that deal specifically with self-government.

Furthermore, while "Aboriginal" generally refers to the Indian, Inuit, and Métis peoples of Canada, I will focus on the testimony of Native Indians, specifically on those who identify themselves as members of what are commonly referred to as First Nations. My analysis is thus concentrated at the level of on-reserve Indian peoples. Of the 811,400 persons who identify with their Aboriginal ancestry, 438,000 are registered Indians.[2] Of these, 254,600 (58.1 percent) live on reserves, while an estimated 183,400 (41.9 percent) live in nonreserve areas, mostly in urban settings. It is therefore important to keep in mind that the on-reserve population on which I focus constitutes a minority of the total Aboriginal population in Canada.

By extension, I will devote limited attention to the specific and often unique political aspirations of the nonidentifying Aboriginal population (375,000), the Inuit (38,000), the Métis (139,000), the off-reserve status Indian (183,400) and nonstatus Indian populations (estimated at 112,600), as well as the 100,000-plus status Indians recently reinstated under Bill C-31, most of whom do not live in reserve communities (recognizing, of course, that there is some overlap between these categories). Where I do discuss off-reserve Indians, I do so almost entirely in terms of their links with reserve-based communities.

As a generalization of the hearings, it can safely be said that many of the Indian, Inuit, and Métis witnesses employed concepts and categories that call for an understanding of self-government based on modified approaches to Aboriginal identity and political power. Where positions converge, I believe that the central insights of political pluralism can be applied to the respective quests for self-government pursued by the Inuit and Métis as well as Indians. Yet there is a real variety of emphasis in the philosophical and historical positions of the three constitutionally recognized Aboriginal peoples as well as in the political interests that flow from those positions. More so than the others, for example, Indians tend to lodge their political claims within the normative language of original occupancy, nation-to-nation equivalency, and treaty entitlement. Taken together, these concepts connote claims to maximum political autonomy for self-governing Aboriginal nations within Canada. It is toward the moral and political questions raised by these kinds of fundamental principles that I will direct my attention. My intent is to demonstrate how the central categories of political pluralism can help us to respond to these fundamental questions.

In Chapter 1, I examine the major existing approaches to the study of ethnic identity and then discuss the three main types of pluralism. I address the question of identity politics from the perspectives of what I call "difference" and "identification" approaches and then seek to relate the findings of these approaches to normative concerns about justice that typically preoccupy pluralist scholars.

Chapter 2 examines some of the theoretical literature that explores the theme of Aboriginal identity. It looks at what it means to have an Aboriginal identity and examines the relative merits of analyzing that identity in terms of difference and identification-based approaches. The first two chapters together provide the theoretical background against which the rest of the book should be interpreted.

I then shift in Chapter 3 to an examination of the politics of Aboriginal identity as expressed in the public hearings of RCAP. This material forms the empirical basis for the remaining chapters. Chapter 3 provides an analysis and critique of the communitarian idea that the Aboriginal claim to self-government possesses normative force because it safeguards an Aboriginal right to cultural and political difference. The focus here is on relations between Aboriginal communities and the Canadian state and on the question of which principles ought to guide those relations.

In Chapter 4, I shift from relations between Aboriginal communities and the Canadian state to relations within Aboriginal communities. I address the problem of political power from the perspective of the individual and evaluate the individualist ideal that, when there is conflict between Aboriginal individuals and the cultural and political projects undertaken by their communities, the individual right to freedom of choice should prevail.

Chapters 5 and 6 advance the idea that Canadians have not been well served by the terms of the present debate on Aboriginal self-government because it so often pits the rights of Aboriginal individuals against those of their communities and the rights of Aboriginal communities against those of the Canadian polity. These chapters then develop an alternative framework based on evaluative criteria that assess self-government in terms of relational pluralism.

Finally, the Conclusion summarizes and evaluates the arguments and data presented and speculates about the future direction of Aboriginal self-government in Canada in light of the fundamental moral and political questions posed in the book. It also includes an assessment of how the experience of Canadian citizenship for Aboriginal peoples can be cast in a more positive light when filtered through the lens of relational pluralism.

SHIFTING BOUNDARIES

CHAPTER I

IDENTITY POLITICS AND PLURALIST THEORY

I begin by examining the major existing approaches to the study of ethnic identity and then discuss the three main types of pluralism. First, I assess two theories of ethnic agency and action: one links the source of ethnic identity to attributes of community difference, and the other links that source to relatively open-ended processes of community self-definition. Second, I demonstrate how the three faces of pluralist theory constitute different responses, at the level of principle, to the demands for political recognition that one often finds at the heart of identity politics. Here I identify the links often forged between the empirical claims of the two main approaches to ethnic identity and the normative concerns of the three faces of pluralism. I then offer an assessment of the accuracy and utility of these links.

IDENTITY POLITICS

The relationship between democracy and what has been variously called the politics of cultural, national, and ethnic identity has become a central concern to political scientists, and for good reason. The emergence of "identity politics" in the form of conflict between the various cultural, religious, and political affiliations that comprise ethnicity is now so visible in many societies that it has become impossible to ignore. Identity is about belonging, about the values that individuals share with other individuals, and about what differentiates one set of individuals from another. Identity is what gives individuals a sense of personal location and stability. But identity is also about conflict. By striving to express one's identity and the deeply felt desires and needs associated with it, individuals and their communities are often drawn into conflict with one another. Political scientists are then left with the challenge of addressing fundamental political questions. What stimulates identity politics? Does identity politics constitute a basic challenge to "existing cultural models, institutionalized social norms, and acknowledged group identities?"[1] Is it possible to achieve a political reconciliation between the universal needs of citizens and the specific needs of individuals as members of diverse communities?

Although the various expressions of this politics of identity take no universal form, they all share the common feature of being constituted by people who perceive their identities to be under some kind of threat. Group members consider their identities to have been, in some way, neglected or discriminated against by governments and society at large. In addition, these groups often lack formal political power when compared with the power exercised by the states in which they are found. Consequently, what group members demand is some form of remedial action from the state. They are often most concerned about creating space in civil society for the expression of their distinct identities − a critical component of their larger effort to gain recognition from the dominant, mainstream society.

The demands that groups make for remedial action are typically of two major types: some demand extensive rights of political autonomy, while others demand particular rights of political inclusion. In the former case, groups seek the right to govern themselves in certain key institutional areas of community existence, while in the latter case groups seek to realize collective interests in specific sectors of civil society. Both types of demands can be regarded as remedial because they are intended to remedy the purported destructive effects of previous governmental policies and societal practices.

In general, groups in search of increased shares of political autonomy from states tend to be united by bonds of kinship, ethnicity, traditional community, territory, or tribal affiliation and are often referred to as "nations," "peoples," or "cultures."[2] Multination states tend to arise when a state incorporates more than one of these so-called nations (defined by Will

Kymlicka as a more or less institutionally complete historical community) either through invasion and conquest by one over another or through mutual agreement when nations "form a federation for their mutual benefit."[3] In contrast, groups in search of specific rights and programs designed to protect some dimension of their particularity are often referred to as "new social movements." These groups are usually organized to advance stated objectives. Rather than sharing a purportedly common culture, nation, or ethnicity, their members typically share disabilities, sexual orientation, gender, or race. They tend, therefore, to be concerned with a limited range of objectives such as employment equity (the disabled), spousal benefits for same-sex couples (gays and lesbians), affirmative action (women), and civil rights (visible minorities). In this book, I am concerned primarily with identity groups of the former kind – that is, with groups typically understood to arise from cultural, national, and ethnic sources.

Once raised by groups, the issue of identity is unlikely to go away: the questions must be addressed if states are to meet their alleged obligations. To make sense of these developments, new theories of agency and action have emerged. In most discussions of historical communities of ongoing cultural, national, and ethnic identity, the term is used in one of two senses. In the first more conventional sense, identity "is used to refer to what is unique, peculiar or specific to a community and distinguishes it from others."[4] Here objective traits of cultural and political difference are said to constitute the ontological foundation of community identity. From this perspective, if identity is not to be lost, the community must retain its fundamental historical traits of difference from all other groups at all costs. In the second sense, identity refers not to ongoing objective traits of cultural and political difference but to the self-defining processes of communities and their corresponding inner structures.[5] While differences remain important in the sense that most communities may be historically, culturally, and politically unique, these differences are also viewed as immaterial and thus ontologically secondary from the point of view of identity itself. What is far more important from this point of view is the idea that identity is constituted by the historical continuity of relatively open-ended processes of self-definition by community members that relate to both what they take themselves to be and how they define their interests or ends over time. While the first sense dominates debates that take their point of departure from cultural and national explanations of community identity, the second sense is more prevalent in identification explanations. It is the second sense that is closer to my position. What follows examines each approach in turn.

The Difference Approach

One important source of work on the politics of identity comes from those who analyze the process of identity building as an ongoing struggle by communities to capture recognition for the distinctive cultural and political attributes of their ways of life. Among leading scholars in this tradition are Will Kymlicka, Patrick Macklem, Charles Taylor, and James Tully.[6] For the sake of convenience, I will refer to this approach as the difference approach. It ties the well-being of individual community members directly to the strength and vitality of their communal cultures and nations. Individuals are said to be able to reach their potential only if the distinctive cultural and political attributes that ground their common existence are given opportunity for free expression.

The difference approach proceeds from the assumption that the foundations of personal identity lie in cultural and national sources. While the concepts of culture and nation are sometimes used interchangeably in these arguments, culture is usually the preferred term of choice. The general argument can be characterized as follows.

In explaining the process of identity formation, commentators in this tradition proceed from the assumption that individuals answer the question of identity by turning to the cultural values and allegiances that come to them as members of their communities. The basic claim here is that personal identity is formed in a symbiotic relationship with a collective identity nourished by the culture that the community shares. As Taylor notes, "I may come to realize that belonging to a given culture is part of my identity, because outside of the reference points of this culture I could not begin to put to myself, let alone answer, those questions of ultimate significance that are peculiarly in the repertory of the human subject."[7] Framed in this way, culture provides individuals with a horizon of meaning that is essential to their being human. Culture helps to identify individuals: it gives them "strategic and stylistic guides to action."[8]

Integral to the difference approach is the idea that culture must be understood as a comprehensive way of life. For example, Kymlicka defines cultures as multidimensional and all-encompassing in the sense that they provide their members with "meaningful ways of life across the full range of human activities, including social, educational, religious, recreational, and economic life, encompassing both private and public spheres."[9]

That culture is comprehensive leads to an important conclusion: the cultural traits of communities are taken as that which differentiates individuals from one another. The reasoning here is straightforward. The more deeply an individual is involved in the life of her community, the more likely it is that she will regard the world through its cultural horizon of meaning rather than that of any other. As a result, culture not only provides individuals with identity but also divides them from one another at the deepest level of human existence.

From this conclusion, a critical further step is taken: some commentators point out that individuals need culture not in a general way but in the specific ways provided by the cultures of their own communities. Their specific culture alone is what gives individuals the distinct content that they need to live life with the meaning and dignity perhaps already enjoyed on a variety of levels.[10] Thus, it is the existence of cultural differences rather than the existence of culture itself that becomes the basis of the identity of a community. Stephen Cornell argues that "the assumptions we make about the world and how to behave in it are more or less the same, and it is this that provides the common ground of our identity."[11] By implication, if communities are to survive, they must maintain and promote those traits of culture that distinguish them from other communities. Failure to do so is said to jeopardize precisely those cultural elements that lend to individual lives their distinctive meaning and dignity.

While cultural identity may be the outgrowth of distinctiveness, the difference approach does not preclude cultures from being dynamic. For example, Jeremy Webber argues that cultures evolve, adapt, and "are continually subject to interpretation and re-interpretation."[12] Macklem argues that cultures are not static but "undergo dramatic transformations," while the individuals within them may "express a plurality of cultural allegiances."[13] And Tully argues that "we cannot grasp the politics of cultural recognition" until we also understand that cultures are "overlapping, interactive and internally negotiated."[14] There is a general acceptance in the difference approach that cultures evolve in response to ongoing assessments of cultural values and customs that are taken up in response to ever-changing historical circumstances. However, while cultures do overlap and can change, the ontological premise of this approach remains the same: individuals rely on their cultures to provide them with the moral, social, and political resources that they need to make meaningful choices in their lives. In this sense, commentators continue to stress that cultures do possess distinct and valuable characters. They merely wish to frame the nature of that distinctiveness in ways that "embrace movement and development, not a rigid constancy or uniformity."[15]

Another feature of the difference approach is that shared experiences of culture are often closely related to those of nationhood. Like cultures, nations are typically identified as communities held together through objective bonds of history, language, and culture, whose members then use those bonds subjectively to create a sense of shared nationhood.[16] These broad characteristics of nationhood are then made the foundation of community identity and, equally important, the sources that serve to differentiate one community from another.

When commentators explain the role of nations in identity formation, they often identify nations as cultural communities of a particular kind. A culture becomes a nation if the members within it think of themselves as entitled to some form of territorial sovereignty and state power.[17] Some communities may well be able to sustain their distinct identities if granted collective rights in sector-specific areas. Demands may aim for control over education, for example, and thus the right to educate children in the history, language, and culture of the people. Other groups, however, may demand political and territorial rights in addition to sector-specific rights on the ground that the former are essential for the preservation of their distinctiveness. In fact, in the case of colonized enclaves within settler states, the point is sometimes made that minorities "maintain themselves at least partially by sustaining a hope for political independence or for the recapturing of lost territory."[18] Paul R. Brass argues that in such cases, "insofar as it succeeds by its own efforts in achieving any one of these goals either within an existing state or in a state of its own, it has become a nationality or nation."[19]

However, while the objectives of nations may be more extensive, the difference approach makes the same ontological claim for nations as for cultures. Like cultures, nations are seen as essential to persons because they provide them with unique ways of life central to their identities. The difference between cultural and national communities relates to the nature of their political objectives: unlike cultures, nations are said to need a measure of territorial control and political power in order to give expression to their distinct ways of life. Tully notes that what nations "share is a longing for self-rule: to rule themselves in accord with their customs and ways."[20] It is assumed that control in these areas gives nations the ability to perpetuate their languages, cultures, and memberships as well as traditional economic, political, and land use practices, elements that, when taken together, are defined in turn as integral to the expression of nationhood.

What often follows is that commentators ascribe to nations a primordial status. Because of the overarching nature of the political project that nations are understood to take up on behalf of their members, those members are said to reach freedom and fulfillment only when they cultivate the peculiar identity of their own nation and when they concede primacy to the nation above all other identities. The nation then becomes the primary focal point for political legitimacy and action. By extension, aspiring or actual nations denied territory, political control, and the means to political action are said to have difficulty sustaining the confidence and sense of well-being of members. As argued by Taylor, a political "community cannot be without achievements in these sectors, because these are the sectors that people value; and a community without realizations of this kind will inescapably come to depreciate itself and thus find its identity undermined."[21]

When the quest for identity is framed in terms of a struggle to preserve national distinctiveness, this understanding also lends a particular character to the approach's argument for self-government. Self-government is understood to be the right of a nation because it is what nations are said to need to survive as distinct societies. Avishai Margalit and Moshe Halbertal express this sentiment clearly: "all persons are supremely interested in their personal identity – that is, in their ability to preserve the attributes that are seen as central to them and the members of their group."[22] Self-government is thus critical to this project because it makes it possible for members of cultural groups to retain their identities – and in particular to retain those attributes of identity that distinguish them from the members of other groups. Self-government, in other words, is the means by which communities maintain their differences and distinct experiences of humanity for their members.

In summary, probably the most commonly held assumption in the difference approach is that individual identity arises ultimately from some sort of cultural or national identity. Culture and nation tend to be seen as kindred concepts since the majority of nations are defined as cultural in character. The analytical distinction made between the two concepts is straightforward: nations are cultures that demand territorial control and political power on behalf of their members. In either case, the approach constructs identity in reference to the structures that surround the individual. Cultural characteristics are thought to define the interests of nations, and the institutions of nations are then viewed as the principal means for advancing those interests.

Nations, in turn, are defined as units created by feelings of nationalism. Nationalism is the idea that nations deserve primary loyalty and attachment not only because they incarnate in some comprehensive way the distinctive cultural and political attributes of community identity but also because the structures of nations are said to be in the best position to protect those attributes. In short, theories in this approach assume that individuals act because of who they are, and who they are flows from the attributes that they share with others in similar cultural and national categories. We see, in other words, in such arguments a clear link between the traits of community identity and the need to preserve those distinctive traits if the community is to survive.

The Identification Approach

The other major approach to discussing the politics of identity begins from the assumption that human identity is derived from "a sense of relatedness that is ascribed to peoples, either by themselves or by others or both."[23] I will refer to this approach as the identification approach to identity. This approach starts from the premise that individuals should not be identified for collective purposes in a deterministic fashion by their cultural or political attributes. Rather, individuals should be identified by their membership in, and political commitment to, their ethnic community and the way of life promoted by that community. The key element here is that ethnicity is a form of identification or relatedness that is either ascribed to or claimed by peoples, usually based on real or assumed bonds of kinship. Because the meaning of ethnicity is associated with the quality of belonging to an ethnic community and not with the individual possession of cultural and political attributes, this approach lends to identity a greater flexibility; it acknowledges that identity can change over time without jeopardizing the integrity of the individual's identity itself or the identity of the community to which that individual is related. Succinctly, an identification approach to identity emphasizes that human identity is malleable and that it can be shaped to meet different kinds of political objectives.

According to the identification approach, ethnicity, broadly conceived, has to do with classifying people and the nature of group relationships.[24] The criteria for membership within ethnic groups are generally seen as the following:

- a collective proper name;
- a myth of common ancestry;
- shared historical memories;
- one or more differentiating elements of common culture;
- an association with a specific "homeland"; and
- a sense of solidarity for significant sectors of the population.[25]

According to P.G. McHugh, the central element in an identification approach is collective solidarity based on rules of descent and the capacity for self-definition. What binds group members together is the shared and ongoing sense of belonging to one another over time. What motivates group members to act together is the desire to participate in the ongoing exercise of group self-definition. Self-definition, in turn, is identified by McHugh as the outcome of groups utilizing the criteria of their identities both to allocate resources internally to their members and to establish relations with other groups and public authorities on their own terms. This approach to ethnicity, then, accentuates the process of self-definition as critical to identity formation. While identity is invariably based on a sense of common ancestry and history, combined with other characteristics such as a shared collective name, culture, and territory, the approach does not link identity to the development of specific cultural or national content per se.

The identification approach does acknowledge that ethnic communities

can possess a relatively stable core that endures. But the larger point emphasized is that pure stability is elusive. This is because ethnic identity is
seen as referring not to the presence of stable cultural and political content
over generations but to a sense of intergenerational continuity forged
around subjective criteria of shared destiny established by those both inside
and outside the group.[26] The stable core of ethnicity can thus be linked
to little more than historical continuity of a common collective self-
consciousness rooted in real or assumed bonds of descent or kinship.[27] And
even here, as Anthony Smith argues, the important component in this understanding remains largely subjective because "it is the myths of common
ancestry, not any fact of ancestry (which is difficult to ascertain) that are
crucial."[28] We see in this argument, then, the claim that, if we are to understand ethnic groups, we must do so not with respect to lists of purportedly
objective and differentiating community attributes (since groups may not
be conscious of these attributes or inclined to use them for social or political ends) but with respect to the nature of the ongoing subjective bonds
that tie individual members to their community.

   In the difference approach to identity, one commonly finds that ethnic
groups are equated with cultural groups; people who share a distinctive culture are considered an ethnic group. The identification approach has determined that this method of classification is difficult to justify. It emphasizes
that cultural attributes are frequently shared across group boundaries and
that people do not always share the same set of cultural attributes with
those to whom they feel ethnically bound. As Thomas Eriksen writes, "one
may have the same language as some people, the same religion as some of
those as well as of some others, and the same economic strategy as an alto-
gether different category of people."[29] For Eriksen, then, if we rigidly insist
that ethnic identity receives its point of origin from cultural attributes, ethnic identity itself would presumably wax and wane as the attributes first
achieve and then recede in distinctiveness and thus importance for group
members.[30]

   A more innovative approach to cultural identity is taken up by scholars
within the difference tradition who insist that culture be understood as a
concept possessing elasticity. Macklem, for example, argues that political
equality is enjoyed only where group-based difference, especially cultural
difference, is taken into account. But he also insists that the nature and ex-

tent of cultural interaction in the modern world mean that there is an elective aspect to cultural membership; individuals "have access to and choice among a range of meaningful options from which to forge their identities," options that often come to them in the form of "fragments from a variety of cultural sources."[31] For theorists within the identification approach, this position still puts emphasis in the wrong place where the source of ethnic identity is concerned. If cultures do "undergo deep transformations over time," and if "cultural identity is an active web of interlocking and intersecting allegiances among individuals and communities," then why insist on preserving cultural difference on the premise that it is a good in and of itself?[32] Those within the identification tradition therefore conclude that the object of attention should be not culture but those bonds of relatedness and loyalty that link individuals to their ethnic communities in the first place.

The difficulties associated with equating ethnic groups with shared culture lead some commentators to conclude that ethnic identity should be determined not by cultural content but by social interaction and organization. For example, the influential work by Fredrik Barth and his followers establishes that there is no necessary correlation between ethnic identity and shared culture at all.[33] They argue that, despite cultural overlap and mutual influence, ethnic identities and perceptions of difference between groups can remain robust. This phenomenon led Barth to suggest that, while culture does remain important to identity, the focus of research in ethnic relations ought to be on the boundaries that separate groups and not on "the cultural stuff they enclose."[34] For him, ethnicity is, above all, a constructed identity: it forms because people who happen to share historical continuity through characteristics of ancestry, culture, or territory decide that it is important to them that they be viewed as members of a distinct group. Consequently, for Barth, groups ought to "be defined from within, from the perspective of their members."[35] What matters from the point of ethnic group membership, therefore, are the understandings that the group itself establishes concerning the essence of their group character and whether a person is in or out. Conversely, if we want to know if someone is or is not a member of an ethnic group, the answer is not necessarily provided by examining the cultural characteristics of persons per se.

The question, then, is whether ethnic identity presupposes any dimension of shared culture. The identification approach provides an affirmative answer if culture is filtered through the subjective lens of self-definition. From this perspective, ethnic groups are who they claim to be not because they possess distinctive cultures but because they use certain aspects (not all) of their cultures in order to mark themselves off from their neighbouring communities. In this sense, culture is understood to function as a subjectively self-conscious tool. Ethnic groups employ rules of descent and kinship as well as cultural and political symbols to create internal solidarity and boundaries between group members and others.[36] Boundaries here are further defined as invisible dividing lines established between groups. Eriksen puts it this way: "Cultural differences relate to ethnicity if and only if such differences are made relevant in social interaction."[37] Ethnicity is thus seen as a relational phenomenon: ethnic groups are defined by the way in which their boundaries (which vary in importance and change over time) are used to stimulate relationships with others.

The same general point is made with respect to national symbols. Ethnic groups are identified as having transformed into nations when considerable effort is made to integrate and then assign political meaning to attributes associated with ancestry, history, culture, language, and territory. Commentators point out that a key element of nationhood is the existence of a territorial home; nations cannot exist if they do not possess territory. Beyond the basic objective requirement of territory, however, the same principle of self-definition and the relativity of ethnic boundaries are applied to nations. It is only when they are deliberately used to make a difference in relations between ethnic groups that national differences are viewed as important for the creation of ethnic identity. In this sense, national identities are also seen as constructions, constituted in relation to others and designed to capture the specific political interests of particular ethnic groups.

In short, the identification approach emphasizes that, while cultural and political attributes may be present in the life of a community, their existence is largely irrelevant from the perspective of whether ethnic identity exists or not. What is relevant is the role that cultural or national symbols play in the claims that ethnic groups make about who they are and how they wish to be seen.[38] Cultural and political attributes are therefore viewed not as intrinsic to ethnic identity but as contingent on it. Beyond the simple assertion of a primary connection to one another through ancestry and historical time, the nature of the contrast (or the boundary that separates groups from one another) will vary depending on what it is beyond ancestry that group members wish to emphasize: "ethnic groups become agents in their own construction shaping and reshaping their identities and the boundaries that enclose them out of the raw materials of history, culture, and pre-existing ethnic constructions."[39]

If ethnic groups use cultural and political attributes for the purposes of self-definition, we might ask to what purpose? There are three interrelated critical purposes that the identification approach establishes.

First, this approach emphasizes that ethnic consciousness often does not emerge until an ethnic group finds itself under pressure from outside forces. As Eriksen puts it, "ethnic identity becomes crucially important the moment it is perceived as threatened."[40] Threats may come in various guises, but Eriksen notes that they are almost always associated with change of some kind, whether it be demographic, economic, or change that results from integration or encapsulation by a larger political system. Because ethnic identity emerges as a response to tension in intergroup relations, the importance of boundary development and maintenance is often conditional upon the degree of pressure exerted on these boundaries by outside groups. As pressure mounts, ethnic groups tend to fortify their boundaries by creating clear distinctions between the categories "Us" and "Them" so as to preserve an enclosed space in which to exercise autonomy over the development of their own identity. Ethnicity is seen in this sense as intimately connected to the individual need for collective continuity in the historical life of the group.

Second, while the identification approach regards the mobilization of ethnic identity as triggered in part by the existence of external threats to the group, the approach also highlights the degree to which ethnic identity is typically used as a tool in political struggles to capture resources (whether political, economic, cultural, or otherwise) from outside the group. Of course, the approach accepts that ethnic identity is always more than purely instrumental in function. Members belong to ethnic groups because such groups are intrinsically important to them – that is, shared ancestry and kinship and ideologies of shared culture are seen as evoking in members the moral conviction that "belongingness" is of intrinsic worth because it provides them with an important source of self-respect and personal authenticity. Yet the sense of identity that attachment to an ethnic group provides is also claimed as an important resource to mobilize a community to fight collectively for scarce resources.[41] Ethnic groups are seen as constructing identities and then deliberately employing them to claim resources on the purported moral ground that, without specified resources currently denied to them, they will be unable to exercise their right to develop their identities according to their own definitions.

Third, the identification approach posits that the capacity of ethnic groups to capture resources inevitably varies. Interethnic relations are often highly asymmetrical with respect to access to political power and economic resources. Differential levels of power are thus identified as key to understanding ethnic diversity. In its simplest form, the argument here contends that ethnic identity is often stimulated in response to existing oppression or anticipated oppression by a rival group. Ethnic assertiveness thereby develops when ethnic leaders rise to challenge the existing practices of ethnic domination and the inequitable distribution of political and economic resources. In this power struggle, the life of the subordinated group will be simultaneously directed toward cultivating inclusive bonds among the membership and projecting robust images of identity externally "so as to mobilize strength for the attack upon the practices which exclude them from privilege."[42] Naturally, the political importance of ethnic identity is greatest when the three purposes reinforce one another and are enacted simultaneously.

Probably the most commonly held assumption in the identification approach is that the source of individual ethnic identity originates from simple identification with a continuing community that makes particular claims about itself. Here ethnic identity tends not to be seen in terms of objective attributes; there is no one-to-one correspondence between ethnic identity and cultural or political characteristics. Rather, the approach tends to stress that ethnic identity is constructed: the primordial identification supplied by ancestry becomes the basis for the development of community identity that is often both highly variable and relatively open-ended and capable of being pushed in different directions over time. A central element in the identification approach, therefore, is that ethnic identity is presented in instrumental or interest-based terms. Ethnic groups are said to use elements of their history, culture, or nation as resources to make demands in the political arena so as to capture resources for their members. Theories in this approach assume that ethnic identity makes sense only in the context of an ethnic group's contemporary circumstances and in light of its contemporary interests. The content of ethnic identity can change, with one or another feature of cultural or political identification becoming more or less salient depending on the social organization of ethnic group relations and the nature of the competition between them.

Comment

The kinds of debate on ethnic identity taking place essentially divide on the status assigned to those aspects of identity that differentiate groups of people from one another. In essence, while the difference approach emphasizes the centrality of certain aspects of ethnic group life (associated with culture and nation respectively), an identification approach emphasizes the importance of the ethnic interest in communal self-definition. The difference approach starts from the premise that the basis of human identity in community is difference, while the identification approach suggests that the basis of community identity is fluid, negotiated, and subject to change. The difference approach advances the idea that community attributes are the source of identity, while the identification approach counters with the idea that attributes are merely expressions of identity.[43] From the difference perspective, then, it is a mistake not to make difference the basis of community identity. Difference is what distinguishes communities, and to ignore difference is to imperil communities at the most important identity-conferring level of their existence. From an identification perspective, however, the relationship is reversed. Here it is a mistake to limit human identity to particular aspects of it and then to reconfigure the political world exclusively in terms of conflicts between those aspects. This is to reify identity and misunderstand the nature of politics.

If we are to understand the nature of identity politics and the conflict generated by it, then we cannot reduce that conflict to the purported desire of ethnic communities to preserve their cultural and national identities as if these were ends in and of themselves. Rather, we have to understand how and why ethnic groups isolate, interpret, and then use dimensions of their cultural and political attributes to define themselves and to press their political claims. Thus, I believe that, despite what claimants may say, the preservation of cultural and national attributes is not really what is at stake in ethnic conflict: indeed, it is simply misleading to state that ethnic groups are identical with cultural or national groups and that shared culture or nationhood is the origin of ethnic identity. Instead, it is critical to understand that identities are negotiable and situational: "the selection of boundary markers is arbitrary in the sense that only some features are singled out and defined as crucial in the boundary process."[44] Hence, attributes of culture and nationhood should be understood as aspects of ethnic identity that are used as a basis for justifying other interests and rights.

THE THREE FACES OF PLURALISM

The current interest in identity politics indicates that many social scientists now regard enduring ethnic, cultural, national, and other forms of identity as important factors in the ordering of social and political relations. Both major approaches to identity politics start from the theoretical position that conflict based on identity is a normal and chronic condition in democratic states. Both offer new interpretations of the social processes and power relations that contribute to identity formation. In this sense, the approaches have stimulated a deeper awareness and understanding of the complexity of human identity and relations. Both approaches, in other words, constitute explanatory theories.

In this context, there has also been a revival of interest in the topic of pluralism. In its broadest sense, pluralism is also explanatory because the starting point for most discussions of pluralism is recognition that we inhabit a world teeming with differences. These differences are identified in moral outlooks, ethnic, cultural, and national identities, religious beliefs, the foundations of law, and even methodological approaches to scholarship.[45] Such differences are perceived as salient in that they will persist for as long as we can reasonably foresee. As Chantal Mouffe argues, "pluralism is not merely a fact, something that we must bear grudgingly or try to reduce, but an axiological principle." Indeed, for her, pluralism is the defining feature of modern democracy, so the challenge is to determine the best way to approach its nature and scope.[46]

What often preoccupies scholars is not the fact of pluralism itself but the question of which conclusions are to be drawn from recognition of this fact. Political theorists typically entertain two specific questions in this re-gard. First, what is the origin of group diversity? And second, how should we respond to these differences individually and politically? In other words, pluralist theory contains explanatory elements, but these elements, in turn, are used explicitly to address normative questions of justice. The first ques-tion has been answered differently by scholars, though most point to the degree of community diversity and the degree of institutional separation into "analogous, parallel and non-complementary segments" within a soci-ety as important variables in their explanations.[47] These explanatory ques-tions will not detain me here. It is the second, more normative question associated with pluralism that is my concern. Here pluralism is used evalu-atively to express an ideal. It stands as a social theory that not only describes and explains the sources of difference in human life but also recognizes that those differences generate tensions, oppositions, and conflicts between peo-ple. The practical problem of having to live together in a world of distinct but overlapping groups in which we get in one another's way all the time is what is at issue. The normative task of political theory is to show how relationships and the conflict attendant upon them can be channelled and accommodated. In contemporary political theory, "pluralism" has come to signify one specific way of channelling and accommodating those relationships.

An associated normative use of the concept of pluralism lies in the do-main of government policy. Here the leading problem that occupies schol-ars and policy makers alike is how institutions of liberal democracy might make room for the recognition of group diversity. The underlying premise here is that the group basis of social mobilization, particularly in cases where hitherto marginalized groups seek to validate and empower them-selves, is both necessary and positive. For Iris Marion Young, for example, the normative ideal of a plural public is one in which "each of the con-stituent groups affirms the presence of others,"[48] while for Charles Taylor it is critical for a polity to provide spaces for the expression of what he calls "deep diversity." For him, recognition of "deep diversity" builds "a country for everyone," because a plurality of ways of belonging is therefore "ac-knowledged and protected."[49] With respect to Aboriginal peoples, Macklem insists that "a unique constitutional relationship exists between Aboriginal people and the Canadian state," so for him recognition "of this relationship is demanded by elementary principles of justice."[50] Tully echoes this concern when he urges "that Aboriginal peoples should be recognized as equal, coexisting, and self-governing nations and accommodated by renewing the treaty relationship."[51] For these authors, pluralism (or multiculturalism, as Taylor prefers to call it)[52] stands as a political principle that requires the state to act in ways to protect group diversity by not discriminating against social groups and, more positively, by acting in the domain of public policy to ensure their ongoing viability. These are commonly referred to as pluralist accommodations.[53]

Where group diversity is addressed by political theorists, they often do so within the context of individualist or communitarian commitments. Throughout past decades, political theory has been dominated by sharp disagreements between liberal and communitarian scholars over the proper relationship between individuals and their socially significant groups. What is fascinating about this debate is the degree to which pluralist themes figure prominently in the scholarship of both camps. Both seek to defend visions of pluralism, though often of radically different sorts.

What I perceive in these recent debates about group diversity among political theorists are three faces of pluralism: communitarian, individualist, and relational. Furthermore, I believe that the communitarian and individualist understandings of pluralism need to be complemented by a relational understanding if pluralism is to be used as a tool to further understanding of Aboriginal politics. This is because communitarian and individualist understandings tend to rely on a difference approach to Aboriginal identity. When pluralism is linked to a difference approach, its normative project tends to be formulated in dichotomous terms: communitarians defend a pluralism in which the Aboriginal community's right to preserve and protect specific cultural and political attributes of difference is upheld at all costs, while individualists defend a pluralism in which the Aboriginal individual's right to freedom of choice is always given priority over the preservation of those cultural and national attributes.

I want to suggest, however, that the communitarian and individualist approaches to pluralism are misleading, and, insofar as they structure our understanding of Aboriginal self-government issues and their resolution, they do so inaccurately. In my view, the framework of relational pluralism is the more helpful of the three because it lends itself more readily to a discussion of Aboriginal identity in terms established by the identification approach. When pluralism is linked to an identification approach, it is seen as a political state of affairs that promotes relations of equality between and within societal groups so that group members can pursue their collective interest in being self-defining in freedom. What follows establishes some links between the two major approaches to identity and the three main types of pluralism so as to prepare the theoretical ground for arguments in later chapters.

Communitarian Pluralism

Several communitarians lend normative justification to what they identify as the critical role that cultural and national communities play in shaping the lives of individuals. There are many diverse points of view encompassed within the tradition, though it is probably best represented in the work of Michael Sandel, Alasdair MacIntyre, Charles Taylor, Michael Walzer, Will Kymlicka, and James Tully.[54] With the exceptions of Kymlicka, Taylor, and Tully, however, communitarian writers have not explicitly addressed the philosophical and practical challenges associated with the existence of indigenous peoples within pluralist nation-states.[55]

In the 1980s, the central topic of debate in the philosophical writings of liberal and communitarian theorists was distributive justice, the principal question being whether people are entitled to the economic and material goods that they possess or whether those goods should be subject to some form of redistribution. That arguments about justice would lead to metaphysical questions about the nature of the self, rationality, and community is not surprising. More recently, however, theorists have begun to place greater emphasis on the significance of diversity, pluralism, and multiculturalism. These debates spring from the perception that forms of inequality and oppression extend well beyond economic relations to include what they label relations between cultural communities as well. The question of justice, therefore, is said to apply just as readily to what is now commonly known as the politics of cultural diversity. Communitarians have been quick to take up this new philosophical challenge.

What principally unites communitarians is the form of critique that they level against the excessive individualism they see as central to recent liberal political theory. Communitarians argue that the quest for identity goes much deeper than individual interest. In identifying the source of individual identity, however, communitarians take a critical though limiting step. A feature of the communitarian approach is that it is simply taken as given that individual identity is in substantive measure formed by the cultural attributes of the communities in which individuals are members. What then follows is an analysis of identity in which cultural difference is made the basis of community identity. Consequently, political conflict is construed in cultural terms. Tully, for example, assumes that the preservation of "authentic" identity depends on recognition of cultural diversity. Consequently, for him, the object of justice must be to protect the distinct cultural characteristics or the unique configuration of cultural attributes of minorities from the pressures applied against them by the larger and more powerful surrounding majority.[56] What this implies for communitarians is that the object of political morality should extend beyond economic redistribution issues to the rights of what they take to be culturally formative identity groups. Markate Daly argues that this critique directly follows from, and is cast in terms of, a distinct social metaphysics. "Instead of such values as individual interests, autonomy, universality, natural rights, and neutrality, communitarian philosophy is framed in terms of the common good, social practices and traditions, character and solidarity, and social responsibility."[57]

On a practical level, communitarians believe that the fundamental principles and corresponding political conventions of the liberal democratic state act regularly to impede the cultural ambitions of ethnic minorities. Put simply, the nature of this political conflict is defined as a case of competing cultural frameworks. While the objective of liberal democracies may be to treat all individuals equally, the standard political conventions that uphold this principle – such as individual rights, universal citizenship, and majority rule – are in fact understood to be discriminatory where cultural groups are concerned. Taylor, Kymlicka, and Tully address specific features of this problem.

In "The Politics of Recognition," Taylor argues that a healthy identity depends on the presence of both dignity and authenticity.[58] While dignity refers to the idea that human beings deserve equal respect regardless of race, colour, or creed, authenticity refers to the idea that each human being has a unique way of being human that is formed in cultural settings with others and that, if left unrecognized, can severely damage an individual's distinct sense of personal dignity. Taylor further argues that, while the politics of authenticity grew organically out of the politics of dignity in that each upholds a common standard of equality, at present they exist in significant tension with one another. The politics of dignity seeks to safeguard a standard of human sameness (universal dignity for all), while the politics of authenticity demands recognition for the unique cultural identities of individuals and their groups – that is, what differentiates them from everyone else.

The advocates of equal dignity claim that individuals should be treated equally and assert that such equality is accomplished by treating everyone as abstract individuals in a "difference-blind" manner rather than as members of particular groups. Taylor accepts that on some level the idea of abstract equality is attractive because it promotes a common standard of nondiscrimination. Individuals should not be discriminated against on the basis of irrelevant characteristics such as age, race, gender, or religion. But at the same time, Taylor points out that the politics of cultural difference construes nondiscrimination in quite different terms: nondiscrimination is understood to involve special protection based on individual and cultural differences. Thus, for Taylor, what is presented by liberal advocates as universal can in fact be culturally particular because, under the guise of ethical universalism, dominant groups can refuse to protect cultural differences on grounds that to do so would be discriminatory.[59] Where cultural minorities are threatened in this sense, Taylor believes that it is imperative their equal worth be acknowledged and protected through access to differential collective rights.

There is another sense developed in the work of Kymlicka that the cultural universalism of the individualist argument is identified as having a negative impact on the cultural identity of ethnic minorities. His discussion is applied directly to the politics of Aboriginal people in Canada. He argues that the purported neutrality of universal individual rights obscures the fact that the integrity of minority cultural differences is often vulnerable to the decisions made by the dominant culture. In his view, democratic devices such as "one person, one vote" and "majority rule" can consistently work against minority cultures if majority cultures use these devices to outvote and outbid minorities for resources critical to their cultural survival. This is a threat, Kymlicka says, that the dominant group need never face given its superior numbers.[60]

Kymlicka argues that the Aboriginal peoples of Canada have been the recipients of precisely such disadvantages. Historically, they were subjected to brutal forms of mistreatment as their ways of life were systematically undermined by colonial and Canadian governments. This situation has changed appreciably, and today Aboriginal individuals are no longer discriminated against since they are now protected by the same regime of universal rights enjoyed by their non-Aboriginal Canadian counterparts. Kymlicka's point, however, is that, because Aboriginal peoples constitute only 2.7 percent of Canada's population, their unique cultural practices remain vulnerable in the marketplace of cultural competition.[61] Governments can continue with impunity to undermine the competitive ability of Aboriginal peoples, and Canadians can more generally continue to outvote and outbid Aboriginal peoples for the resources that they need for their communities to develop and flourish. For Kymlicka, "special political rights ... serve to correct this inequality by ensuring that Aboriginal communities are as secure as non-Aboriginal ones."[62]

Tully, in turn, uses the liberal ideals of civic and individual freedom and responsibility in relation to that of self-respect to advance the case for cultural rights. He argues that individuals need a basic threshold of self-respect if they are to engage in citizenship and exercise personal freedom. If individuals are to be the confident and effective citizens that liberalism promotes, then they must be assured that their participation in politics and in life more generally will be regarded by others as worthwhile. But, he adds, many liberal theorists now also recognize that what individuals say and do and how they contribute to public life are "partly constituted by their cultural identity."[63] Consequently, the precondition for the existence of self-respect is a society in which cultural diversity is not only recognized and affirmed but also protected in cases where cultural minorities are vulnerable to the decisions of the majority. Not to offer such protection, argues Tully, is to undermine the ability of individuals "to be citizens and autonomous individuals in work and private life."[64] Yet these are precisely the conditions under which Aboriginal peoples in Canada have suffered: "the disastrous effects of successive policies of cultural destruction and assimilation on the self-respect of Aboriginal peoples proves this obvious point beyond a reasonable doubt."[65] Tully's remedy is thus identical in form to those of Kymlicka and Taylor. Tully insists that, if Canada is to provide an environment for Aboriginal persons to enjoy their civic and personal liberties (which, he adds, are the most important liberties of a liberal democratic society), it must enable Aboriginal persons "to participate in governing their societies in accord with their own laws and cultural understanding of democracy, to overcome alienation, and to regain their dignity as equal and active citizens."[66]

The arguments of Tully, Kymlicka, and Taylor about the corrosive cultural effects of an un-nuanced liberalism on minority communities only make sense when lined up against the difference approach to individual and community identity. For them, cultural differences are the basis of ethnic identity in community. As advocates of cultural difference, they attack the idea of liberal universalism on the grounds that it constitutes a cultural imposition of the hegemonic culture that, in turn, threatens vulnerable minorities with cultural extinction. Because the cultural practices of groups are viewed by all three as constitutive of individual identity, when those practices are compromised or destroyed, those who have shared in them are said to be either left in a partial or complete identity vacuum or forced to undergo a difficult process of identity adaptation.

Communitarian scholarship in Canada seeks to expand the horizons of liberal theorizing by creating a vision of justice in which ethnic groups are allowed free cultural development on the premise that not doing so will hinder the self-development of their members. The result is a form of communitarian pluralism. A just society, for communitarians, is one in which the cultural autonomy of these distinct communities is respected and not subject to threats from other cultural ways of life.

Furthermore, for communitarians, Aboriginal peoples are communities in precisely this sense. Aboriginal claims for rights are said to rest on specific reasoning about the rights of Aboriginal peoples as colonized peoples. For them, these rights are not simply about the need for material compensation but more profoundly about the need to respect the original sources of Aboriginal tradition and to preserve differences in cultural practice. Thus, for communitarians, at the heart of the cultural identity of Aboriginal communities is contrast: the belief that Aboriginal people are in important cultural respects different from non-Aboriginal people. Moreover, what communitarians suggest is that the nature of the contrast between Aboriginal communities and non-Aboriginal Canadians goes to the deepest epistemological and normative levels of life. Consequently, at the critical identity-conferring level of core cultural commitments, communitarians believe that there remains considerable distance between Aboriginal and non-Aboriginal peoples. This distance then means that communitarians place a high premium on the significance of assimilative pressures on Aboriginal people and what they see as the corresponding desire of Aboriginal communities to place their identity-conferring attributes beyond the potentially all-enveloping reach of Canadian society.

Individualist Pluralism

Individualist pluralism can be understood in large measure as both a refinement of and a reaction to the central claims of communitarian pluralists. Importantly, however, numerous theorists in the individualist tradition also accept the premise that individual identity is a function of the cultural characteristics that one shares with others in a community. Hence, the explanatory and normative thrust of individualist pluralism also relies on the difference approach to identity. Where it parts ways with communitarian pluralism is in its assessment of the priority that ought to be given to protecting cultural distinctiveness. For individualist pluralists, priority must always be given to the principle that individual rights together with provisions for nondiscrimination must come before collective cultural goals.

In contemporary Canadian politics, particularly among the anglophone community, there is considerable skepticism when it comes to governmental recognition of what has come to be understood as the cultural interests of collectivities. For some, "this scepticism extends to any attempt to promote a particular culture through the use of law,"; "for others, opposition is more tightly focused on legislation potentially affecting what they see as important individual rights."[67] Claude Denis explains that this concern for the individual arises out of "modernity's self-glorification as uniquely respectful of individual rights."[68] Liberal democracy's most basic commitment is to the freedom and equality of individual citizens. Thus, when the quest for community identity is construed in terms of a desire by that community to enhance or cultivate distinct cultural traditions, any ensuing conflict between individuals and their communities is inevitably interpreted in dichotomous terms. The nature of the conflict is posed in the following way. Individual rights are said to have empowered the individual against the state. But if communities are then empowered against the state as part of a commitment to uphold their distinct cultural characteristics, what guarantee is there that individuals will not be totally engulfed by the cultural demands of their communities?

One important response to this line of questioning as it relates to Aboriginal peoples in Canada is offered by Tom Flanagan in his *First Nations? Second Thoughts.*[69] His proposition is classically liberal. He argues that, while individuals naturally form associations in order to achieve their ends, it is imperative from the perspective of justice that these associations be voluntary. He is thus highly critical of government policy that places people into categories that entitle them to different legal rights, "especially when those categories are based on characteristics such as race or sex."[70] Flanagan is convinced that Aboriginal peoples have fallen into precisely this trap. First, he argues, Aboriginal leaders make claims about Aboriginal original occupancy, traditional nationhood, and historical cultural equivalency with Europeans that are dubious at best because they simply cannot be supported by historical and political evidence.[71] Second and more grievous, Aboriginal leaders then rely on these claims to argue for legal rights to property and self-government powers that Flanagan believes will only further serve to lock most Aboriginal persons into conditions of welfare dependency, political powerlessness, and ongoing social dysfunction.[72] It would be far better, he says, to recognize that Canada is made up of earlier and later immigrants, that all ought to be contained within one political community under a single rule of constitutional law, and that, while Aboriginal ethnic loyalties are to be encouraged, the ties that bind Aboriginal persons to one another should always be subservient to "social processes based on free association" that encourage Aboriginal integration into the Canadian "liberal society, political democracy, and market economy."[73]

Flanagan's desire to safeguard the Aboriginal individual against the potential hazards of the overbearing cultural practices and institutions of his or her community is informed by three powerful liberal assumptions: the importance of individual autonomy, the instrumental role of groups, and the priority of individual choice. Not only are these liberal democratic beliefs deeply embedded in Canadian political life, but they also regularly emerge in discussions about Aboriginal self-government. It is therefore important that each assumption be addressed in turn.

First, according to standard liberal accounts, the individual is the basic unit of society, standing at the centre of all relations of power, trust, and cooperation. Individuals are given pride of place in this liberal scheme for the simple reason that they are defined as rational actors – beings taken to be the best judges of their own circumstances and thus in the best positions to calculate their own priorities. At the heart of liberal doctrine stands the belief that individuals must be free to pursue their rational self-interest without interference from the state, societal groups, or other individuals. Markate Daly summarizes this liberal sentiment as follows: "as an individual, each person has a unique identity defined by a subjective consciousness, forms and carries out projects that unfold in a personal history, holds an inalienable right to pursue this life plan, and follows universal principles of morality in relationships with others."[74]

The political world of liberalism is directly harnessed to this liberal view of human nature. The task of the state is to balance and contain self-interest so that no individual harms the interests of others. Yet the active arm of the state must also be minimized so that it does not unduly interfere in the private lives of individuals. The power of government is therefore to be constrained by devices such as constitutions. Not only do constitutions protect the rights of minorities against the power of majorities, but they also protect basic individual freedoms such as the right to life, liberty, speech, religion, and association. A political system should thus be principally concerned about the well-being of its individual citizens; its task is to create a civil society based on equal respect for individual rights.[75]

Modern liberalism's political morality can thus be said to encompass a number of essential ingredients. Liberals regard individual autonomy, broadly understood as the capacity for self-direction, to be intrinsically valuable and so deserving of respect. Liberals also place priority on the right of individuals to exercise autonomy in instances where autonomy conflicts with other values. It is for this reason, for example, that Ronald Dworkin argues that the state must remain neutral with respect to what he calls different conceptions of the good, because if it does not it will inevitably promote a conception of the good that may override the autonomous and prior right of an individual to pursue an alternative course.[76] Finally, the priority that liberals place on individual autonomy translates into their general reluctance to regard a particular course of life as essential for everyone. Liberals accept that many activities and life choices have value, and by extension there are a composite number of ways and means by which individual lives can flourish.[77]

Second, while liberals champion the centrality of individual freedom, this does not mean that they ignore the importance of community for political life. Indeed, much liberal theory recognizes that individual political behaviour is largely a reflection of the influences of group affiliations on the lives of individuals.

One stream of liberalism in which groups are featured prominently is American pluralist writing. According to this tradition, established by the mid-twentieth century, individuals are not the rational, independent political actors of classical liberal theory. Writers such as Arthur Bentley, David Truman, and Robert Dahl argued that such understandings of politics are excessively abstract and hopelessly unrealistic for complex and technologically advanced liberal democratic societies such as the United States.[78] Purely on the level of political power, for example, individuals realize that they are essentially powerless if they act alone. Indeed, the research of American pluralists demonstrated that individuals have a natural capacity to act together with others to achieve common purposes. What American pluralists showed, in other words, is that groups empower individuals because they give them the standing and influence that they need to have their positions heard and considered by the state and other societal groups.

American pluralists also observed that it is a feature of democratic societies that groups tend to compete, negotiate, and strike compromises with other groups as they seek to influence governmental decision making. Consequently, a realistic depiction of politics ought to incorporate an analysis of both group interests and the capacity of groups to exercise power in order to act on those interests. By implication, the quality of democracy itself was judged by American pluralists in terms of group freedom. For them, the spirit of democracy exists where there is evidence of competitive and flexible group interaction. The defining characteristic of democratic politics is the process whereby the state acts to adjust and adjudicate the competitive advantages and conflicting interests of groups. Rand Dyck argues that the term "brokerage politics" is often used to characterize this political activity "because in a pluralist system the authorities engage in wheeling and dealing with the various groups in an effort to keep them content."[79]

More recently, some liberal theorists (though notably not Flanagan) have begun to ask whether the competitive disadvantages consistently suffered by some groups in democratic contexts can justify a system of group-differentiated rights. Will Kymlicka is a leading theorist in this camp and answers in the affirmative. He argues that it is perfectly consistent with liberal principles of individual freedom and equality to offer certain minorities rights to land, language, representation, and self-government that other groups do not have. His justification for such rights is thoroughly cultural in its origin. Minority rights are justified in his view because they provide individuals with a context in which to use the cultural attributes of their communities to make choices about the direction of their lives. Cultural attributes are thus a primary good in the same sense that rights and liberties, powers and opportunities, income and wealth, and the basis for self-respect are primary goods for John Rawls.[80] Each is said to contribute a crucial element to the larger project of individual identity development. Given the pivotal role that cultures are said to play in helping individuals determine their life plans, it is only just in Kymlicka's view that minority communities be granted protection in instances where they are threatened by the superior power of the majority society that surrounds them.

In short, liberals do not object to the presence of groups in the lives of individuals. Indeed, liberals of all stripes recognize that groups play a central role in capturing resources for individuals that they could not capture acting alone. Some, such as Flanagan, argue that the existence of groups is not in and of itself a ground for granting them rights, particularly so when the normative foundation for those rights rests on what they see as dubious myths that fail to stand up to close scrutiny. Other liberals adopt the opposite approach. Some, such as Kymlicka, argue that, because groups play a central role in the lives of individuals, they should enjoy group-differentiated rights, especially in cases where their ability to capture resources for their members is consistently compromised. At the same time, however, liberals generally stand united in their commitment to the individual above all. Groups exist to serve the interests of individuals because the individual is the bottom line in what has value. As a result, while most liberals accept that democracy rests on the existence of strong, vital groups, they also insist that democracy requires individuals to be free from the demands of groups where they perceive those demands to be in conflict with their most basic interests. Hence, the form of pluralism that liberals support is individualistic at its foundation.

Third and finally, while liberals defend the right of communities to exist, what some object to is a particular defence of community by communitarians that is directed at them as a form of criticism. In general, communitarians allege that the priority liberals place on individual choice creates an individualistic ethos that impoverishes the civic and moral life of democratic culture. The net effect "is a decline in the practice of community values" and a corresponding breakdown of commitment by individuals to the public good.[81]

As distinct from liberal analysis, communitarian writing tends to flip the moral priority of individual versus community. In much communitarian analysis, individualism is never the bottom line that has value. Instead, what has value are different cultural forms of life, each of which is seen to carry its own norm for human self-creation.[82] What communitarians emphasize is that individuals are always embedded within certain cultures and traditions. Their claim is that the moral and political development of individuals is dependent on the rich cultural frameworks in which individuals are situated. Culture thus has ultimate value because cultural communities provide individuals with what is essential to their health: norms for human conduct that inspire political and moral commitment to the common good of the community.

In response, some liberals claim that communitarian arguments give prestige to community life in a way that may threaten the individual. These liberals charge that communitarians emphasize the significance of different cultures as though they were sacrosanct and in need of protection at all costs. What they fail to consider, however, is that for some persons belonging to cultural communities may not always be a positive experience; while cultural ties can give support and security, they can also restrict and entrap.[83] The problem that liberals identify, in other words, is that the mandate to preserve culture can also become the basis on which all sorts of practices and traditions are imposed on individuals against their will. As Daly argues,

"Liberals fear that a community-centred political philosophy could lead to government intrusion in private affairs and suffocating conformity in social life."[84]

On the one hand, then, some present-day liberals acknowledge with communitarians that group-differentiated rights for minority communities should be endorsed "where they promote fairness between groups."[85] But on the other hand, these liberals argue that, in most cases of conflict between community and individual liberties, the priority of individual choice should prevail. The notion of liberty defended by liberals is not intended to deny individuals their constitutive attachments. Instead, liberty is seen as a tool that individuals can use to question constitutive attachments and revise cultural norms if they become oppressive. As expressed by Jeremy Webber, "While we value our cultures ... we also value individual autonomy, the ability to take a path different from our ancestors or our neighbours, to reflect critically on our societies, to struggle to transform them, perhaps even to reject them outright."[86] Liberals argue that we must preserve the possibility of changing cultural communities for the sake of enhancing individual freedom. For this reason, they place a premium on individual autonomy so that individuals can exercise freedom of choice. All the while, however, the assumption that identity relates to cultural difference goes unchallenged. The political challenge, instead, is construed in terms of retaining the right to individual autonomy over cultural integrity in cases where the two conflict.

Relational Pluralism

The relational face of pluralism approaches group diversity less in terms of the cultural attributes of groups and more in terms of subjective self-identification, relationships, and the formative role that power has in shaping individual and communal identity. What matters from this viewpoint is not cultural difference per se but the sorts of relations that establish identity and, more pertinently, who actually wields power in defining those relations. There is thus a natural link between the identification approach to ethnic identity and the kind of analysis of group relations offered by relational pluralism. The relational approach is informed by a number of assumptions relating to the ontological basis of human subjectivity and the political ethic of plural relations that follows from this conception of sub-jectivity. I will discuss each in turn.

Individualist pluralism is informed by an understanding of human sub-jectivity in which the individual is stable, marked as such because the ra-tionality of the individual enables her to make autonomous choices based solely on her preferences. In reaction, communitarian pluralists turn their attention toward cultural and political structures and institutions, pointing out that human subjectivity is a derived property, formed in response to the effects of relevant structures on it. What is decisively relevant in each case is the notion of stability; either individual identity is stable as a result of au-tonomous choice, or it is stable as a result of deterministic and predictable patterns of cultural and political socialization.

These positions are at odds with the view of human subjectivity accen-tuated by relational pluralism.[87] Here the developmental nature of both in-dividual identity and social structures is emphasized. Relational pluralists deliberately sidestep the individual agency/social structure dichotomy by arguing that what is key to human subjectivity is the fact that "structures are constantly being made by individuals and individuals are constantly being made by structures," each mutually influencing the development and behaviour of the other.[88] There is no stability in this model of human sub-jectivity but only change, possibly significant change, over time. Individual and group identities are seen to be made and then remade in the never-ending process of interacting with other individuals and groups.

Not surprisingly, the ontology of subjectivity that informs relational pluralism is one of beings in relation, where the identities of individuals and the groups to which they belong are the products of social relations.[89] People are said to acquire their identities in relation to both other people and social structures, so they are understood to be in part a product of so-cial processes, not the origin of those processes. However, because social processes are defined as fluid by nature, they are also understood to be in a continual process of being developed and redeveloped by the individuals who act upon and within them.

That individuals can act upon social processes is most obvious with re-spect to voluntary associations. Here, as Carol Gould notes, individuals can "choose or create many of the relations into which they enter."[90] Yet even where relations are given or not open to choice, as in the case of ethnic groups, relational pluralists argue that choice is not out of the question. They point out that it is individuals who give ethnic structures such as tribes and nations their form. Just as individuals are caught up in constant processes of change and development, so too are the structures in which individuals are situated. Martha-Marie Kleinhans and Roderick A. Macdonald make the same point with respect to law: "legal subjects are not wholly determined: they possess a transformative capacity that enables them to produce legal knowledge and to fashion the very structures of law that contribute to constituting their substantive particularity."[91] In other words, even where structures are relatively enduring, those structures should not be seen as ends in themselves. Rather, for relational pluralists, they are constructions expressed in the way they are because they are deemed representative of identity in given periods of time.

Relational pluralists also emphasize that social groups, like individuals, are derived from the relational character of life. The work of Iris Marion Young is particularly instructive. She argues that social groups are collectives, differentiated from other groups by virtue of the specific affinity that members have "with one another because of their similar experiences or way of life." Young accepts the common understanding that social groups are the products of "cultural life forms, practices, or ways of life." But she is convinced that both social theory and philosophy neglect the degree to which the same cultural life forms, practices, or ways of life are always developed in the context of, and in response to, social relations with other groups. As she puts it, "group identification arises ... in the encounter and interaction between social collectivities that experience some differences in their way of life and forms of association, even if they also regard themselves as belonging to the same society."[92] So, for Young, a social group exists and achieves identity only in response to the interactive relations that it has with other groups and not by virtue of some independently derived attributes that it may possess.

Now if individual and group identities derive from an interactive process of relations, it stands to reason that power would constitute a substantive component of a political theory analyzing those relations. Relational pluralism places social groups at the heart of its political analysis because individual identities are largely determined not just by the activities of individuals but also by the relations implied by the operation of group power on them. Under these circumstances, group power has two important roles to play.

First, the political power required for genuine self-definition is far more likely to come to individuals as members of groups than as individuals standing alone. Given the significance of group membership for individual development, therefore, relational pluralism attends to questions of equalizing power between groups where identity-conferring groups are powerless and subject to marginalization.

Second, because group power mobilizes relations that shape individual identity, it is critical that groups promote the active participation of their members. Groups may be powerful relative to other groups; however, if they employ that power to shape members' identities in ways that are stifling, then the exercise of group power cannot be considered legitimate. Equalizing power between groups, in other words, needs to be complemented by the requirement that power within groups also be equalized in relevant respects.

In short, while social groups need power to shape their members, members also need power to shape their groups. From the perspective of relational pluralism, the social process of self-definition is simply incomplete unless these two levels of power are advanced in a mutually reinforcing and complementary fashion.

There are thus two normative principles for intergroup relations that follow from the relational pluralist characterization of human subjectivity: one emphasizes the political idea of equality, and the other emphasizes freedom from domination.

Relational pluralism accentuates the idea that, if individual development is to be promoted, individuals must be able to contribute to their identity-conferring groups. Moreover, if this purpose is to be concretely realized, what is required in the first instance is a commitment to equality at both individual and group levels.

All individuals are equal in the sense that each possesses an equal entitlement to define himself or herself in the context of his or her relations with others. While individuals need access to a fair distribution of social goods to accomplish this objective (e.g., the human need for food, shelter, nurturance, education, leisure, companionship, and self-esteem), they also need access to power.[93] It is this need for an equitable distribution of power that relational pluralism draws into focus.

Relational pluralists believe that individuals have a vested interest in the question of power because the development of their identities puts them in relationships with others and with social structures that involve the use of power. Consequently, when equality is understood as an equal right to define oneself, this right necessarily carries with it the right to jointly participate with others in the development of these identity-conferring relationships.[94] The rationale of the position here is straightforward: if individuals have a responsibility to define themselves, and if who individuals are is largely worked out in the context of the common activity that they undertake with others, then individuals should have an equal right to shape the objectives and directions of this common activity. Young expresses this sentiment as follows: equality "refers primarily to the full participation and inclusion of everyone in a society's major institutions, and the socially supported substantive opportunity for all to develop and exercise their capacities and realize their choices."[95] Relational pluralists also apply this principle to politics; for them, political institutions should be structured so as to encourage open dialogue, thus enhancing the possibility that, in decision-making processes, the views of all relevant stakeholders will be represented.

While relational pluralists argue that individuals need equal access to power within their identity-conferring groups, they also stress that these groups must be given room for development if the self-development of their members is to occur. These pluralists present this process of group development through the metaphor of boundaries.

To ensure the survival of a particular identity, relational pluralists argue that groups need political authority to construct boundaries around their members. These boundaries, in turn, are thought to give groups protected public space so that members can develop and then express their identities according to their own priorities. Most vexing from the perspective of relational pluralists, then, are situations in which groups find themselves to be relatively powerless in their capacity to protect their boundaries when in relationships with other groups. Penetration by outside influences is one thing, but what must be resisted are attempts at domination. Young's response in such settings is to argue for a type of social equality that requires the specific experiences, cultures, and social contributions of groups to be publicly recognized and affirmed.[96]

Young points to a strong correlation between the level of power that groups exercise in society and the capacity of group members to define themselves. As a normative theory, relational pluralism requires one to confront substantial differences in levels of power exercised by groups as a potential or actual political problem. Fundamentally required in such cases is an absence of domination. Groups should be granted that degree of independence from public authorities and one another, and that degree of self-determination over their internal affairs, to fulfill the unique functions for which they have been commissioned by their members. Of course, what groups require to be free from domination will vary depending on their functions, and this need can be assessed only on a case-by-case basis. While allowing for the different functions of groups is critical, the broader point of relational pluralists is that groups may need to maintain boundaries between themselves so that the collective existence and values of each can be safeguarded and preserved against the encroaching views of the other.

What precisely is required to promote equal relations between groups is differently identified by relational pluralists, though the objective of each amounts to the same thing. Michael Rustin, for example, argues "that particular ways of life and spheres of value need to be defended from invasion,"[97] while Michael Walzer argues that "the aim of political egalitarianism is a society free from domination."[98] Danielle Juteau, meanwhile, employs the metaphor of "boundaries" as I have done to argue that, where First Nations are concerned, they focus their claims "less on the recognition of diversity per se than on increased control over their boundaries, that is, over economic, political and socio-cultural institutions."[99] Whether the reference is to freedom from invasion or domination, or control of group boundaries, the thrust of the argument in each case is that a pluralist society is marked by its capacity to leave to groups the power to decide their own internal affairs. Groups must not be denied the capacity to develop, on their own terms, according to the lives that group members choose to lead. The standard of justice in this scheme remains purely relational. One judges the justice of a political system by the degree of independence and self-direction permitted to social groups of all kinds as they take up their relations with one another.

To summarize, relational pluralism derives its purpose from analyzing complex sets of interrelations within groups and between groups. For group identity to be accepted as an authentic form of self-expression, two evaluative standards must be met. First, adjustments must be made to the self-definition of a group in cases where external groups attempt to exercise influence for the purpose of asserting control. Groups must be able to declare who they are from their own standpoints rather than from that of another, more powerful group. Second, adjustments must be made to curtail assertions of dominance made by group members from within. Members can only be expected to accept the identities that their groups provide if they possess the power and thus the option (though some may choose not to exercise their option) to help shape those identities. Relative equality of relations and freedom from domination are thus the key normative standards of this theory. Embedded in a relational pluralist framework are principles that lay the groundwork for persons to listen to one another and treat one another as equals both as individuals and as members of groups.

Finally, there is no requirement here that pluralism needs to be both defined and measured by the degree to which groups are culturally, politically, or socially different from one another. This point bears reinforcing. Instead, group difference is established as a function of relations; it exists in places where relations among people result in choices being made about establishing boundaries between people so that certain ties of group identification can be nurtured (e.g., ancestry) and objectives fulfilled (e.g., community development). What boundaries do is relate two or more distinct groups of people together who, despite sharing some or perhaps many cultural and political attributes, nevertheless find it important to remain distinct. Relational pluralism accentuates the idea that, in the exercise of drawing boundaries, those who relate across them are not necessarily concerned about preserving unique cultural and/or political content. Instead, what they seek to do is establish a relationship in which the members of distinct communities accept that neither side will invade or attempt to dominate the other as each pursues its respective self-defining processes. What makes this form of pluralism "relational" is the fact that the degree of separation between groups is the product of an agreement secured between them; it can be greater or lesser depending on the respective aspirations of the group members involved.

In general, then, a relational understanding of pluralism rejects opposition and exclusion. From its vantage point, overlapping experiences and porous cultural boundaries between groups need not be regarded as threats to group life. It is not so much what persons agree on as the cultural character of each group that is important. Instead, it is the distinctive structure of the fundamental relations within and between groups that gives groups their unique identities. Consequently, what is a threat to groups are instances where groups and the members within them lose their capacity to remain together (i.e., identification) and where groups lose their capacity to define their own identities in their relations with other groups "in positively supportive ways."[100]

CONCLUSION

While the analytical tradition of pluralism possesses several faces, it is held together by the presupposition that group diversity is a permanent feature of most societies. Beyond simple recognition of the empirical fact of group diversity, however, pluralists are also bound together by a shared normative concern. Each wants to establish principles of justice to channel and accommodate the tensions and conflicts that inevitably arise when societal groups come into contact with one another. Where pluralists differ is in emphasis. Individualist pluralism emphasizes the importance of individual freedom and spontaneity within groups, while communitarian pluralism emphasizes the importance of preserving the common understandings and shared norms that differentiate groups from one another. Relational pluralism, meanwhile, establishes guidelines for relationships between individuals and communities in terms of criteria that uphold the right of groups to be self-defining with respect to one another while also maintaining the capacity for individual self-development within the group. The individualist, communitarian, and relational faces of pluralism employ different concepts, objects of analysis, and political emphasis, yet they are not incompatible in principle. In the final analysis, across all its faces, pluralism refers to the dispersion of power and the need to harness it in ways that contribute to human development in both group and individual settings.

Nevertheless, I believe that, in the context of this triad of pluralisms, the contemporary manifestations of Aboriginal self-government are best analyzed from the relational perspective. It is an appropriate perspective because it leads me to situate the current crisis in Aboriginal-Canadian state relations in terms of the relationship between communal identity development, group power, and equality at collective and individual levels. Framed in this way, the process by which Aboriginal political interests is advanced is placed in a broader perspective than that provided by communitarian and individualist approaches. Communitarian and individualist strategies adopt a difference approach to Aboriginal identity, which means that they situate the source of Aboriginal identity in cultural and political attributes. The process of self-government is then understood to involve a demand for that which is considered central to Aboriginal identity: the nation's right to political autonomy, cultural preservation, or both.

When relational pluralism is coupled with an identification approach to Aboriginal identity and politics, the nature of the analysis changes. Here Aboriginal identity is regarded as inherently dynamic. Thus, while attributes of nation and culture can undoubtedly be said to constitute dimensions of Aboriginal identity today, those dimensions are also regarded as capable of change over time. Consequently, what is important from this perspective is not that certain cultural and political attributes of Aboriginal identity be protected but that the Aboriginal right to be self-defining be protected. This interest in self-definition is then linked to relational pluralism's attention to the normative use of power. When linked to power, claims to self-government are said to emerge out of Aboriginal people's desire for significantly enhanced communal power so that they can choose the direction of their communal self-development, free from external domination and constraint. It is this coupling of the identification approach with relational pluralism that will inform my efforts to answer some of the fundamental moral and political questions raised by the Aboriginal struggle to be self-governing in Canada.

CHAPTER 2

APPROACHES TO ABORIGINAL IDENTITY

The challenge created by the Aboriginal emancipatory movement is usually discussed as an issue of cultural preservation or political self-determination. Both approaches accentuate the oppositional character of relationships by pointing to the multiple forms of cultural domination and political inequality that mark historical and present encounters between Aboriginal people and the Canadian state.[1] This chapter first sets the relations between Aboriginal and non-Aboriginal people in historical and contemporary contexts. Then it substantiates the claim that the field of Aboriginal political studies is dominated by a discourse that equates Aboriginal political identity with cultural and political difference. Finally, in the third and fourth parts, it introduces an alternative approach that relies on an identification approach to Aboriginal identity. I apply the identification approach to the concept of "Aboriginality" and the quest for self-government respectively.

THE HISTORICAL AND CONTEMPORARY CONTEXTS

Aboriginal claims for recognition in recent decades have precipitated a realignment of power relations between Aboriginal peoples and the Canadian state. Previously, however, and despite Aboriginal resistance, the aspirations of the settler society had largely set the terms for the relationship. Settlers did recognize that Aboriginal peoples were already present on North American soil and established in the form of societies when they arrived. Nevertheless, the colonial relationship was a dominant one in which Aboriginal peoples were unilaterally, and without consent, subjected to the superior power and influence of the settler society. Colonial and later Canadian governmental domination of the Aboriginal-state relationship flowed directly from colonial assumptions about the nature of state sovereignty and liberal democratic governance. Essentially, Canada developed a practice of dealing with Aboriginal peoples that it had inherited from the British Crown.

As the settler population increased from the mid-eighteenth century onward, demand for Aboriginal land compelled the British Crown to fashion an Aboriginal policy. This early policy was most clearly enunciated in the Royal Proclamation of 1763. By its provisions, settlers could not occupy Aboriginal territory until formally surrendered to the Crown by duly constituted and recognized Aboriginal leaders. A simple declaration of British sovereignty, therefore, was not viewed by imperial authorities as in and of itself sufficient to remove Aboriginal rights to, or interests in, the land. Instead, Aboriginal title to the land had to be formally extinguished before non-Aboriginal settlement could occur. The Royal Proclamation thus formalized two main types of conflicting relations. On the one hand, by acknowledging both that Aboriginal peoples possessed their lands and that those lands could not be arbitrarily taken, the Crown accepted the premise of Aboriginal proprietorship. But on the other, the idea that legal title could be extinguished in exchange for small and often inadequate Crown reserves, annual annuities, and limited hunting, fishing, and trapping rights points to a colonial dynamic in which Aboriginal autonomy was also denied. One can conclude, therefore, that the British were principally interested in extinguishing Aboriginal title through treaties in order to use the land for their own occupancy and profit.

Despite conflicting themes, and though largely imposed by the British, the treaties did acknowledge the reality of Aboriginal land ownership and the ongoing interest of Aboriginal peoples in preserving their distinct ways of life. Largely for this reason, many Aboriginal leaders now point to this early policy period of rough reciprocity and consent as the normative prototype for present-day claims to traditional lands, political sovereignty, and cultural rights. This early colonial history, however, was severely qualified by new policy directions adopted by the Canadian government in the late nineteenth century.

This was the period in which the Canadian state was born. Although the act of confederation committed Canada to a regime of divided sovereignty between federal and provincial governments, no constitutionally guaranteed powers were set aside for Aboriginal peoples. The doctrine of state sovereignty adopted by Canada decreed that all constitutional authority was exhaustively accounted for in the division of powers between federal and provincial legislatures. Colonial interests simply dictated that plenary power be centralized in the location of the Constitution. Consequently, Aboriginal peoples were denied any of the original or residual independent political power recognized in the Royal Proclamation's treaty process. The outcome was that Section 91(24) of the British North America (BNA) Act made Indians the sole responsibility of Parliament.

Control over "Indians and lands reserved for Indians" was exercised through laws and a series of regulations collectively contained within the Indian Act (1869).[2] An amendment to the Indian Act in 1880 established a separate Department of Indian Affairs. With acquisition of Aboriginal land for settlement and resource development purposes largely complete by the early twentieth century, the new department's goal became one of benign neglect coupled with social control and assimilation. Throughout the late nineteenth century, then, the doctrine of sovereignty that the Canadian state adopted allowed it to constitutionalize what was by then an established political practice: the Constitution Act, 1867 (BNA Act), gave the Canadian government the juridical means to dominate in its relations with Aboriginal peoples.

With juridical domination established, the original themes of political sovereignty and land appropriation gave way to new themes of religious and cultural conversion. Especially after the Second World War, the tenets of liberal democracy in particular were aggressively pursued in relations between Aboriginal peoples and Canadian society. While the themes of this cultural offensive varied, political, educational, and religious objectives of the department and the religious establishment alike were united by the assumption that Indians could be incorporated into the Canadian community of politically equal citizens only if assimilated into the general population. This assimilationist objective was to remain dominant for the better part of a century. Even as late as 1969, for example, the White Paper on Indian Policy proposed to eradicate all legal protections and measures designed to uphold the distinct status of Indian peoples on the liberal grounds that these were discriminatory and thus undesirable.[3]

It is against this historical background that present-day Aboriginal claims must be understood. The relentless and regularly aggressive assimilationist policies of the Canadian government stimulated within Aboriginal communities a deep sense of injury and injustice. Although active protest and resistance against government policy were undertaken by Aboriginal leaders throughout the past century, only in recent decades has Aboriginal protest had any appreciable effect. The introduction of the 1969 White Paper was undoubtedly the impetus that generated a new phase of far more antagonistic and contentious relations. This paper had a way of crystallizing Aboriginal protest because it threatened to obliterate Indian special status and, by extension, Indian identity in one fell swoop.

The legacy of the White Paper profoundly changed the relationship between the Canadian government and Aboriginal peoples. As P.G. McHugh points out, however, the realignment of relations that this modern protest movement set off follows the same trajectory as that established by the colonial relations of the past. Relations continue to be depicted in the dichotomous terms of colonized and colonizer, of oppressed and oppressor.[4] This dynamic is manifested in many Aboriginal leaders' propensity to depict their relations with the Canadian state in oppositional terms. The rights of the Crown are contrasted with those of Aboriginal nations, most often in the form of competing cultures and sovereignties. Colonialism is thus defined by Aboriginal leaders in vertical terms: cultural distinctiveness and political sovereignty are said to have been denied to Aboriginal nations by the Canadian state's unilateral and illegitimate exercise of authority over them.

McHugh also argues that the solution that Aboriginal leaders advance to overcome colonialism is often no less oppositional. Aboriginal nations are said to have been dispossessed, so the key element in Aboriginal leaders' political claims is restitution. Restitution is then identified in the dual form of reappropriation of traditional lands and resources and restoration of original political sovereignty. The picture that emerges is one in which

Aboriginal leaders seek to shift the fulcrum of power from a vertical one of colonizer and colonized to a horizontal one of co-equal cultures and nations. As in the past, however, opposition and antagonism remain at the centre of the relationship. The difference in the new age of revitalization is that Aboriginal leaders have been able to rehabilitate the concepts and themes associated with their subjugation to their own advantage. Reappropriation and sovereignty are now conceptual tools that Aboriginal leaders employ "to attack the state institutions that have been the source of their discontent."[5]

I believe, however, that to cast the relationship between Aboriginal peoples and the Canadian state in terms of an opposition between competing cultures and nations is to participate in a form of binary reductionism. It is undeniable that the leaders of Aboriginal peoples and the Canadian state compete for available resources and political power. Moreover, this competition is often fierce since Aboriginal leaders regularly wish to expand their access to territorial and political resources that Canadian governments are reluctant to relinquish. However, the presumption that this oppositional struggle forms the core of the Aboriginal revitalization movement is both undersophisticated and inaccurate if not conjoined to a second set of struggles.

In recent years, the antagonistic nature of Aboriginal-state relations has been complicated by struggles within and between Aboriginal nations as well as by struggles that Aboriginal persons take up outside the formal structures of their nations. Thus, while nations remain a central locus of Aboriginal identification, McHugh argues that depicting relations in the dichotomous terms of Aboriginal nation versus the Canadian state fails to reflect the increasing complexity that Aboriginal identity has undergone in response to demographic and other influences that have shaped Aboriginal communities in recent decades. Chief among these influences are the effects of urbanization and the growth of Aboriginal feminist and youth movements. While many of the affected individuals remain within the formal structures of their nations, many others find themselves outside these structures, often not by choice. Moreover, for those on the outside, a significant proportion do not regard themselves as any less Aboriginal for being so.

These changes have considerably complicated the Aboriginal revitalization project. In addition to working out the contrast associated with

Aboriginal-state relations, Aboriginal individuals are forced to struggle among themselves for power and influence. Most identify with the project of decolonization. But depending on one's location, position, or ideological predisposition, the visions of self-determination that Aboriginal leaders hold for their people can vary considerably.

ABORIGINAL IDENTITY AS DIFFERENCE

Most approaches that provide normative justification for Aboriginal rights, and the right to self-government in particular, are deficient in their ability to deal simultaneously with these two sets of struggles. At present, one finds two prominent emphases with respect to justification of Aboriginal self-government, both of which take their point of orientation from the difference approach to identity as discussed in the previous chapter. The emphases share the same approach to Aboriginal identity: elements of Aboriginal identity are said to be found in the attributes associated with Aboriginal culture and nationhood. These attributes of identity are then understood to undergird historical and moral claims to self-government: it is justified because it sustains an Aboriginal right to cultural survival and because it restores residual powers of Aboriginal sovereignty. Such approaches one finds, for example, in authoritative works by Taiaiake Alfred, Menno Boldt, Will Kymlicka, Patrick Macklem, James Tully, and Jeremy Webber. Explaining the relation between these purportedly fundamental cultural and political elements of identity is what then characterizes the analysis of those engaged in the study of Aboriginal politics.

According to Alfred, Aboriginal leaders single out attributes associated with culture and nation because they are thought to emphasize in the starkest possible terms the unique character of their individual and collective identities from the non-Aboriginal mainstream.[6] Macklem argues further that notions of cultural difference and unique historical nationhood are used by Aboriginal leaders to premise their "demands for greater control over their individual and collective identities and a restructuring of the Canadian state to accommodate indigenous difference."[7]

Others accept the significance of both culture and nation for Aboriginal communal identity but then tend to use one or the other concept as the lead in their analysis. For example, Webber argues that Aboriginal peoples seek, above all, to reclaim their cultural heritage because they want to "re-build their confidence as Kwakiutl, Ojibway, or Métis, and to carry that identity with them in their engagement with contemporary Canadian society."[8] Webber recognizes the significance of nationhood for Aboriginal communities, but he argues that nationhood and associated claims for self-government should be understood as attributes used principally to preserve culture. For him, elements of culture are central because together they constitute a comprehensive way of life, defining all that is important to Aboriginal people, including their activities, occupations, and most important relationships. As he puts it, Aboriginal peoples do not want their identities washed out in a sea of undifferentiated Canadian citizenship.[9]

Consequently, Webber believes that when Aboriginal leaders utilize the language of nationhood, they do so because they want to preserve their cultural identities as distinct peoples as well as safeguard the uniqueness of their own social institutions.[10] From his perspective, it is incumbent upon Canadians to recognize Aboriginal communities as distinct cultures because not doing so amounts to denying them the right to express their cultural differences and thus, by extension, their identities.

Tully also employs culture as the lead concept in his analysis of Aboriginal identity. While he accepts that cultures overlap, are interactive, and are internally negotiated, he also ascribes to culture an irreducible role because he sees culture as constitutive of identity.[11] Aboriginal communities have governed themselves "by their own institutions and authoritative traditions of interpretation" for centuries, says Tully, and in doing so they give expression to the distinct cultural "customs and ways" that lie at the heart of what it means to be Aboriginal.[12]

With the source of Aboriginal identity framed in this way, the political question of paramount concern for Tully becomes how we are to render justice to the demands for cultural recognition. One thing that we ought not to do, he argues, is build a constitutional order that seeks "to impose one cultural practice" on everyone; to do so would effectively undermine those distinct cultural resources that Aboriginal individuals need to form their own sense of self-respect.[13] Rather, the constitutional solution lies in mutual recognition of both parties (Canadian and Aboriginal) "as independent and self-governing nations."[14] Why is this his proposed solution? Because, for him, self-government is a tool that Aboriginal peoples need if they are to express the particular variant of cultural diversity central to their identity. Thus, it seems that for Tully cultural recognition is the ontological need of first order, and self-government receives its justification because it constitutes the instrumental means by which that need is met.

Alfred, on the other hand, tends to switch the relationship between culture and nation around. He argues that Aboriginal leaders' political activity ought to be characterized in terms of efforts to reconstruct elements of Aboriginal nationhood. In his view, explanations that begin here possess the necessary depth to see that what Aboriginal persons are actually doing is reacting against historical patterns of Western political and cultural hegemony.[15] In other words, Alfred understands assertions of Aboriginal nationhood to constitute struggles for political independence so that Aboriginal communities can use that independence to revive cultural traditions "eroded through the operation of Western colonialism."[16]

Situating Aboriginal cultural identity within the framework of nationalism in the way that Alfred does encourages non-Aboriginal persons to see Aboriginal identity in a slightly different way. For him, Aboriginal people want to exercise a degree of political authority over their traditional lands, resources, and communities because it is control in these areas that he believes gives Aboriginal communities the ability to preserve their distinct cultural identities. Alfred's point, in other words, is that the principal source of Aboriginal communities' distinctiveness resides in this attribute of nationhood: "the distinct culture, identity, and indigenous institutions" are the core elements that, when taken together, comprise Aboriginal nationality.[17] From this perspective, what Aboriginal people are said to want is to be "recognized and respected as equals in the community of nations."[18] Consequently, it is incumbent upon Canadians to restore and respect those remnants of sovereignty still left to Aboriginal communities.

Macklem uses the concepts of culture and nation as central to his analysis of Aboriginal identity as well; however, rather than give one or the other priority, he regards them as mutually supportive and representative of distinct interests and realities. He argues that Aboriginal difference or identity corresponds to "interests associated with culture, territory, sovereignty, and the treaty process."[19] He sees each as deserving constitutional protection but for different reasons. Cultural and territorial interests deserve constitutional protection because they sustain a shared intelligibility to Aboriginal existence and sustain the unique spiritual connections to ancestral lands that "shape the formation of individual and collective identities."[20] Political sovereignty and interests associated with the treaty process, in turn, deserve constitutional protection because doing so guarantees Aboriginal lawmaking power and guarantees the "terms and conditions of Aboriginal and non-Aboriginal co-existence."[21] These four "complex social facts," as Macklem calls them, inform and sustain Aboriginal identity in both its cultural and its national manifestations.[22] Thus, for him, culture and nation are equivalent attributes in the same Aboriginal communal identity.

These commentators do not agree about whether Aboriginal communal identity should be conceptualized in terms of culture or nation. Nor do they agree about what kind of recognition Aboriginal communities require from the state if they are to flourish in the Canadian context.[23] The arguments within this debate are not what is important here. What is important for my purposes is the general character of the debate itself. Commentators not only accept that Aboriginal peoples define themselves politically with reference to selected attributes, but they also lodge with those attributes the most significant aspects of Aboriginal identity. According to this line of reasoning, if we are to understand Aboriginal political activity, then we must frame it in terms of the desire of Aboriginal persons to rebuild traditional elements of their cultures and nations. What follows is the construction of a claims-based model patterned on the difference approach to Aboriginal identity. Since Aboriginal communities are said to have a moral right to rebuild the attributes of their distinctive cultures, nations, or both, and since Canadians are not letting them do so, this moral right should be safeguarded through the provision of legal and constitutional rights. The literature is then dominated by themes fixated on appropriation, dispossession, and the Aboriginal right to restitution through land claims and political self-determination.

While resolution of historical grievances is both a necessary and a critical component in the renewal of relations between Aboriginal communities and the Canadian state, there are also significant limitations associated with explanations that rely on a difference approach to analyzing Aboriginal identity.[24]

The first consequence of analyzing Aboriginal identity in terms of claims that flow from attributes is that doing so projects the image that

Aboriginal people are preoccupied with the assertion of the properties of their groups. The properties of culture and nation are taken both as fundamental declarations of who Aboriginal people are and as normative claims "to right the injustices which those identities help to make visible."[25] Now, while this interpretation is by no means false, it remains incomplete, and in my view much more is at stake. It assumes that for Aboriginal persons at least the terms of their identities are largely settled. Aboriginal persons simply share cultural and political markers of identity that have been "transformed into [a] subjectively felt basis for social identification."[26] The object of theoretical interest then lies in analyzing how these attributes are employed by Aboriginal persons as a basis for changing the existing rules between themselves and non-Aboriginal society. Unwittingly, however, this approach precludes from serious discussion the fundamental and prior question of how and under what terms Aboriginal persons adopt the attributes associated with culture and nation as the principal markers of their identities in the first place.

Moreover, the approach promotes the view that Aboriginal identity is coterminous with historical and not present forms of cultural and political organization. Colonialism is understood to have thwarted traditional expressions of Aboriginal life. The emancipatory goal is then crafted in rehabilitative terms; Aboriginal communities should be given opportunities to reconstruct the residual sources of their cultures and historical nations interrupted by European settlement. However, to focus on the representational carrying capacity of historical "cultures" and "nations" may be to imbue these understandings with too much legitimacy for the present day. Aboriginal societies have been irrevocably changed as a result of contact and the associated history of demographic change. Urbanization in particular has profoundly affected Aboriginal persons, placing many outside the traditional structures of their cultures and nations. So, while the historical attributes of culture and nation and their associated claims may have been important for bringing Aboriginal issues back into the collective consciousness of Canadians, a significant broadening and deepening of relations between Aboriginal peoples and the Canadian polity are also taking place. It is this dimension of flux and process, of ambiguity and complexity, normally associated with relationship building that is missing from the analyses of the commentators cited above.

A second consequence of framing identity in terms of culture or nation is that relations between Aboriginal communities and the Canadian state are identified in terms of unequal access to power. What results is an image in which Aboriginal people and the Canadian state are locked in an adversarial and acrimonious relationship. Naturally, the capacity of majority groups to grant or withhold recognition to the identity-conferring attributes of Aboriginal communities involves the exercise of power. Indeed, one could argue that Aboriginal leaders feature attributes of culture and nation as central to their communal identities precisely because the differences implied by their use demand certain kinds of objective results. For example, on a fundamental level, the meanings associated with "culture" and "nation" demand equivalency: because Aboriginal communities constitute cultures and nations, they are justified in demanding equitable standing and resources with the other constitutionally protected cultures and nations that make up Canada.

Yet this emphasis on equivalency encourages the development of a claims-based relationship with the Canadian state that is largely adversarial. Each side attempts to acquire as much as possible or give up as little as possible to the other on the purported premise that gains or losses at the other's expense jeopardize the ability of each to function as a culture or nation to its respective constituency. Claims are therefore disputatious and the resulting relationship tense. Relations are analyzed with respect to confrontation – typically culture versus culture, nation versus nation, and nation versus individual. What gets lost in the process is the possibility of developing models of politics that are less antagonistic and identities that are more complex, layered, and overlapping: a condition that economic circumstances seems to require and that political circumstances could promote.

Furthermore, characterizing relations in terms of a struggle over resources and political standing perpetuates the colonial relationship of oppressor and oppressed. In making a claim, Aboriginal peoples cast themselves on the goodwill of the Canadian state since it can either accept or reject the claim. So, while claims to cultural and political standing imply equivalency, they can actually reinforce unequal power relations. The rehabilitation of Aboriginal peoples' cultures and nations demands of the Canadian state a concurrent willingness to rehabilitate itself from its historical relations of cultural and political domination. According to Claude

Denis, the fact that the state possesses the political ability to refuse to engage in this enterprise of rehabilitation "is what makes Canada, still today,
a colonialist society."[27] The question is whether Aboriginal peoples and the
Canadian state are well served by the perpetuation of images that lock both
into adversarial rather than cooperative relations.

A third, closely related outcome of the difference perspective is that, because the concept linked to the attribute remains constant (i.e., culture and
nation), the identity associated with the attribute is sometimes regarded as
primordial and fixed.[28] Obscured in the process is that assertions to culture
and/or nationhood are normally stimulated by the political climate of the
period; they emerge, recede, and reconfigure themselves in response to external pressures and opportunities. For example, the construction of identity involves individuals who sometimes struggle against one another in
their attempts to create and maintain different kinds of cultural and political categories as well as meanings and relationships within their shared social world. Consequently, Aboriginal communities should not be thought
of simply as concerned with the preservation of their cultural and political
identities. Rather, they should be seen as communities whose members
struggle with one another to mobilize attributes for the explicit intent of
defending special interests, whether they be political, economic, cultural, or
otherwise.

So one distinct outcome of linking Aboriginal identity to the attributes
of culture and nation is that doing so can reify Aboriginal identity and accentuate Aboriginal difference in the form of adversarial relations with the
Canadian state.[29] However, the dichotomization encouraged by this approach is, in my view, simply too stark because it fails to capture the significant complexity of contemporary Aboriginal life. The approach perpetuates
the idea that Aboriginal individuals are completely ensconced within and
constituted by the cultures and nations of which they are a part or that they
are not. Within this framework, there is seemingly little option for cultural
or national involvement to a greater or lesser degree or that cultural or national identity can be possessed in greater or smaller measures. With identity so rigidly codified in this way, it is therefore not surprising that
Aboriginal cultures and nations alone are able to demand a monopoly on
the Canadian state's attention.

ABORIGINAL IDENTITY AS IDENTIFICATION

In the previous chapter, I showed how the identification approach to identity defines ethnicity in terms of particular kinds of relationships within and between groups. A central element in this analysis is that ethnic groups exist because individuals identify with them, not because of "any intrinsic characteristics that they may possess."[30] Here, in other words, there is no objective requirement that a group must exemplify certain cultural or political attributes to qualify as an ethnic group. What, if anything, happens to an analysis of Aboriginal identity in Canada if we regard that identity as a particular manifestation of ethnicity in this way? Does this approach shed any light on the question of how the cultural and national aspects of Aboriginal identity might be understood? Here three critical points come to mind.

In the first place, because ethnicity is defined as an aspect of relations, Aboriginal identity only makes sense in the context of the presence of a non-Aboriginal "other." As Paul Tennant argues, "Aboriginal" is a word used to distinguish people already established in a place from those who came later as colonists.[31] Seen this way, all Aboriginal peoples are products of the interrelationships between Euro-Canadian settlers and the original occupants of the land.

The political meaning of Aboriginality, moreover, is given particular urgency because the concept emerged in response to colonial relations. That is, Aboriginality is a special form of ethnicity because it contains the twofold suggestion that Aboriginal peoples were both prior and original occupants of the land and that they have suffered as a result of the settlement of their territory. In this vein, Tennant argues that the essential difference implied by the relationship between Aboriginal and non-Aboriginal peoples "relates to political power and influence, for by its very nature colonialism subjugates aboriginal peoples without their consent."[32] The term "Aboriginal" thus carries with it the idea that the group of people to whom the term applies were subordinated by the settler state, treated as outsiders, and regarded as inferiors.

This condition of original occupation coupled with subjugation without consent is in turn the origin of the idea that a people already in place retain rights even after others have taken over their land. By linking the

concept of "Aboriginality" to ethnicity in this way, Aboriginal peoples' political position in Canada is thus seen to be strengthened. The relationship
implied by the concept demands of the settler state remedial obligations to
Aboriginal peoples in the form of fulfilling their rights.[33]

The experience of Aboriginality is thus understood to be a product of
the relations that exist between colonizing and colonized groups. But being
Aboriginal is also understood to be a product of internal relations. The key
element here is identification. The bond that Aboriginal identity provides
individuals is understood to be based on a shared connection through ancestry to the original occupants of the land and a shared history "of having
to deal with the effects of colonialism (racism; prejudice; loss of culture,
land, and population)."[34] David Mayberry-Lewis notes that the salient
characteristic of Aboriginal peoples "is that they were marginal to and
dominated by the states that claim to have jurisdiction over them."[35]
Conspicuously absent in this formulation of identity is any formal requirement that identification by individuals with their Aboriginal communities
must be based on shared attributes of culture or nationhood. Of course,
Aboriginal individuals may share one or more attributes of culture or nationhood, and those attributes may well serve to differentiate them from
non-Aboriginal people. But the point is that the character of the relationship and the strength of the boundaries between Aboriginal communities
and the Canadian state need not by definition be connected to the resiliency
of cultural and national differences.

This identification approach to Aboriginal identity is a slight departure
from the understanding of identity adopted by most. Commentators are
often loath to link ethnic identity to spurious notions of "race" and "blood"
that dominated earlier historical efforts to identify Aboriginal people. To escape notions of race and blood, commentators often use criteria of cultural
competence instead. Will Kymlicka, for example, insists that, with respect to
national groups, membership should in principle be open to anyone regardless of race and colour provided that prospective members are "willing
to learn the language and history of the society and are willing to participate in its social institutions."[36] For Kymlicka, then, descent-based approaches to membership possess racist overtones and are therefore
manifestly unjust.

The identification approach contains a built-in challenge to Kymlicka's assumption. Some note, for example, that most Aboriginal peoples in Canada employ some form of descent-based criteria for community membership to little controversy.[37] Descent from a precolonial people also constitutes a standard judicial requirement for entitlement to Aboriginal rights in Canada.[38] Descent-based criteria, in other words, need not be ruled out if they depart from a strict blood-based quantum and instead allow for possibly nonracial, nondiscriminatory factors.

When employing the identification approach, then, Aboriginal identity is defined as the outcome of a threefold experience. The experience of colonization both shapes and reinforces the awareness of Aboriginal identity as a form of ethnic identity. Aboriginal identity is furthermore the outcome of a process of self-definition by those linked to one another through the experience of colonization. Having been marginalized in the past, the political project of Aboriginal peoples is often presented as their desire to survive as distinct communities, a process said to involve their right to control the building of their community identities. And where Aboriginal peoples look for some qualification of community identification over and above the desire to be self-defining, there is the added factor of connection through descent.

Removing cultural and national difference from the centre of Aboriginal identity leads directly to the second point of the identification approach. When we consider where Aboriginal identity is derived from, we ought to look at the self-defining processes of Aboriginal peoples themselves.[39] Their associations with elements of their cultures and nations ought to be viewed not as ends in themselves but as manifestations of a process of ongoing relations in which they make both conscious and unconscious choices about the individual and communal directions of their lives.

Thus, from the perspective of community, Aboriginal identity is said to exist because persons who happen to share ancestry, historical elements of culture and politics, and experiences of colonization decide that it is important to be members of the same communities. Aboriginal communities are then understood to use their rules of descent and elements of traditional culture and politics to develop points of identification within the community and boundaries between group members and the larger Canadian society. All such efforts are further identified as part of the larger Aboriginal interest to defend territorial rights and the right to define their own ways of life.

In practice, most such communities will be what are commonly referred to as First Nations.[40] In principle, such communities could develop as urban Aboriginal persons of diverse ethnic backgrounds, as tribal councils, as organizations at local and provincial levels, or as Aboriginal persons at the pan-Canadian level, such as the Assembly of First Nations (AFN). However, existing First Nations communities are central to my analysis because

- they have long-established relations with the Canadian government;
- they have a distinct constitutional status and are the bearers of Aboriginal rights, including that of Aboriginal self-government however recognized or implemented;
- they have a continuing or former identity as an Indian Act band that provides members with common experiences and perceptions;
- they have a unique location and a land base that infuse their identity;
- they have a governing structure;
- they provide both political and social settings in which individuals can gain and maintain their personal Aboriginal identities; and
- they have fiscal resources enabling them to carry out community activities.

Many First Nations are small in both population and reserve size, making it difficult and perhaps unrealistic for some of them to administer the services and financial resources necessary for self-government. First Nations may therefore choose to delegate authority to political entities such as tribal councils in functional areas beyond their capacity such as policy development, higher education, and human resource training. However, it is First Nations at the band level that are invested with statutory political authority, and for this reason they are the focus of my attention.

It is in the light of this ongoing identity development that current Aboriginal aspects of culture and nation are situated. Those who employ the identification approach see them less as single and universal sources of Aboriginal identity than as particular expressions of that identity crafted to meet and repel external pressure applied against the boundaries of Aboriginal communities. Of course, it is generally accepted that Aboriginal persons often do possess a deep historical sense and that many have struggled hard to preserve traditional cultural and political institutions in the face of unrelenting adversity. But the larger point that the identification approach draws into focus is that, whatever the status of their continuity with the past, of greater interest is how elements of culture and nationhood are used to secure resources for Aboriginal communities so that their members can safeguard and develop the experience of identity for Aboriginal individuals in the present.

The third and final implication of the identification approach is that, because the attributes of groups are seen to constitute aspects of identity rather than their origin, the scope of Aboriginal identity need not be confined to cultural and/or national attributes alone. What is regarded as primary here, in other words, is the experience of Aboriginal identity itself and not any one particular cultural and/or national manifestation of that identity.

Of course, it is recognized that Aboriginal individuals may choose to draw greatest political attention to the fact that they are members of nations, but this does not mean that national attributes have to monopolize all identity options. Rather, central to the identification approach is simple evidence of individual attachment to an Aboriginal community as a primary source of personal identity.

One can illustrate what is at issue here by thinking of Aboriginal identity in terms of a continuum. At one end of the continuum are those Canadian citizens who possess Aboriginal ancestry but for whom this fact has little if any appreciable effect on their identities. Some of these individuals may have Aboriginal ancestry but be unaware of it, while others may know that they have Aboriginal ancestry but choose not to make it a basis for identifying with a functioning Aboriginal community. This category can also include persons who may belong to a First Nations community but who choose not to identify with it in any meaningful way. Given the importance of individual community attachment for the identification approach, this category of persons will receive little attention in the chapters that follow.

At the other end of the continuum are those Aboriginal persons who would consider themselves Aboriginal in identity and would identify themselves as Aboriginal in most if not all situations. Many of these Aboriginal individuals may live on reserves, while many others may live off reserves. This distinction concerning location is largely irrelevant in my view since there is no necessary connection between Aboriginal identity and location of residence as far as many of these individuals are concerned. What is crucial for my purposes, however, is that in almost every case these persons will identify with, or aspire to attain membership in, a local Aboriginal community. In practical terms, Aboriginal persons who leave their First Nation for employment or other purposes will say that their "home" remains within their community. It is to this category of persons that I will direct my attention.

ETHNICITY AND ABORIGINAL SELF-GOVERNMENT

This is a good place to approach one final theme: the relation of the concept of ethnicity to Aboriginal self-government. Many Aboriginal leaders argue that the starting point for future relationships between Aboriginal peoples and the Canadian state must be recognition of the Aboriginal right to self-government. Importantly, this right has moved today from the realm of discourse and advocacy into the realm of emerging political practice. The federal government, for example, has not only indicated a willingness to negotiate self-government agreements but has also recognized the right as an "existing Aboriginal right" under section 35(1) of the Constitution Act, 1982.[41]

On one level, it is undeniable that the relative success of the Aboriginal self-government movement is because Canadian governments now make qualitative distinctions between ethnic and national groups and the kinds of claims advanced by each.[42] Ethnic groups are usually defined as immigrants who typically carry with them a shared language and culture and who are interested in having Canadians recognize some manifestation of their diversity per se.[43] At the same time, ethnic communities are understood to be content to integrate into mainstream Canada provided that they can preserve some degree of their ethnocultural distinctiveness.[44]

It is further generally accepted that what differentiates national groups such as Aboriginal nations from ethnic groups is the fact that they possess a fundamentally different status based on a very different relationship. Aboriginal nationalism is essentially seen as a response to colonialism: Aboriginal nations existed prior to European settlement and never consented to become subject to the political rule of the non-Aboriginal majority.[45] Understood in this way, ethnic communities simply do not possess many of the characteristics of nations. They represent fundamentally distinct historical formations. While ethnic groups wish to retain their cultural integrity, they accept the authority of the larger society. Nations, on the other hand, aspire to a separate power base reinforced by the acceptance of parallel institutions. It seems, then, that to regard Aboriginality in a way that links Aboriginal nationhood to that of ethnicity is to commit a considerable conceptual error. Indeed, as Alfred argues, given the history and the kinds of claims that Aboriginal leaders advance, much more can be learned if we regard Aboriginal political activity as a manifestation of nationalism.[46]

So, given the unambiguous assertion of power that apparently flows from a national identity, why might one want to categorize Aboriginal identity in terms promoted by the identification approach? Why not rigidly insist that, outside nations, Aboriginal persons cannot retain Aboriginal identity? One answer provided by the identification approach is that through it one can build in greater flexibility where Aboriginal political identity is concerned. As a form of identification, Aboriginality alerts us to the fact that what is paramount is that Aboriginal persons bound together through shared history, location, and communal ties of ancestry and culture be given room to define themselves across the range of identity options that might occur to them. In other words, Aboriginal peoples and Canadians should recognize one another as equals who coexist as communities and who possess the right to be self-defining across the many relations that draw them together. There is no requirement here that this process of self-definition must occur from behind the boundaries of nations for it to be authentic or result in distinctive cultural practices for it to possess legitimacy. Furthermore, insisting that Aboriginal peoples' political activities be understood as manifestations of nationalism can also typecast state-Aboriginal relations in confrontational and incompatible terms. The images associated with "radical challenges" and "upheavals" in relations, for example, as sometimes used so provocatively by some commentators, carry with them the idea that the sovereignty of Aboriginal peoples can be won only when wilfully set against the sovereignty of the Canadian state.

The clearest expression of this kind of confrontational approach arises from the ongoing question about the origin of the Aboriginal right to self-government. In the "delegated" version, Aboriginal peoples exercise governmental authority because they have been granted powers from the Canadian state. Here all power is concentrated in the hands of the state, to be both distributed and rescinded according to the priorities set by the Canadian government itself. In the "inherent" version, Aboriginal peoples exercise governmental authority immediately. Here Aboriginal peoples are the self-authorizing source of their own political power by virtue of their precontact status and history as autonomous nations. By implication, they exercise their right to self-government independently of any permission granted to them by the Canadian state or authority conferred on them by the Constitution.

What these images of "delegated" versus "inherent" sources of political authority convey is that there are two distinct political systems in competition. The federal government asserts dominance over Aboriginal peoples, while Aboriginal peoples counter with their own claim to political independence. When claims are rigidly set against one another in this way, it is difficult to see how relations of interdependence could be both necessary and beneficial to both partners.[47]

The identification approach can be seen as providing an avenue for softening this kind of confrontation. It preserves the possibility that Aboriginal identity is not rigidly confined to attributes of traditional culture or nation but is a more evolving dynamic that can shift and change in response to the reconfigurations of Aboriginal political practices and interests over time. From this perspective, nations should be seen as political tools that Aboriginal leaders use to establish boundaries between their communities and the Canadian government for the purpose of capturing the resources that they identify as central to their communities' capacity to be self-defining. This means that, just as Aboriginal community identity is complex, evolving, and nuanced, so too is the potential range of expressions of Aboriginal political relationships. Naturally, this approach does not provide a guarantee against political confrontation, nor should it when to engage in confrontation delivers to Aboriginal communities precisely those resources that they need to sustain and develop their communities. It does, however, highlight the degree to which different kinds of political choices can be made, thus creating room for moving from confrontation to cooperation. I will say much more about the implications of this approach for the politics of Aboriginal self-government in Chapter 5.

CONCLUSION

Two conclusions can be drawn from an identification approach to the study of Aboriginal identity. First, the approach links Aboriginal identity to the experience of belonging to and identifying with a community of shared ancestry and historical continuity. Conspicuously absent from this approach is any formal requirement that the criteria for having Aboriginal identity lie in cultural and/or national attributes. Aboriginal communities, in other words, do not need to be culturally distinct or have political accomplishments as nations to be considered Aboriginal. Second, the approach highlights the degree to which Aboriginal identity development is inherently dynamic, always a process rather than a result. The assumption here is that, because Aboriginal communities change, so too will their political forms. By framing the development of identity in this way, the perspective provides a way of broadening relationships within and across Aboriginal communities; the integrity of Aboriginal identity is defined as much by the nature of the relations that they have with others as it is by any specific characteristics that are uniquely their own.

I noted in the previous chapter that pluralism constitutes an analytical tradition that not only conceptualizes politics in terms of the group basis of life but also devises strategies for its recognition in democratic contexts. When applied to Aboriginal politics, what assumptions do the various faces of pluralism incorporate into their assessments of Aboriginal identity? How do they regard Aboriginal identity in its origins? Furthermore, how do these assumptions bear upon the normative justification that each offers in support of a right to self-government? The chapters that follow take up the communitarian, individualist, and relational faces of pluralism in turn and seek to answer these questions.

CHAPTER 3

ABORIGINAL CULTURE, NATION, AND THE POLITICS OF DIFFERENCE

My empirical point of departure for the communitarian view that Aboriginal political boundaries should be coterminous with cultural boundaries will be the hearings and the report of the Royal Commission on Aboriginal Peoples (RCAP). In carrying out my assessment, I first identify a number of the central organizing concepts and terms that some Aboriginal witnesses used before RCAP to define their general situation within Canada as well as to justify their political aspiration for self-government. I then assess the extent to which communitarian assumptions are embodied in the report of RCAP and thus shape its policy proposals and recommendations. Finally, I discuss the implications that flow from the idea that Aboriginal communities are entitled to self-government because of their cultural and political differences.

IDENTITY AND BOUNDARIES

The Hearings

Released on 21 November 1996, the Royal Commission's report consti-tutes the capstone of a remarkable five-year process in which an enormous mobilization effort was undertaken through both public hearings and re-search to examine virtually every facet of Aboriginal life in Canada.[1] Negotiations leading to the Charlottetown constitutional accord immediately preceded and ran parallel to the public hearings of RCAP. However, unlike the Charlottetown Accord, which involved highly specialized Aboriginal elites negotiating the terms of abstract constitutional principles with non-Aboriginal specialized elites, the hearings of RCAP were organized to get closer to the Aboriginal grassroots. Indeed, this was the intention of the hearings; RCAP was told that it must "travel extensively to Aboriginal communities and ... let Aboriginal persons tell their stories in person."[2] RCAP was interested in hearing from anyone who wished to express views on Aboriginal issues in Canada and provided every available means for individuals to do so.

What made the widespread public hearings phase of RCAP so distinctive was the degree to which they were expressive of a breadth of Aboriginal identity claims unprecedented in Canadian history. Persons who came forward ranged from presidents and grand chiefs of major Aboriginal organizations, to executive directors, research directors, and staff of smaller organizations, to chiefs of bands, nations, and tribal groups, and in some instances to individuals speaking on their own behalf.[3] Never before within a single set of public hearings had so many Aboriginal persons and organizations articulated the range of aspirations for their future and the forms of recognition that they demand from Canadian society. The report and the transcripts of the public hearings phase thus provide an unparalleled lens through which to examine the modern identity aspirations of Canada's Aboriginal peoples afresh.

RCAP conducted more than half of its hearings in northern and Aboriginal communities, away from urban Canada.[4] While witnesses "came from different backgrounds and cultures and spoke of differing experiences, interests, needs and desires ... most agreed on the need for a dramatic change in the relationship between Aboriginal and non-Aboriginal people."[5] There is a remarkable consistency across Canada in the concepts and categories that many witnesses used to tell their stories of past experiences and of present and future aspirations. These concepts and categories can be reduced to five key themes: a tragic and heroic past, exploitation, resistance and healing, cultural contradiction, and nationalism.[6]

A TRAGIC AND HEROIC PAST Foremost among themes in the testimony of some witnesses is the emphasis placed on history. These witnesses repeatedly portray precolonial history as a golden age; it is characterized by harmony and peaceful living with Mother Earth, self, others, community, and nations. Contact with European powers is then described as having turned this Aboriginal world upside down. What then follows in a number of these accounts is the charge that colonial governments are responsible for obliterating much of the social, political, economic, and spiritual fabric of Aboriginal societies. In fact, witnesses sometimes state that they believe colonial governments sought to undermine Aboriginal nations simply because they were seen as obstacles to European development. In this rendition of history, the overall impression one gets is that, for many Aboriginal persons, colonial and Canadian governments are seen as deceitful and destructive because they deliberately refused to recognize what those witnesses take to be the rightful place and dignity of Aboriginal nations.

A lightning rod for much testimony in this genre is the perceived duplicity of governmental action with respect to treaties. Witnesses generally insist that treaties were intended to uphold European recognition that Aboriginal societies were nations with entitlements to political standing equal to that of European powers. Yet some of the same witnesses say that treaties were often interpreted by Europeans as proxies for wholesale Aboriginal consent to the extinguishment of their sovereignty, traditional governments, and rights to control lands and resources. As expressed by one, "The strategy was clear, but yet we were naive to believe that their intentions were good. We thought they were here to improve the well-being of their people as well as the well-being of our own. We didn't know that they came to destroy our land, but more importantly, to destroy our nation."[7] This theme of historical deceit is regularly reinforced by corresponding expressions of anger: "if our ancestors could have seen in the future when they welcomed early explorers to this land, they would never, never have let them land."[8]

EXPLOITATION In places, witnesses use catastrophic adjectives to describe what they see as ongoing damage to Aboriginal communities suffered at the hands of the dominant society: "deterioration almost to the point of extinction";[9] "victims of a stubborn and destructive federal bias";[10] "endured the repression of cultural genocide";[11] to "lose our languages [will be to] have lost everything";[12] and "development has brought nothing but disaster to our people."[13] In this context, witnesses make frequent references to Aboriginal communities' loss of all but a fraction of their traditional territories and with it the means to their own livelihood.[14] The result of loss of livelihood is said by some to have entangled vast numbers of Aboriginal individuals in the dehabilitating snare of the welfare state, itself described as only a temporary way station on the route to crushing poverty.

Many see the roots of this tragedy going even deeper. In much testimony, witnesses link loss of land to loss of connection to the source of Aboriginal spirituality since "the Creator has made us the caretakers of the land."[15] This disconnection, coupled with the suppression and outlawing of Aboriginal languages, religions, and social and political institutions, removed for many what they identify as Aboriginal peoples' most stable anchors in life. The claim that follows in the testimony of many witnesses is that they have suffered grievously from colonially instigated violence. It is a violence in which Aboriginal identity is often said to have been literally beaten out of an entire generation through instruments such as the child welfare system and church-run residential schools. Indeed, some witnesses say that the removal of thousands of children from their families and cultures into the child welfare and residential school systems left their people culturally, spiritually, and emotionally crippled.[16]

In aggregate, the testimony in this genre leads one to an inevitable and disturbing conclusion: numerous Aboriginal witnesses see their people as having been exploited from every conceivable angle. The results of exploitation are a "broken culture and a broken spirit"[17] and a people who "became ill, spiritually, mentally, physically."[18] Against this background, witnesses then often outline in detail the predictable litany of social problems that now exist in so many Aboriginal communities: violence, abuse, suicide, and alcohol, drug, and gasoline fume addictions. Moreover, these witnesses often describe this violence as ongoing.[19]

RESISTANCE AND HEALING While numerous witnesses attribute many of the present difficulties of Aboriginal communities to the colonial past, many also stress the importance of sustaining a spirit of survival and resistance. Witnesses regularly applaud the ability of Aboriginal communities to withstand the pressures of assimilation for so long. Moreover, many seem to share the sentiment expressed by one witness that Aboriginal persons must now use the strength associated with their endurance "to strengthen and re-build Aboriginal cultures as the foundation for self-assured and self-respecting peoples and communities."[20]

Political leaders in particular say that political healing must be a prior-ity. They blame the Indian Act not only for undermining traditional struc-tures of Aboriginal leadership but also for placing band chiefs and councils in what they say is the impossible situation of having to be accountable to both the Department of Indian Affairs and Aboriginal constituents.[21] Leaders say that what results is a disturbing loss of legitimacy for chief and council within many communities. The testimony of the Assembly of First Nations (AFN) is particularly instructive in this regard.[22] The AFN argues that the band council system "has severely undermined our traditional gov-erning systems and attacked our consensus form of democracy, which is al-most universal for First Nations peoples."[23] To this end, the AFN argues that political healing should involve the resuscitation of governments based on Aboriginal traditions, including hereditary systems, clan systems, and new institutions that combine traditional and contemporary approaches.

Evidence of interest in healing extends well beyond the realm of poli-tics. Some witnesses repeatedly use concepts such as pride, struggle, sur-vival, and voyage of rediscovery. Ancestry is regularly pinpointed as the common denominator here, and, when combined with community heal-ing, it is said to be the best hope for rebuilding positive Aboriginal self-images. Witnesses sometimes connect healing to the idea of the traditions of community teachings, spirituality, and the role of elders in community and family life. To be Aboriginal with confidence today, some say, it is crit-ical that parents and children are taught what being Aboriginal has histor-ically meant, and for that they need the traditions. Knowledge of the traditions is then identified as a buffer that will help to insulate Aboriginal peoples from falling further into crises of identity: "healing must come, not from the outside, not from the short-term health and social programs de-signed in Ottawa and elsewhere, but from Aboriginal people, their tradi-tions and values."[24]

CULTURAL CONTRADICTION In some testimony, witnesses emphasize the importance of what might be termed contradictions between "white soci-ety" and Aboriginal "regulations." A particularly apt illustration of this is contained in the words of an elder who introduced the AFN's commissioned study to RCAP: "We cannot function with white society's regulations ... because it doesn't work for us. We have our own regulations that we can live with, because we are different people. We are not the same as white society, and we will never be. It doesn't matter what we do, we will never be that race of people, because we were given the gift of being different people. We are special people."[25] In this vein, witnesses draw attention to what they characterize as a contrast between the Western conception of land as exploitable resource, subject to alienation, division, and private holding, and the Aboriginal view of land as spiritual sustainer, conceived in terms of trusteeship, integral in its relationship to the entire cosmos, and held in common with all people.[26] Similarly, some witnesses point out the contrast that they see between Western political authority based on legislative supremacy, centralized decision-making power, and majoritarianism and Aboriginal political authority based on a spiritual pact of communal belonging, consensual decision-making power, and direct participation.[27]

In essence, one can infer from the testimony that the basis for the contrast between Western Euro-Canadian and Aboriginal worldviews rests on what some witnesses say are fundamentally different understandings about humanity's place within the world order.[28] While Euro-Canadians are said to define the human being as an "autonomous, rational, self-interested entity, possessed with a number of unspecified natural or inherent rights," Aboriginal persons are said to define the human being as an entity whose status is determined in reference to the cosmic whole (including land, animals, plants, water, and rocks), of which it is no more than a part.[29] Ovide Mercredi, former Grand Chief of the Assembly of First Nations, summarizes this sentiment as follows: "this new journey we are involved in ... is really about acceptance of our way of life, acceptance of our world view, and acceptance of the basic principle we grew up with: respect for the right to be different."[30]

NATIONALISM Aboriginal nationalism has existed in Canada since at least the 1970s when, in reaction to the 1969 White Paper on Indian Policy, Aboriginal leaders began to "craft an ideology of opposition which rejected the dominant political ethos and the place of Aboriginal people within it."[31] The public hearings of RCAP provide a poignant illustration of how this "ideology" has matured into a complex and robust defence of Aboriginal power. At the centre of the ideology stands the now familiar demand for recognition of the inherent right to self-government. This recurring demand for recognition of the Aboriginal right to self-government is regularly framed by witnesses in ways that parallel the language employed by one witness: "First Nation peoples of this country had self-government prior to contact, governments that were democratic, consensus seeking and very workable ... We are original caretakers, not owners of this great country now called Canada, never gave up our right to govern ourselves and thus are sovereign nations. Our responsibilities to Mother Earth are the foundation of our spirituality, culture, and traditions."[32]

Embedded within this justification I perceive two different kinds of arguments, one historical and the other cultural. On the one hand, it appears that witnesses view the right as flowing from historical precedence, captured in ideas such as "had self-government prior to contact," "never gave up our right," and "thus are sovereign nations." But on the other hand, it also seems that witnesses see the right as flowing from the source of Aboriginal cultural differences. Here witnesses point to justifications based on being responsible "to Mother Earth," becoming "original caretakers," and living in ways consistent with "our spirituality, culture, and traditions." In short, one cannot help but notice that Aboriginal witnesses tend to offer arguments that make Aboriginal communities both unlike and like the Canadian society to which they relate. On one level, their communities are said to be culturally distinct, while on another they are said to enjoy complementarity of status as equal nations.

SUMMARY The impression that one takes away from a reading of Aboriginal testimony before RCAP is twofold. On one level, Aboriginal testimony often reads as a litany of exploitation and marginalization: here Aboriginal witnesses seem to depict a world in which relations between Aboriginal and non-Aboriginal peoples are unsettled at best and fraught with enmity and strife at worst. On another level, one also encounters significant elements of hope and signs of improvement in Aboriginal testimony: here Aboriginal witnesses seem to be saying that, despite assault from every conceivable angle by what they term an aggressive, interfering society, their communities have managed to retain (though some barely so) distinct senses of communal identity. Community survival is then often accompanied in testimony by calls for the development of a wide range of approaches to community healing. Some of these approaches to healing contain overtly political elements. Here numerous witnesses seem to be demanding, in part, a return of the political power that they once exercised so they can rebuild their communities according to their own priorities.

Implications and Analysis

This testimony can be read in a number of ways. Two of the more important take their points of departure from the theories of identity politics discussed in Chapter 1. The first, which tends to dominate Canadian discussions, I have called the difference approach. In this reading, both the problem and the solution remain simple on the surface. That Aboriginal people draw so much attention to the enduring existence of their cultural and political differences is taken as demonstration that Aboriginal identity is equivalent to its current cultural and political expressions. From this assumption, a relatively small but critical further step is taken: the symbols of Aboriginal cultural difference linked to art, economic pursuits, political organization, spirituality, and so on are equated with the criteria that validate individuals and communities as Aboriginal. From this perspective, then, to be Aboriginal is, by definition, to be culturally and politically distinct.

The related assumption is that Aboriginal nations exist to preserve culture. Governance by what is taken to be a culturally alien society is understood to have done violence to these unique cultural identities; thus, Aboriginal peoples should govern themselves. It therefore stands to reason for those who hold this view that each Aboriginal nation should have its own government. The idea here is that the enhanced power that self-government brings would provide Aboriginal communities with the resources they need to lead in the revival of their distinct cultural, spiritual, and political traditions.

The second reading of Aboriginal political rhetoric does not so much reject the first reading as go beyond it to provide context and perspective. This reading follows from the identification approach. In this version, the five organizing themes should be understood with respect to community boundaries. The Aboriginal revitalization movement is seen as trying to establish a new kind of relationship with Canadian society, one in which

Aboriginal peoples are no longer measured by the standards of Canadian society but act as a people, distinct from and equal to other Canadians, empowered to determine their own future. To ensure the survival of their identities, however, Aboriginal communities are understood to need political authority to fashion boundaries. That is, they need access to political space fenced in by boundaries so that they can develop their identities free from external interference.

From the vantage point provided by this second reading, the three themes of a tragic and heroic past, exploitation, and resistance and healing contribute to the larger Aboriginal enterprise of creating boundaries between Aboriginal communities and the larger Canadian society. This reading elevates the significance of Aboriginal identity precisely because it is related to a historical dynamic that sought its extinguishment. Aboriginal persons are seen as bound together through their universal experience of colonialism, which dramatically acts to separate them from the Canadian mainstream. They are unique among Canada's population in that only they suffered a full-scale institutional assault on their right to be self-defining. The boundary here could hardly be more visible: it is created through retelling the story of this tragic and heroic past.

Similarly, the second reading leads one to see the theme of cultural and political contradiction as providing countervailing pressure against the pressure already being applied against Aboriginal communal boundaries. Here cultural attributes of difference are not regarded as having intrinsic importance in and of themselves, nor are they equated with the source of Aboriginal identity. Rather, they are seen as expressions of Aboriginal identity, used to forge and maintain individual and group identities so as to further separate Aboriginal communities from the non-Aboriginal mainstream. The boundary here is thus rendered that much more visible: it is created through the strategic and emblematic use of cultural and political symbols.

What follows from this second reading is an understanding of the Aboriginal motivation for self-government that is strikingly different from the one assumed by those who hold to the difference approach. What testimony by Aboriginal witnesses before RCAP is understood to demonstrate is that, despite pressure against their community boundaries, individual identification with Aboriginal communities remains strong for many. Consequently, testimony on self-government is taken to illustrate that

Aboriginal individuals want to be able to choose their own political authorities and administer their internal affairs according to their own priorities. This reading concludes, therefore, that what is important for Aboriginal community survival is the preservation not of cultural and political differences per se but of the boundaries that separate Aboriginal and non-Aboriginal communities from one another. With community boundaries thus protected, Aboriginal persons can exercise their communal interest in being self-defining across a whole range of identity options that might occur to community members.

However, the idea that Aboriginal political credentials are best established by cultural distinctiveness remains the dominant view. Indeed, Aboriginal leaders regularly contribute to this view: they often point to the ongoing existence of distinct cultural practices and traditions in situations in which doing so will strengthen their political claims. This stance is not surprising because many Aboriginal persons are genuinely interested in resuscitating the sources of their traditional cultural customs and practices, a natural response to a colonial history in which so many of these practices were arbitrarily suppressed.

The problem with the difference approach in my view, however, is that it can confuse specific time-bound attributes of Aboriginal cultural and political identity with their source, which is better located in the more elemental reality of ancestry, shared history, and community identification. The subsequent danger is that the moral strength of the claim to self-government can diminish the moment Aboriginal communities lose aspects of their cultural and political distinctiveness. Yet it is precisely this first reading's approach to self-government that one finds at the core of RCAP's five-volume final report. In fact, at crucial points in its analysis, the report echoes themes that I identified in Chapter 1 as central to communitarian pluralism. Just how it does so, and what implications follow for its justification of an Aboriginal right to self-government, are what I turn to next.

THE REPORT OF THE ROYAL COMMISSION ON ABORIGINAL PEOPLES

The final report of the Royal Commission on Aboriginal Peoples (RCAP) comprises five volumes containing over 400 policy recommendations. Its formidable length, coupled with enormous amounts of testimony and research, make it the most comprehensive examination of Aboriginal issues in Canada undertaken to date.[33] Undoubtedly, RCAP's prescriptions will not settle questions of principle relating to Aboriginal people's future within Canada; indeed, despite assurances from Indian Affairs ministers Ron Irwin, Jane Stewart, and then Robert Nault that they have been guided by the report, many of its central recommendations have yet to be implemented.[34] Nevertheless, the sheer scope of RCAP's work suggests to me that some of its central ideas are worthy of examination. I assess a number of those key ideas in this section.

The ideas contained in the report are firmly rooted in the soil of the past. RCAP organizes history into four stages: the precontact stage of "separate worlds" followed by three contact stages. The first contact stage RCAP characterizes as "contact and cooperation." Here initial relations between Aboriginal peoples and European colonists are analyzed in terms of nation-to-nation equality. The second and longest contact stage RCAP defines as "displacement and assimilation." This stage is defined as the dark chapter in Canadian history because during it Aboriginal ways of life were encroached upon, Aboriginal peoples marginalized, and Aboriginal rights ignored and trivialized. The third contact stage, "negotiation and renewal," is the current one, beginning with the Aboriginal rejection of the 1969 White Paper.[35] RCAP defines this stage as a turning point because, with the repudiation of the assimilationist model by Aboriginal peoples, Canadians must accept the challenge to design and build a "relationship between Aboriginal and non-Aboriginal people in Canada" on new foundations.[36]

RCAP proceeds to explore why initial relations of cultural and political equality based on what it terms mutual respect, recognition, sharing, and responsibility gave way to a colonial relationship of exploitation and domination. With history defined in this way, the path toward a renewed relationship is regarded as relatively obvious, at least in principle. As the title of the first volume of the report suggests (*Looking Forward, Looking Back*), one can only look forward by first looking backward and restoring what was so wrongfully taken away. For RCAP, historical practice sets the norm for both the present and the future. Herein lies RCAP's central organizing idea for Aboriginal revitalization. Aboriginal communities can be restored to health only when they are given licence to develop their cultures and exercise political power as they did in the precolonial and early contact past. According to RCAP, the institutional route to such revitalization must be through the recognition and restoration of historical Aboriginal nationhood.

Nations are privileged in the report as central to a new relationship between Aboriginal communities and Canadian governments. On this score, the report is single-minded; all governments in Canada are to recognize that "Aboriginal peoples are nations vested with the right of self-determination" as "recognized and affirmed in section 35(1) of the Constitution Act, 1982," and as originally arising "from the sovereign and independent status of Aboriginal peoples and nations before and at the time of European contact and from the fact that Aboriginal peoples were in possession of their own territories, political systems and customary laws at that time."[37] Only nations, with their resident populations of 5,000 to 7,000 and with the foundation of a land base, possess the institutional capacity "to preserve and transmit the core of language, beliefs, traditions, and knowledge that is uniquely Aboriginal."[38]

A commitment to cultural strength and "the right of other people to be different" stands at the centre of RCAP's report.[39] In its words, what makes Aboriginal people unique are "their rights as peoples, their languages, their belief systems, their values, their family structures – in short, their very cultures."[40] Beyond attachment to elements of distinctive culture, in other words, RCAP is of the view that Aboriginal persons will be hard pressed to remain Aboriginal. For it, identification with a nation is essential for Aboriginal persons because, through the structures of nationhood, individuals are provided with the unique cultural elements of identity that make them Aboriginal. The implication here is clear: for RCAP, to be Aboriginal is to be culturally and politically distinct.

With the central organizing concept of nation thus established, RCAP proceeds to outline in detail how this new regime of self-governing nations is to be brought into existence and sustained into the future. Each measure and policy recommendation builds upon the others to provide an interlocking institutional design that would significantly enhance Aboriginal peoples' symbolic status and political power in Canada. Measures include a new Royal Proclamation and companion legislation. Together they would supplement the recognition granted to Aboriginal peoples in the Royal Proclamation of 1763 by setting out a clear regime of principles to govern not only the nation-to-nation relationship between the Crown and Aboriginal treaty nations but also the treaty-making, treaty implementation, and treaty renewal process. The further combination of an Aboriginal Nations Recognition Act, capacity building for self-government, new federal departments, treaty commissions, an Aboriginal Lands and Treaty Tribunal, an Aboriginal House of First Peoples, and an Aboriginal Peoples Review Commission to monitor progress would contribute to the project of rebuilding and re-equipping Aboriginal nations to govern.[41] RCAP pushes for an equality of governmental status and bargaining power that would allow Aboriginal nations to take a place alongside federal and provincial governments in a reconstituted multinational federation.

RCAP's argument for recognition through the lens of nationhood raises a basic question: why this route? Why, in the commissioners' view, are nations the only political vehicle capable of resuscitating, preserving, and developing Aboriginal culture and, by extension, Aboriginal identity? Two reasons can be inferred from the report, one normative and the other more practical.

On a normative level, the commissioners faced the question of how to mobilize Aboriginal persons to fulfill obligations to other community members as well as protect their communities as a whole. Their understanding is that political communities need prepolitical background assumptions or common cultural identities for individual members to assume a basic threshold of trust and to establish mutual relations and common goals. RCAP claims that, because Aboriginal nations are already existing, and because testimony by Aboriginal witnesses suggests to RCAP that nations cohere in a morally satisfactory way for many of their members, they are the best means to address this challenge. Aboriginal persons often share ethnic origins, cultural beliefs, historical experiences, and national characters that are said to give them common grounding. The importance of nation-based Aboriginal communities here "is simply that they are encompassing communities which aspire to draw everyone who inhabits a particular territory" by giving each member a legitimate way of understanding his or her political place within the world.[42] In RCAP's reading of the situation, identification with nations is what principally binds Aboriginal persons to one another. Common identification with a nation is taken to breed obligation, obligation in turn is understood to breed trust, and trust is then said to provide the foundation for the further development of a communal cultural identity.

The second reason why RCAP privileges Aboriginal nations is more practical. RCAP documents that many Aboriginal persons already see themselves as members of nations, both in the historical past and in the present, though present versions often exist in severely compromised forms. Rather than dispense with the past and begin afresh, RCAP uses the structures of the past as a model to reinvigorate the present. Put simply, self-governing nations on a land base are already in place, so RCAP sees no reason not to use them. Indeed, according to RCAP, all that nations need are the resources to fulfill the cultural functions for which they were created. Moreover, given the sweeping nature of the functions that nations normally perform for their members, rebuilding Aboriginal nations can contribute more so than any other option to multidimensional individual and communal Aboriginal cultural development, or so the report indicates. To this end, RCAP names three key institutional building blocks that need to be strengthened.

First, RCAP links the institutions of nationhood to a wide range of cultural artifacts. In its report, RCAP underlines the idea that members view their nations as established and familiar frameworks for the development of their cultural attachments. Of course, the report goes to considerable length to show that cultural suppression of Aboriginal identity in the past was both aggressive and wide-ranging. But this fact, supposedly, only reinforces RCAP's argument for robust, activist Aboriginal governments. For RCAP, only Aboriginal governments possess the institutional sophistication to resuscitate distinct cultural practices that still serve to bind Aboriginal communities together. RCAP thus calls on Aboriginal governments to provide leadership in launching a whole battery of cultural initiatives. Among them are establishing Aboriginally governed schools, residential colleges, and a university; developing languages; supporting the literary, visual, and performing arts; creating healing centres and lodges as well as youth centres and camps; protecting cultural artifacts and heritage sites; and integrating traditional Aboriginal knowledge in the development of health science, educational, environmental, and social services research and service delivery.[43]

Second, this connection of culture to community is what compels RCAP to situate territory for Aboriginal nations at the centre of its recommendations. It is undeniably the case that Aboriginal nations are closely linked to traditional territories. But RCAP goes beyond this truism. For it, the fit between nations and territory is much closer: RCAP claims that the cultural survival of Aboriginal nations depends on it. As stated in the report, "Possession of a land base is vital to the full exercise of nationhood, especially Aboriginal nationhood, which has always been intimately connected to the land."[44] Elsewhere the report indicates that Aboriginal people regard their reserves and settlements "as the heartland of their culture. For most living off the reserve or settlement and in the towns and cities is like being in a diaspora."[45]

In RCAP's view, Aboriginal nations look for territory because in a sense they already have it or because they harbour memories of once having had it: the link between Aboriginal people and the land is understood to be a critical component of Aboriginal identity. The political problem that RCAP means to solve is control over sufficient land as well as political power and economic resources to make Aboriginal nations self-reliant. For this reason, treaties are RCAP's preferred instrument for bringing about reconciliation between Aboriginal and non-Aboriginal peoples. From the point of view of RCAP, not only can treaties comprehensively address the Aboriginal need for land, resources, and political autonomy, but they can also elevate the status of Aboriginal nations to that of equals in the federal partnership of governments that makes up Canada.[46]

Third, while Aboriginal nations already have their own distinct elements of culture as well as lands, RCAP also reinforces the idea that nations have the means to control people entering or exiting their communities. Only if Aboriginal nations can determine and then enforce decisions about membership will their ways of life and communities be secure. The commission points out that Aboriginal nations, as political and cultural entities, already possess acceptable membership criteria. Rules of descent, coupled with historical links to Aboriginal peoples' collective life, "cultures, values, traditions, and ties to land," are what establish whether individuals are, or can plausibly claim to be, citizens of Aboriginal nations.[47] These criteria of citizenship illustrate further why, in RCAP's view, Aboriginal nations are the best route to Aboriginal emancipation. In claiming a right to self-determination, Aboriginal nations assert the capacity to establish cultural and territorial boundaries as well as the citizenship criteria that flow from them. Both boundaries and citizenship can then be employed to protect Aboriginal communities from domination by the Canadian state.

There are, then, two reasons why the concept of Aboriginal nationhood is placed at the centre of RCAP's report. The first reason is normative: RCAP is of the view that Aboriginal persons need their nations for community and solidarity. Where the right to self-determination exists, Aboriginal nations can develop and regulate a set of institutions that distributes entitlements and responsibilities to people in a way consistent with the ongoing development of their distinct cultures. The argument here is that only a common nationality, with its attendant capacity to give institutional form to obligations, can make this sense of reciprocal cultural solidarity possible.

The second reason is more practical and builds on RCAP's understanding that Aboriginal nations are not only the most appropriate form of political community but also the only possible form in which the overall aspirations of Aboriginal people can be met in contemporary Canada. RCAP believes that Aboriginal communities think of themselves as nations, and because they do so they should be given what they want, the right to self-determination. What justifies the want are the credentials of the claim itself. Where Aboriginal communities can demonstrate that their identities are distinct as a result of ancestry, history, culture, and land, they are entitled to make a claim for self-determination. Such a claim is justified on these grounds because the powers associated with the right are the best means to guarantee the continuation of the distinct attributes of Aboriginal cultural identities.

The guiding ideal of RCAP's report is that Aboriginal peoples reproduce their national identities and together make decisions about matters of concern to them, particularly where culture is concerned. To achieve this, Aboriginal nations need political institutions with adequate authority, though RCAP is careful to point out that what the scope of that authority might be will depend on the particular identity of the nation in question and on the aspirations and objectives that each wishes to pursue. It is therefore next to impossible for RCAP to set a priori limits on the scope of authority that each Aboriginal nation will exercise on its own behalf.

Nevertheless, because RCAP invests so much in national structures as the route to Aboriginal emancipation, it exhibits no qualms whatsoever in establishing a minimal threshold for viable nationhood. To this end, RCAP recommends in its report that the right of self-determination be vested in Aboriginal nations rather than in local communities or Indian bands. RCAP simply disqualifies small communities and bands because they do not possess the necessary institutional sophistication or resources to make the running of modern, complex governmental organizations viable. RCAP defines an Aboriginal nation as "a sizeable body of Aboriginal people with a shared sense of national identity that constitutes the predominant population in a certain territory or collection of territories."[48] Numbering between sixty and eighty and containing populations of 5,000 to 7,000, these nations include the former Indian nations now fragmented into bands by the Indian Act, the historical Métis nations of the prairie west, and the Inuit nations of the North (when and where the term applies to them).

While there is no guarantee of success even under these terms, the report provides a battery of recommendations to ensure that aspiring Aboriginal nations get off to as good a start as possible. For example, although RCAP believes that Aboriginal nations possess an inherent right to self-government, it nevertheless recommends that they meet a series of criteria before they exercise their "inherent self-governing jurisdiction."[49] As set out in an Aboriginal Nations Recognition and Government Act, Aboriginal nations would receive recognition from the government of Canada once they demonstrate that they share common ties (of language, history, culture), are of sufficient size to support a self-governing mandate, have completed a citizenship code consistent with international norms of human rights and the Canadian Charter of Rights and Freedoms, and have drawn up a constitution through a wide process of consultation and ratification.[50] RCAP also recommends that additional lands and resources be allocated to aspiring self-governing nations to enhance their economic prospects.[51] Resources and land are further bolstered by recommendations for adequate fiscal support.[52] Among the types of funding that the report outlines are own-source funding (e.g., user fees, resource royalties, gaming, Aboriginal corporations), transfers from other governments, entitlements from treaties and land claims, and borrowing.[53]

These stringent criteria demanding both competence from aspiring self-governing nations and support from Canadian governments make sense when held up against the significant responsibilities that Aboriginal

nations could take up on their own behalf. RCAP recommends that
Aboriginal nations should be able to exercise jurisdiction with respect to
"all matters relating to the good government and welfare of Aboriginal
peoples and their territories."[54] For nations possessing exclusive territories,
a partial list of the kinds of powers that RCAP envisages them exercising
includes the right "to draw up a constitution, set up basic government institutions, establish courts, lay down citizenship criteria and procedures, run
its own schools, maintain its own health and social services, deal with family matters, regulate many economic activities, foster and protect its language, culture and identity, regulate the use of its lands, waters and
resources, levy taxes, deal with aspects of criminal law and procedure ...
generally maintain peace and security within the territory" as well as regulate "many substantive Aboriginal and treaty rights."[55]

The report's overwhelming focus on self-government as the route to
Aboriginal emancipation demonstrates just how profound RCAP's faith is
in the structures of Aboriginal nations. For RCAP, no other structures rival
Aboriginal governments in the potential to protect and foster elements of
common culture, to build institutions of reciprocal obligation so as to generate trust among Aboriginal citizens, and to grant Aboriginal citizens the
power to solve collective problems and thereby determine the destinies of
their communities. Only nations and their attendant structures can provide
Aboriginal peoples with the sense of solidarity that makes their emancipation within Canada possible.

EVALUATING THE CULTURAL FRAMEWORK

Communitarian pluralism lends philosophical justification to the premise
that culture is constitutive of identity; hence, where group members cling
to collective goals in the name of preserving their cultural differences in the
face of overwhelming odds, they are justified in demanding collective
rights. The RCAP report supports this premise almost without qualification. RCAP places Aboriginal nations at the centre of its concerns because,
in its view, nations exist to protect culture, and it is culture that makes
Aboriginal communities distinctive. One can conclude, therefore, that for
the commission "nationalism is primarily a cultural doctrine or, more ac-
curately, a political ideology with a cultural doctrine at its centre."[56]

In this section, I discuss the implications of the idea that Aboriginal communities are entitled to self-government because they are culturally distinct. What follows explains, first, why cultural justifications for self-government contain contradictory elements and, second, why these contradictions are politically dangerous when they become the basis for arguments supporting Aboriginal rights. I then identify how cultural justifications rely on an understanding of Aboriginal identity that is seriously incomplete.

The central difficulty with placing so much political value on cultural differences is that it tends to subvert its own justification for group-based protection. RCAP's report promotes a doctrine suggesting that, when healthy, culture forms the basis of all important differences and similarities between Aboriginal and non-Aboriginal peoples. RCAP tailors its recommendations to build institutional support so that Aboriginal nations will be able to "preserve and transmit the core of language, beliefs, traditions, and knowledge that is uniquely Aboriginal."[57]

I would argue, however, that the ontological security of RCAP's defence of Aboriginal identity is predicated on bounded conceptions of cultural and political systems that are difficult to sustain within a technologically advanced and socially heterogeneous society such as Canada's. In fact, to follow the line of reasoning of its report is to raise the spectre of an Aboriginal identity that may be "a helpless subscriber to the dominant conception of value," suggesting that individuality is purely a determined product of a person's "circumstances, social conditioning, and community culture."[58] A realistic portrait should not depict Aboriginal identity in this way because Aboriginal communities by nature are fluid, changeable, subject to influence, and riven by internal pluralities. As Katherine Fierlbeck observes, "Given the ability of modern technology to collect and dissipate widely disparate ideas and practices, very few cultural groups are now clearly 'separate and distinct'; and few individuals within any cultural grouping are 'totally in' or 'totally outside' their cultural group." Indeed, empirical observation of minorities readily reveals that they "gradually adopt norms and practices and vocabularies both from the 'mainstream' practices and from other minority groups."[59]

In places, RCAP does acknowledge the inevitable influence of modernity on the lives of Aboriginal persons, and it accepts those influences as edifying ones. In this sense, RCAP promotes contradictory themes. It documents with little anxiety the fact that Aboriginal communities have joined the popular world culture of mass media and transnational industries as active participants.[60] Furthermore, RCAP argues that, if Aboriginal communities are to survive economically, they must equip their young people with the skills necessary to compete in the "global economy."[61] To that end, RCAP embraces a vision of equality in which Aboriginal adults attain education and training to enjoy careers comparable "to that of any other segment of the population." Careers specifically mentioned include "doctors, engineers, carpenters, entrepreneurs, biotechnologists, scientists, computer specialists, artists, professors, [and] archaeologists."[62]

But RCAP's spirit of optimism for modernity is qualified in its report by a profound suspicion of the homogenizing and destructive effects that it assumes modernity has on Aboriginal cultures. Thus, while Aboriginal individuals must participate in the modern economy to survive, it is no less important from the perspective of RCAP that Aboriginal individuals "sustain their cultures and identities, and [that] they see education as a major means of preparing their children to perceive the world through Aboriginal eyes and live in it as Aboriginal human beings."[63] Given this analysis, one can conclude that for RCAP there is an inevitable tension between the forces of modernity and Aboriginality. Moreover, given the superior power of the former, when the two conflict the integrity of the latter must be protected. For RCAP, then, Aboriginal identity is firmly planted in the soil of cultural distinctiveness.

The propensity to tie Aboriginal identity to culture is politically dangerous because it qualifies arguments for Aboriginal rights in two important respects. First, by conceiving of culture as internally distinct, RCAP inadvertently promotes the idea that Aboriginal rights are best reserved for those Aboriginal communities whose cultural identities are significantly different from the mainstream.[64] The logic here is that Aboriginal rights rely on the existence of cultural practices that existed prior to contact and that remain integral to Aboriginal culture. By implication, the more the cultural practices of an Aboriginal community have been assimilated into those of the non-Aboriginal culture, the less it needs Aboriginal rights since the Aboriginal community in question will have lost the basis of its cultural differences and thus the need for special protection.

What this cultural difference test ignores, however, is that the longer and more sustained the nature of contact, the less likely it is that Aboriginal cultural practices will have remained completely culturally distinct. Interaction with colonial forces has undoubtedly left lasting impacts on Aboriginal communities, the inevitable outcome of a long and sustained process of cohabitation on the same soil. Indeed, as Patrick Macklem argues, the ongoing existence of Aboriginal communities is in part a result of Aboriginal peoples assimilating cultural practices of the more powerful non-Aboriginal society into their own on their own terms. Macklem observes, for example, that, if Aboriginal peoples had been unwilling to participate in the fur trade or had refused to incorporate elements of European beliefs into their religious practices, it is unlikely that Aboriginal communities would have survived at all.[65]

Today the dividing line between Aboriginal and non-Aboriginal lives continues to blur. Families blend Aboriginal and Western understandings of life in the context of intermarriage, Aboriginal youth desire skills to participate in the modern wage economy, Aboriginal businesses accept the economic premises of capitalism, and Aboriginal persons raised as Christians often wish to remain so. The elements of traditional Aboriginal culture now constitute one choice among several, a choice that individuals can judge on its own merits and in terms of how it will enrich their lives. Consequently, it is patently unfair that, where Aboriginal cultural practices are both similar to and different from the practices of their more powerful non-Aboriginal counterparts, they may make claims for Aboriginal rights only on the basis of their cultural differences. To pursue this path is to disregard the critical question of power and how Aboriginal peoples have been compelled to adapt to the fact that Aboriginal societies are no longer alone on this continent.

The second danger jeopardizes Aboriginal rights from precisely the opposite direction. In this scenario, a preoccupation with attributes of cultural difference can act to sever ties with the non-Aboriginal society that Aboriginal communities need for their own survival.

In this line of reasoning, Aboriginal rights are based on requirements of cultural difference because it is largely Aboriginal leaders themselves who argue that the expression of traditional elements of cultural distinctiveness forms the necessary foundation for the continuation of their communities.

The source of this argument is identified as originating from the fact that Aboriginal societies were previously repressed and undervalued. Given that the dominant society was a source of oppression for Aboriginal peoples, Aboriginal interest in their own cultural resuscitation is taken as containing a fundamental antagonism toward the cultural practices of their Euro-Canadian counterparts. The conclusion is clear: the freedom and self-development of Aboriginal societies will best be pursued if they separate as much as possible from the dominant society by establishing their own culturally distinct and independent political, economic, and social practices and institutions.

This oppositional approach to cultural self-understanding is not without its virtues. The approach promotes the idea that Aboriginal communities inhabit a distinct world of cultural practices that can be used to generate political solidarity among group members. Such solidarity, in turn, can lead to the construction of political institutions and practices that could appreciably improve the lives of Aboriginal persons as well as give them political leverage in their confrontation with the dominant Canadian society.

Nonetheless, Samuel LaSelva writes that, when the quest for self-government is understood in these confrontational terms, Canada becomes a country of solitudes, and federalism "ceases to be an option for the resolution of Aboriginal issues."[66] Alan Cairns reinforces this sentiment by suggesting that it is unfortunate to structure the contemporary debate concerning the future of relations between Aboriginals and non-Aboriginals with reference to difference because it precludes the possibility of shared citizenship.[67] Why should this matter? Because, as David Miller astutely observes, in the absence of a shared identity, Canadians "are being asked to extend equal respect and treatment to groups with whom they have nothing in common beyond the fact of cohabitation in the same political society."[68]

Without a doubt, the oppression that Aboriginal peoples have experienced is considerable. But on some level, RCAP assumes "that simply to expose an injustice is already to have created a constituency willing to abolish it."[69] Along with Miller, I believe that something more is needed. For Canadians to combat the forces that perpetuate injustice against Aboriginal peoples, there must be trust and a common sense of belonging to the same political community. Put differently, for Canadians to meet the just demands of Aboriginal peoples now, they should reasonably be able to expect that Aboriginal peoples will be responsive to the just demands of their non-Aboriginal counterparts if and when they arise. But this responsiveness requires trust, and trust requires solidarity "not merely within groups but across them." Miller points out that such solidarity "depends upon a common identification of the kind that nationality alone can provide."[70]

This danger of undue isolation impacts directly on the question of Aboriginal communal survival itself. Aboriginal communities that regularly average 1,000 members or fewer are simply incapable, by virtue of small populations and limited resources, of building communities independent from the Canadian mainstream. Aboriginal communities are in constant discussions with Canadian governments, ranging from treaty negotiations to social service delivery agreements, transfers of monies, and investment in reserve-based capital expenditures. Clearly, Aboriginal communities remain reliant on the non-Aboriginal majority for resources critical to community development.[71] Promoting cultural strategies that isolate Aboriginal communities from their Canadian counterparts, in other words, may well jeopardize the relations of interdependence that now serve as the life blood for Aboriginal communal existence.

Undoubtedly, culture can be used as a tool to build political community. But to ask it to provide the answers to fundamental crises in Aboriginal identity is to demand too much of it. Yet, as has been shown, RCAP resolves the question of Aboriginal identity decisively in favour of the cultural nation. For RCAP, the distinct attributes of culture associated with language, religion, art, history, and homeland are made the basis of Aboriginal identity. The principal task of the Aboriginal nation, in turn, is to protect and cultivate these distinct cultural attributes. The nation is thus depicted as offering its members security of identity. It is the nation that is said to generate the common cultural attributes that define the identities of the individuals within it, and for this reason the nation deserves primacy of loyalty and attachment. Framed in this way, Aboriginal identity depends on individuals having a strong association with a nation. I would define this way of framing Aboriginal identity as a form of cultural nationalism.

In my view, when the cultural nation is given priority in this way, the multiple identities of Aboriginal persons (as women, professionals, gays, urban dwellers, youths, Christians, Canadians) are either suppressed or defined as manifestations of the cultural nation. However, even if one can show in the manner that the public hearings of RCAP do that real psychological and physical damage has been wrought upon Aboriginal persons as a result of colonialism, it is not necessarily the case that all those affected will (or even can) turn to traditional attributes of Aboriginal cultural difference for identity. Reasonable people of good faith can disagree on what it means to be Aboriginal. Moreover, for many, ties to the cultural attributes of their nations may be both tenuous and distant as a result of living in cities and towns, to cite but one example. Many of these individuals will have formed conceptions of their lives that do not involve a direct association with the distinct cultural attributes that their nations purportedly exist to protect. Rather, their lives may derive greater meaning from sources related to their gender, age, profession, education, or urban location. The point, then, is that, outside ancestry and a shared experience of communal historical continuity, what it is to be Aboriginal cannot be resolved by referring to some obvious or universally agreed upon culturally authoritative source.

It is not my intention to dispute the importance of Aboriginal identity associated with elements of cultural nationalism. As testimony by witnesses to RCAP made clear, many Aboriginal persons identify themselves with respect to precisely such elements. What does not follow in my view, however, is that these communal elements are in and of themselves worthy of protection. Yet this is precisely what communitarian theory justifies and what many of the policy recommendations of RCAP propose.

The conceptual problem stems from the propensity to confuse aspects of Aboriginal identity with their source. In this sense, the philosophical justification of communal identity developed by communitarian scholars and the analytical framework reflected in RCAP's report suffer from the same methodological problems attributed to the difference approach to Aboriginal identity outlined in Chapters 1 and 2. Similarly, analysis in both theory and policy settings focuses on Aboriginal attributes and then reifies or absolutizes them. By "reify," I mean the tendency to grant to an aspect of identity a permanency that it either does not possess or possesses only temporarily. By "absolutize," I mean the assumption that one or another aspect of Aboriginal identity (in this case, the cultural nation) is primary and therefore has greater significance than any other potential aspect. The communitarian approach is to accept Aboriginal political rhetoric at face value and then insist that Aboriginal communities must be nations if they are to attain cohesion of purpose to make the cultural emancipation necessary for identity security possible.

CONCLUSION

The strength of the communitarian understanding of pluralism also contributes to its essential weakness. The perspective teaches us that Aboriginal collective existence is necessary because Aboriginal individuals need customs and traditions as points of orientation to make sense of their world. At the same time, it takes those customs and traditions of cultural identity and equates them with the criteria that validate individuals and communities as Aboriginal. The result is that cultural identity is both reified (taken as given and permanent) and absolutized (taken as fundamental and primary).

But cultural identities are not given, nor are they necessarily primary. Cultures are above all "constructed." Their content is reconfigured and changed in response to the relations that communities take up with one another over time. We need, therefore, to look at culture in a different way – not as a noun but as a verb that, among other things, can be used selectively for the political purpose of establishing boundaries between groups of people. Anything less would be to rid Aboriginal identity of precisely the feature that makes it political: namely, the ability to evolve as a result of communal choice, decision, association, and so on. Because communitarian commentators consistently miss this point, their justification for Aboriginal self-government is unduly restrictive.

Yet much of Aboriginal people's political capital for self-government rests on arguments that relate the right to their cultural distinctiveness. Interesting for my purposes is that these arguments in turn have generated a specific form of critique rooted in the presuppositions of individualist pluralism. Both communitarian and individualist faces of pluralism accept the proposition that the cultural and political sources of Aboriginal identity are at root primordial and fixed. Where they differ is in their normative responses to the political implications of this proposition. While communitarian arguments defend the Aboriginal right to cultivate cultural difference, individualist arguments defend the individual Aboriginal right to freedom of choice in cases where collective and individual projects conflict. The question is whether these arguments do justice to the complexity of the politics that takes place within Aboriginal communities. The multiple theoretical and practical problems raised by conflict between Aboriginal communities and individuals are most clearly illustrated in the politics of Aboriginal women and youth. It is to this topic that I now turn.

CHAPTER 4

ABORIGINAL WOMEN, YOUTH, AND THE PRIORITY OF INDIVIDUAL CHOICE

Here I assess the individualist view that the right to Aboriginal self-government should not be allowed to prevail over the individual right to freedom of choice. In carrying out my assessment, I return first to the public hearings of RCAP. This time I focus on the testimony of Aboriginal women and youth and identify the primary concepts and themes that they use to define their circumstances and to articulate their political objectives. Then I demonstrate how individualist pluralism structures assumptions about what is at stake in policy. An apt example here is provided by Aboriginal women and the Charter debate. Finally, I confront the question of relevance by addressing both what an individualist perspective on Aboriginal identity illuminates and what it obscures.

INFLUENCE AND POWER

The Hearings

Many Aboriginal women and youth participated in RCAP, submitting briefs as part of its Intervenor Participation Program and giving oral presentations to the commissioners in the public hearings process.[1] In this section, I identify the primary concepts and themes that these witnesses used to describe their political aspirations to RCAP, in particular their aspirations for Aboriginal self-government.

While Aboriginal women and youth are commonly referred to as "minorities," this is a distortion of reality. Recent statistics indicate that 51 percent of Aboriginal persons are women[2] and that 56.2 percent are youth under the age of twenty-five.[3] For my purposes, minority status refers to relations of power. The question that I will address is whether, compared with the power exercised by their male and adult counterparts, Aboriginal women and youth lack power and thus opportunity to set priorities for the directions of their communities as well as their own places within those communities.

Aboriginal women and youth should also not be viewed as internally uniform groups with identical interests. With respect to women, for example, RCAP notes that "the idea of a separate voice for women in any political context is always fraught with controversy, because not all women see themselves as having interests distinct from those of men, and even when they do, many people of both sexes deny the usefulness of such distinctions. Still ... women do have a unique set of circumstances to address, and a unique vantage point from which to see their own – and the general – interest. This argument was made to us by many Aboriginal women."[4] The same qualification can be applied to Aboriginal youth. While no perspective can be universally applied to youth, their testimony suggests that they often do have distinct experiences that give them unique vantage points from which to evaluate the Aboriginal self-government process.

Yet the concepts and themes prevalent in the testimony of Aboriginal women and youth do not move in lockstep with one another. Each category of witnesses has very different life experiences and perspectives and thus different "issues and concerns, problems and solutions."[5] Nevertheless, what binds these witnesses together is the fact that both regularly raise hard questions about the ways in which self-government plans are being developed by what might be called "mainstream" Aboriginal political organizations and local tribal and band council leadership. Five themes formed the basis of numerous presentations by Aboriginal women and youth: cultural resuscitation, outstanding issues associated with Bill C-31, political accountability, violence and healing, and bicultural identity.

CULTURAL RESUSCITATION A common theme in much testimony by female witnesses is the tendency to attribute the source of Aboriginal women's present inequality to what they identify as patriarchal structures imposed on Aboriginal societies by colonial powers – in particular, patriarchal political structures that they say stimulated the development of an Aboriginal male elite. In this rendition of history, witnesses repeatedly portray colonial powers as violent perpetrators of injustice against women. Notably, witnesses blame the Indian Act for imposing Victorian standards of patriarchy and race on Aboriginal societies that are then said to have fundamentally disrupted relations between men and women.

Some Aboriginal women also emphasize that many Aboriginal men now accept the premises of patriarchy – a behaviour that they often attribute to men's own experience of abusive indoctrination in residential schools and socialization in Canadian society more generally.[6] While these female witnesses make it clear that they do not condone abusive male behaviour, there is often a corresponding refusal to hold men entirely responsible for their actions. As I see it, the rationale here seems to follow a consistent logic: while Aboriginal men are now involved in the subjugation of women, they do so not because Aboriginal societies have traditions of violence but because this is "learned behaviour, part of a practice of cultural genocide."[7] With the problem viewed in this way, what often follows is that female witnesses identify solutions to male violence in terms of repudiating what they say are the "foreign" patriarchal assumptions that have infiltrated the Aboriginal way of life.

Strict dichotomizations also play a prominent role in the testimony of some female witnesses. Precolonial relations between men and women are often depicted as having been dignified, respectful, and harmonious. Witnesses then describe the postcolonial situation as one in which women are devalued, displaced, and often denied legal standing in their own communities. What often follows are arguments about how precolonial gender relations ought to be resuscitated and made the norm for the present. Witnesses in this genre consistently say that, as Aboriginal women, they have a special responsibility to show their men the discrepancy between colonial images of male-female relations and precolonial images in which women enjoyed a full measure of dignity. As one woman noted, "We don't want the colonial, European style of government, with inequality of representation. We as Aboriginal women want to share in the decision-making, as in traditional times."[8]

Some Aboriginal women also equate rejuvenated female roles with cultural images of traditional femininity: "in our community, the woman was defined as nourisher"; "Woman has had a traditional role as Centre, maintaining the fire"; "She is the Keeper of the Culture."[9] These witnesses seem to imply through the use of these images that women were revered in times past because they possessed roles that were uniquely their own – as givers and sustainers of life, as educators, as keepers of the sacred sources of knowledge. Some witnesses also add that these roles were "destroyed by outside forces coming from European society," which, by extension, is said to have destroyed much of Aboriginal society itself.[10]

Finally, there is a tendency among female witnesses to establish strong connections between expressions of precolonial femininity and prospects for Aboriginal community revival. Women often say that, just as families cannot be healthy and secure apart from the active roles of women, so too are communities doomed if women do not participate fully in the development of self-government. These witnesses then generally insist that, if they do not have their important social, economic, and political roles restored to them as in precolonial times, their societies will lack the "wisdom-keepers," the teachers, the "healers," and the "decision-makers" they need to survive.[11] One woman notes, "Their responsibilities stretch all the way from the cradle to the grave. Our women are the mothers, the providers, the wife, the decision-maker, community leader, and these many roles require them to keep a careful balance."[12]

One can conclude from this testimony that for a good number of female witnesses cultural images of traditional femininity constitute symbols of community and nation. For them, it appears that gender equality is a normative requirement because they seem to regard themselves as the origin of all that nurtures and sustains Aboriginal people.

BILL C-31 While many female witnesses discuss the colonial origins of their inequality, they are no less preoccupied with issues of the political present. A lightning rod for considerable commentary in this genre was Bill C-31. Prior to 1985, Aboriginal women with Indian status under the Indian Act who married nonstatus men lost their status and all the rights that flowed from it. These rights included being able to live on the reserve, being able to be politically active band members, and being able to confer Indian status on their children. Bill C-31 was enacted by the federal government to repeal these discriminatory provisions and thus make the act consistent with the equality provisions of section 15 of the Charter of Rights and Freedoms. However, in the hearings, some Aboriginal women drew attention to what they identified as a new round of inequalities set in motion by the bill.

The importance of the Charter of Rights and Freedoms for Aboriginal women figures prominently in testimony that addresses Bill C-31. Some witnesses note that the availability of Charter rights gave them and their children the constitutional leverage they needed to have the discriminatory s.12(1)(b) of the Indian Act removed. These witnesses say that the 1985 legislation provided for the reinstatement of women and their children who had lost Indian legal status when they married non-Indians. In addition, the benefits that witnesses say they now enjoy as a result of the 1985 legislation include the reacquisition of treaty rights, access to free education and health care, and eligibility to have band membership restored.[13] However, these witnesses also emphasize that gains made with the passage of Bill C-31 have simultaneously created new conditions for their inequitable treatment. The problematic areas that witnesses identify relate either to ongoing legal inequities or to difficulties experienced in receiving services or returning to communities after regaining status.

Some witnesses point out that, while no one now gains or loses status through marriage, problems of sexual discrimination still exist. For example, while many women who have reacquired Indian status cannot pass it on to their children, the same rule does not apply to men.[14] As one woman mentioned, "[I] am a member of the Lower Nicola Indian Band. Though I regained my status under Bill C-31, my children were denied status. The children of my male cousin, who traces his descent from our common grandmother through the male line, have full status."[15]

Much is also made of the fact that both the federal government and reserve communities often deny reinstated persons the means to enjoy their rights. Two issues repeatedly mentioned by witnesses are educational grants for youth and housing on reserves for women. Some witnesses allege that reinstated youth are often subject to discrimination because they are "given low priority when bands allocate post-secondary funding."[16] Women wishing to return to reserves, meanwhile, say that they are discriminated against

because they are regularly denied housing. While witnesses generally acknowledge that reserve housing is scarce and waiting lists are long, their
words also convey an underlying suspicion that they are habitually placed
at the bottom of the list of priorities:

> *I thought by applying and receiving my [Indian Act status under Bill C-31]
> I would have the same benefits as other status Indians. [But] I don't have
> equal rights and, in fact, I have less identity than before ... I can't have a
> home on my reserve ... The reserves at present could possibly house us, the
> Bill C-31 minority Aboriginal people, but refuses to ... I will probably have
> a resting place when the time comes, but why should I accept to be buried on
> reserve land after I die, when I could also enjoy sharing all the services that
> are being kept away from me today ...*[17]

Thus, one element in the testimony of some women and youth is a general concern that gains made through Bill C-31 have still not given them
full equality. Some of these witnesses blame the federal government for this
problem. They say that the disadvantages of women, youth, and children are
a direct result of the federal government's failure to provide adequate resources for Aboriginal communities to resettle and provide for their
reinstated members. At the same time, these witnesses often express considerable cynicism toward the Aboriginal leadership itself. There is simply
little confidence expressed by many that male-dominated organizations and
band councils will uphold women's equality or provide the means for
women and youth to enjoy their rights.

POLITICAL ACCOUNTABILITY Some Aboriginal women and youth say that
power is often concentrated in the hands of a few in Aboriginal communities, a situation that regularly leads to patronage. What follows in their testimony are significant expressions of concern over how self-government
would be implemented.

Some witnesses accuse chiefs, band councils, and Aboriginal organizations of exercising arbitrary power, failing to consult with the general
membership, and blocking efforts by some to exercise influence over self-
government negotiations. This concern is most often expressed by female
witnesses. Some question the wisdom of implementing self-government if

it is to lead to the empowerment of Aboriginal men only. "Presently the women in our communities are suffering from dictatorship governments that have been imposed on us by the Indian Act. We are oppressed in our own communities. Our women have no voice, nowhere to go for appeal processes ... We are penalized if we say anything about the oppression we have to undergo in our community."[18]

A number of witnesses outline in considerable detail how implementation of self-government would likely perpetuate existing abuses of power, elitism, and infringement of individual rights. Testimony in this vein is filled with examples of how current "power brokers" in Aboriginal communities all too often dispense favours to their next-of-kin in the form of limited reserve employment, housing allocations, housing repairs, and other band-administered services.[19]

In response to these conditions, witnesses repeatedly emphasize the need to make the Aboriginal leadership politically accountable "to the grassroots in their operations and policies."[20] In fact, some witnesses say that self-government will remain politically dangerous until meaningful safeguards against abuse are put in place: "In order for self-government to become a reality, our own leadership at all levels must change their ways, their attitudes, their behaviour and be more accountable to the people who elected them and start including them in the decision-making process. The youth and the women must be invited, encouraged, educated and supported to become part of the whole process."[21]

The solution to the accountability problem outlined by many witnesses is to develop consultative processes that involve families, women, youth, and urban dwellers in the political decision-making processes of their communities.[22] More immediately, however, a number of witnesses add that some kind of mechanism should be put in place to protect the rights of individuals and to hold the leadership accountable.

Some women's organizations, such as the Native Women's Association of Canada (NWAC), the Indigenous Women's Collective, and the Tobigue Women's Group, recommend that protection of Aboriginal individual rights should come in the form of the Charter. These organizations claim that the Charter is an important tool because it provides a guarantee that vulnerable minorities will have the external protection of the Canadian state to rely on should their local governments prove abusive.[23] Other proposals identified to promote greater accountability include "limiting the number of terms of elected Aboriginal officials, allowing all members to vote in band elections whether they live on or off reserve," establishing "conflict of interest guidelines for elected officials," and creating "a strict system of checks and balances for public moneys going into band councils and Aboriginal organizations."[24]

VIOLENCE AND HEALING Some witnesses representing a number of leading women's organizations place dealing with violence against women and children at the top of their agendas.[25] The spokeswomen for these organizations say that there is a general unwillingness by the male leadership to acknowledge or address issues of family violence. This reluctance is seen not only as putting women and children at risk but also as failing to represent the agendas of women and children in decisions that male politicians make as part of Aboriginal self-government discussions.[26] In response, the leaders of these organizations address family violence as a political matter, one that they say possesses greater magnitude and urgency than any other political issue facing Aboriginal communities: "Most women supported fully the move toward self-government and yet had many concerns and fears about the fulfilment of that right for Aboriginal peoples. Why? Why do women feel such ambivalence toward the idea of self-government? The answer is clear to women ... We have to change our priorities. We must have personal and community healing."[27]

Emphasis on violence is accompanied by emphasis on the need for healing. Here some witnesses say that the need for healing should take priority in Aboriginal communities, even if "it means delaying the move to self-government."[28] Indeed, some witnesses suggest that failure to make community healing the first priority will have devastating consequences: it will result in a self-governing nation that "will oppress the very people it set out to liberate. It will be corrupted, it will be visionless, and it will be heartless."[29]

Given the magnitude of the problems associated with individual and community violence that a number of witnesses identify, references to healing are almost always made in holistic terms. These witnesses regularly explain that the healing process should be approached in terms of counselling the individual, family, community, and nation. In this context, witnesses identify healing as a lifetime communal process in which Aboriginal individuals should help one another to cope with the harmful effects of both structural and personal violence. The priorities that witnesses identify include suicide prevention, support for victims of violence, adaptation of resources to make them culturally relevant for victims, anger and stress management intervention, and money for training so that Aboriginal persons can undertake their own counselling and healing.[30]

BICULTURAL IDENTITY A final theme of considerable importance for some Aboriginal women and youth living in urban environments is the need to expand and strengthen the meaning of Aboriginal identity. Aboriginal youth in particular regularly stress how Aboriginal societies are in transition, cut off from many of the sources of their traditional culture as a result of "cultural genocide, racism, and poverty," while also trying to make their way in an increasingly sophisticated and technologically advanced modern world.[31] Women and youth generally insist that an Aboriginal identity continues to lie at the heart of Aboriginal existence: they say that it is central to rebuilding Aboriginal self-esteem and to strengthening and enriching Aboriginal communal life more generally. But given the colonial influences of the past, and the need to come to grips with the modern world, they regularly ask what currently constitutes Aboriginal identity.

Witnesses are ambivalent in their answers. Sometimes they give accounts of Aboriginal persons who feel hopelessly strung between two cultures and psychologically at home in neither. Witnesses identify many in this predicament as falling "into patterns of despair, listlessness and self-destruction."[32] They "carry a heavy burden of pain and self-doubt that undermines their cultural identity."[33] Witnesses also report, however, that some are able to "see across this great divide."[34] In these cases, witnesses say, Aboriginal identity flows from an Aboriginal self empowered by both resources of traditional Aboriginal culture and skills necessary to succeed in the modern world.

A number of witnesses also note that Aboriginal youth, and urban dwellers in particular, are the most likely to meet the modern Aboriginal identity challenge. Most persons in these groups are identified as wanting "to achieve an adequate standard of living and participate in the general life of the dominant society, while at the same time honouring and protecting their own heritage, institutions, values and world view."[35] Many Aboriginal

youth and urban dwellers are identified as working at reacquiring their cultural identities, which they then blend with elements of non–Aboriginal
culture. One witness mentions that, "While our communities are going
through difficult times, our culture remains vibrant and capable of adapt-
ing. Our 'cultural glue' is strong, and a future which combines the best of
the old with the best of the new is not just a cliche – it is achievable."[36]

In short, witnesses that broach the subject of Aboriginal identity often
emphasize that many youth and urban dwellers are on the cutting edge of
revitalizing Aboriginal culture in cities and towns across Canada. In its report, RCAP defines this revitalization process as the development of bicultural identities.[37] There is a firm rejection by some witnesses that Aboriginal
persons must choose between traditional and modern ways of life on the
purported ground that there is no way to accommodate the two. Instead,
these witnesses tend to see both as complementary. What they emphasize is
the need for freedom to creatively adapt and develop Aboriginal cultural
resources so that Aboriginal individuals can take their place as strong and
self-confident people in the modern world.

SUMMARY Testimony to the Royal Commission by many Aboriginal
women and youth emphasizes concerns about land, resources, governance,
health, education, justice, and the well-being of Aboriginal families, communities, and nations. What differentiates much of the testimony of women
and youth, however, is their additional emphasis on the need for accountability: Aboriginal leaders and governments must be accountable to their
members through mechanisms that uphold standards of fairness and equality: "I firmly believe that self-government based upon the inherent right to
be self-determining must hear the weaker voices as well as the stronger
voices. Self-government must be built upon the foundation of all Aboriginal
people ... [and] must provide for those people in need. Self-government
must be built upon fairness and equality."[38]

The testimony of Aboriginal women and youth is frequently filled with
demands for an equality of influence and power in the decision-making
processes of their communities. Aboriginal women appear to seek "equal
participation in the social, economic, cultural and political life not only of
their communities but of Canadian society as a whole,"[39] while Aboriginal
youth appear to seek empowerment through "healing, education, employ-

ment, culture and identity, and recognition of and involvement in the institutions that affect their lives."[40] The arguments in statement after statement play as variations on the same theme: Aboriginal self-government can
only be effectively developed when women and youth have the opportunity to fully participate in Aboriginal community power structures.

Implications and Analysis

While this testimony can be read in many ways, two of the most important
parallel those associated with the testimony summarized in Chapter 3. The
first, which again tends to dominate Canadian discussions, might be called
the "competing rights" perspective. In this reading, the actions of
Aboriginal women and youth who resist tribal and band council leadership
tend to be labelled as conflicts between collective and individual rights.
Women and youth are seen to be defending their rights and interests as
individuals against the purported interest of the collective for self-
government. Fear of self-government is stimulated by what the testimony
itself is taken to demonstrate: tribal and band council leadership does not
always act in the best interests of Aboriginal women and youth.
Consequently, if the Aboriginal collective right to self-government is given
priority over the rights of individuals within the collective, vulnerable
women, youth, and children may lack adequate safeguards against their
governments.

These competing individual and collective rights claims defy easy resolution, however, because of a related assumption adopted by the first reading. This assumption, in turn, is informed by the difference approach to
Aboriginal identity and the related communitarian-like justification for
self-government. Here Aboriginal identity is equated with particular expressions of cultural nationalism; indeed, these expressions are taken as the
criteria that validate individuals and communities as Aboriginal.
Consequently, self-government is regarded as important because it is the
collective right that Aboriginal communities need in order to preserve their
cultures and to arrange their political lives in ways consistent with their traditions. Seen in this light, an appeal to an outside authority such as the
Charter in conflicts between individual and collective rights poses a potentially serious threat to the security of Aboriginal communities. Why?
When individual rights are placed over the right of the collective, doing so

"diminishes the autonomy of the community/nation, imperiling the strug-gle for self-determination and diminishing traditional culture and decision-making processes."[41]

This first reading thus sets up a significant dilemma. On the one hand, the vulnerable cultures of Aboriginal communities are seen to be worthy recipients of collective rights. Aboriginal nations should be protected be-cause they allow Aboriginal individuals to live their lives according to communal customs and traditions that both precede and constitute the in-dividual. But on the other hand, some Aboriginal individuals may believe that their freedom of choice is compromised by the cultural standards of their communities. Consequently, Aboriginal individuals should also be protected because they should be able to live their lives according to their own priorities.

This dilemma is heightened by the stock reply that to impose liberal standards of justice on traditional cultural forms of Aboriginal govern-ment is to participate in an act of colonial arrogance. To do so would be to violate "principles of cultural integrity, abrogate inherent rights of self-determination and weaken the collectivity in favour of the individual."[42] Within the dilemma posed by this reading, then, we are confronted with the troubling and seemingly irresolvable double life of culture: "its poten-tial to give radical recognition to the humanity of its subjects, as well as its potential to keep the individual within such tight bounds that the capacity to experiment with one's self – which is equally a mark of one's humanity – comes to be severely at risk."[43] It is this dilemma that advocates of the in-dividualist face of pluralism seek to address. They generally accept the premise that the cultural and national expressions of Aboriginal identity are empirical givens. At the same time, however, they insist that Aboriginal per-sons should have the right to differ from those expressions when they per-ceive it to be in their interests to do so.

In treating dissension between Aboriginal minorities and community leadership as a contest over "competing rights," however, the first reading overlooks a critical issue, one rendered more visible by the second reading. This reading is informed by the identification approach to Aboriginal iden-tity and then builds in a perspective on self-government that relies more heavily on the assumptions of relational pluralism. According to this read-ing, framing the testimony of Aboriginal women and youth in a competing rights framework obscures their political intent: namely, that the five organizing themes of political resistance should be understood with respect to the desire of Aboriginal women and youth for community power. The second reading suggests that individual freedom is important to many Aboriginal women and youth not because it gives them the right to dissent from overbearing cultural traditions (although this may be true for some) but because it gives them the political leverage they need to exercise power and influence within their communities.

From the vantage point of the second reading, the social and political agendas of Aboriginal women and youth simply cannot be reduced to an individual rights campaign. Women and youth are seen to share core issues with the entrenched Aboriginal leadership – most importantly, the desire to establish boundaries between Aboriginal and non-Aboriginal communities so that the former can develop in freedom from external interference by the latter. What the reading emphasizes is that, in the context of freedom from external interference, all Aboriginal citizens should have the same political rights behind community boundaries: to vote, to run for office, to assemble, to speak freely, and, most significantly, to exercise influence in the communal self-definition process.

The related assumption is that many Aboriginal women and youth lack these conditions of equal power in two respects. First, the testimony of Aboriginal women and youth is read in terms of exclusion: many women and youth are seen to be excluded from the most important Aboriginal decision-making institutions, whether nation, tribe or band council, or national political organization. Without participatory rights, Aboriginal women and youth are regarded as lacking equal standing in their communities and, by extension, the economic, social, and political opportunities that other Aboriginal persons take for granted. Second, where Aboriginal women and youth do possess participatory rights, their testimony is read in terms of marginalization. To be marginalized is regarded as no less a denial of standing because community standing is seen to carry with it the critical element of respect: the expectation not only that others will listen to you but also that you will exercise influence in the communal decision-making process.

Hence, the two readings offer rather different interpretations of the same testimony by Aboriginal women and youth. The first identifies struggles between Aboriginal women, youth, and the entrenched elite of Aboriginal communities as a conflict between individual and collective rights. Here political resistance is equated with a desire by Aboriginal women and youth to protect a right to freedom of choice against potentially overbearing Aboriginal cultural practices and traditions. The second identifies the same conflicts as a struggle by women and youth for power and influence within the Aboriginal communal self-definition process. Here conflict between individual liberty and cultural expressions of identity is not what is primarily at issue. Rather, political resistance is understood to reflect a general desire by women and youth for inclusion in community power structures.

Of course, one could argue with justification that it is important to protect a wide space for individual expression within Aboriginal communities. My point, however, is that reducing claims made by Aboriginal women and youth to fundamental conflicts between collective and individual rights is simply too narrow an approach. Yet it is precisely this understanding of conflict that not only informs but also on occasion overwhelms policy discussions of Aboriginal self-government in Canada. Nowhere is this clearer than in discussions about the appropriateness of applying the Charter to Aboriginal governments. Therefore, it is to the assumptions that inform objections against self-government made on behalf of individual liberty that I now turn.

THE CHARTER OF RIGHTS AND FREEDOMS

For many Canadians, the Charter has become an important symbol of Canadian citizenship. Its liberal democratic provisions for individual freedom and equality represent for many what citizenship in Canada is all about. These deep commitments to liberal democratic beliefs, in turn, contribute to the character of the debate about Aboriginal self-government: many assume that, at the substantive core of the relationship between Aboriginal peoples and the Canadian state, there is a fundamental value conflict between Aboriginal cultural traditions and the kinds of liberal values represented in the Charter. Yet it is generally argued that, if Aboriginal self-governing communities are to retain their ties with Canada, they must accept certain commitments to shared citizenship, among them the Charter. The cost of Canadian citizenship to Aboriginal peoples, in other words, is the requirement that Aboriginal governments forgo those cultural practices that violate basic Charter rights.

Before RCAP, Aboriginal leaders regularly argued that their cultures are wedded more closely to group-differentiated than to individual rights. The problem that some liberals immediately associate with group-differentiated Aboriginal rights is that they can be put to use to restrict the liberty of Aboriginal individuals "in the name of group solidarity."[44] Undoubtedly, Aboriginal governments would have considerable latitude to shape the identities of Aboriginal individuals if the authority that Aboriginal governments exercise over individuals is based on the need to preserve and develop culture. Kymlicka argues that this kind of governmental power raises the possibility of individual oppression.[45] All sorts of values could be imposed on Aboriginal individuals in the name of preserving culture.

It is precisely this kind of discrimination that the Charter is said to address. Its general purpose is to clarify the nature of the relationships between citizens and their governments. In standard liberal fashion, the Charter reflects a form of individualism in which the individual is considered autonomous, rational, self-interested, and capable of free action. This assumption, in turn, informs a view of society in which individuals share a range of agreed-upon collective interests but who nevertheless remain at base self-interested and thus hold entitlements to protect their capacity for free decision "against the political authority of that society."[46]

These liberal ideals provide a powerful justification for a set of guarantees to protect individuals from the potentially overbearing hand of the state. The Charter is said to fulfill this basic need. It is designed "to shield individuals from governmental actions restricting or suppressing their basic human rights and freedoms."[47] So, for example, in exercising freedom of thought, belief, opinion, and expression under section 2(b) of the Charter, "individuals should be able to speak freely anywhere in Canada without fear of unwarranted interference or sanctions from any governmental source."[48] Where individuals are convinced that a government has violated their rights, the Charter guarantees their right to a third-party appeal process so that they can petition for redress (section 24[1]).

The same principles of freedom would hold true if applied against Aboriginal governments. Where Aboriginal residents have Charter rights, they could petition the Canadian state for redress of Charter violations perpetrated by their local Aboriginal governments. Thus, while Aboriginal rights may be legitimate (and not all Canadians accept this premise), many insist that appropriate measures also be put in place to ensure that Aboriginal individuals are empowered against their governments. Most point to the Charter as the clearest line of defence against what is often identified as the potential for heavy-handed tactics by Aboriginal governments against their citizens. Through it, Aboriginal individuals would be assured protection from discrimination and domination by their own collectivities.

Although acceptance of the Charter varies among Aboriginal persons, those who do object to it almost always do so on cultural grounds. RCAP puts it this way: "some Charter provisions reflect individualistic values that are antithetical to many Aboriginal cultures, which place greater emphasis on the responsibilities of individuals to their communities."[49] The idea implicit in this view is that Aboriginal governments exist largely to preserve distinct Aboriginal cultures. Accordingly, if the Charter were to apply to Aboriginal governments, it could undercut what some take to be one of the most important reasons for self-government: the desire to restore and revitalize Aboriginal cultural values and traditions. Arguments of this kind usually contain both practical and normative elements.

On a practical level, some Aboriginal leaders indicate that the democratic rights provisions of section 3 of the Charter could be used to block the possibility of restoring traditional Aboriginal forms of governance. In its testimony before RCAP, for example, the AFN argued that the Charter might undermine its collective right to reinstate "traditional forms of governance such as those based on clans, confederacy, or hereditary chiefs."[50] Here Charter requirements such as Western-style elections and majority rule are seen as antithetical to traditional Aboriginal leadership selection processes.

On a deeper, more normative level, some see the Charter as an "unwitting servant of the forces of assimilation and domination." RCAP notes that interpretation of the Charter "lies ultimately in the hands of judges who are often unfamiliar with Aboriginal ways" and who "are likely to prove unsympathetic to them when they depart from standard Canadian approaches."[51] As summarized by Menno Boldt, the fear here is that with time a series of Charter-based judicial decisions that uphold individual over collective interests may lead to a "snowballing of individualism" and thus to the eventual cultural disintegration of Aboriginal communal societies.[52]

The application of the Charter to Aboriginal governments is regarded by some as presumptuous and by others as the ultimate form of colonial arrogance because it assumes that Aboriginal and non-Aboriginal societies share the same liberal view of human nature. According to this view, then, the fundamental issue raised by the Charter debate is that of cultural conflict. The individual rights found in the Charter allegedly do not fit with the conceptions of human nature and the expectation for human behaviour found in many Aboriginal societies. Nevertheless, liberal beliefs about individual freedom and equality are deeply rooted in the political landscape of Canadian culture. As a result, despite the forceful manner in which cultural arguments against the Charter are often advanced by Aboriginal leaders and their supporters, Canadian governments generally insist that any institutional recognition of Aboriginal governments must go hand in hand with Charter accountability by those governments. The general principle advanced here is simple. No government is immune from perpetrating abuse and injustice against its citizens, Aboriginal governments included. On this ground alone, Aboriginal persons are said to need the protection of the Charter.

Furthermore, advocates of the Charter point out that many Aboriginal persons themselves are strong supporters of the Charter. Indeed, the testimony of women and youth summarized earlier is taken as ample evidence that many Aboriginal individuals already suffer from a disturbing lack of individual freedom. The visible signs of lack of freedom are said to be obvious: unwillingness on the part of leaders to accept women and children back into their communities under Bill C-31, failure to address domestic abuse as a political priority, and lack of responsiveness to demands from women and youth for political accountability. The position of the Native Women's Association of Canada (NWAC) is perhaps clearest on this point. In its 1994 report to RCAP, members of NWAC expressed concern about the danger of sexual discrimination in their communities and argued that the decisions of Aboriginal governments should be subject to the Charter.[53] When non-Aboriginal Canadians are alerted to the presence of political opposition within Aboriginal communities in this way, many insist that arguments upholding the alleged superiority of collective over individual interests wear thin.[54] What they see are cultural arguments being used by Aboriginal leaders as a shield to protect practices that in fact oppress Aboriginal individuals.

Nevertheless, when the Charter debate is framed in terms of individual versus collective rights, one can see how a cultural dilemma can emerge. Boldt describes the dilemma in this way: "If the Charter is imposed on Indian communities, then inevitably the two sets of incompatible standards – Western liberal individualism and traditional Indian communalism – will not only create tension and conflict within Indian communities but will destroy what is left of … communalism."[55] The challenge in his view, therefore, is not to try to balance individual and collective rights but to design mechanisms for the protection of individual Aboriginal persons that are "consistent with Indian communal cultural traditions."[56]

RCAP accepts the terms of this cultural dilemma almost without qualification. Its strategy is to try to resolve the dilemma within the framework of section 25 of the Charter. Two elements characterize its approach. First, RCAP points out the obvious – that application of the Charter to Aboriginal governments is necessarily "moulded and tempered by the mandatory provisions of section 25."[57] This means, in its view, that the Charter cannot be used to attack the basic institutions of Aboriginal governance or undermine basic Aboriginal political powers. Second, RCAP insists that section 25 should also be viewed as a constitutional instrument that Aboriginal governments can use to protect traditional governmental practices from potential Charter challenges. For it, section 25 is not only an interpretive rule but also one whose principal function is to protect "distinctive Aboriginal philosophical outlooks, cultures and traditions."[58] In general, then, RCAP argues that the section exists to prevent "Aboriginal understandings and approaches from being washed away in a flood of undifferentiated Charter interpretation."[59]

The Charter debate thus provides a vivid illustration of how the philosophical assumptions associated with communitarian and individualist pluralism relate to one another in the domain of Aboriginal policy. While communitarian assumptions sustain an Aboriginal right to cultural survival, individualist assumptions sustain individual rights to liberty. When conflict ensues between the two forms of rights, however, the Charter is seen by many non-Aboriginal Canadians in particular as a legitimate device for safeguarding the individual right of freedom of choice over that of cultural integrity. This state of affairs leads Boldt, among others, to conclude that at bottom "Canadian federalism at present is designed to accommodate pluralism based on 'individualism,' not 'communalism.'"[60]

THE QUESTION OF RELEVANCE

I turn now to assess the relevance of applying liberal assumptions about conflicts between individual freedom and cultural security to the Aboriginal self-government debate. What follows explains first why individualistic arguments contain problematic elements and are thus politically misleading when they form the basis for supporting limitations on Aboriginal power. I then draw a distinction between voluntary and nonvoluntary aspects of Aboriginal identity in order to explain the complex ways in which Aboriginal individuals can belong to their communities.

The central difficulty with the Charter debate is that it links the normative defensibility of Aboriginal self-government to those governments upholding standards that, by their nature, represent divergent traditions. The general character of the debate is that it frames conflicts within Aboriginal communities in terms of fundamental struggles between individual and collective rights. Here the collective rights of Aboriginal nations to cultural autonomy are pitted against the individual rights of Aboriginal women and youth to individual freedom.

I would argue, however, that the philosophical starting point of the Charter debate is predicated on a dichotomy that fundamentally misconstrues the nature of the most important identity claims that Aboriginal individuals level against their communities. What results is a philosophical and practical divide at the level of analysis that simply fails to do justice to the complex ways in which Aboriginal individuals and their communities relate to one another. This divide is evident in two respects.

First, the "culture versus individual freedom" approach to identity-related claims trades in the language of normative absolutes. On the one hand, there are those who see the imposition of individual Charter rights on Aboriginal peoples as a violation of Aboriginal cultural integrity. Jodi Cockerill and Roger Gibbins point out that, from this perspective, the Charter is regarded as a "symbolic affront to traditional principles."[61] In this sense, the application of the Charter is seen as yet another attempt at assimilation, an attempt, moreover, to once more deny Aboriginal peoples the right to practise their traditional cultural values.

On the other hand, there are those who see individuality as everything, so "the rights and freedoms of individuals must be protected even at the risk of group interests and values, including cultural survival."[62] From this perspective, consent is critical, and, if cultural obligations are conferred on individuals without their consent, the obligations that ensue can only be regarded as an imposition. In such cases, any defence of cultural traditions will be regarded as a source of coercive power applied against an unwilling membership.[63]

When conflict in Aboriginal communities is framed in terms of a fundamental competition between individual and collective rights, the values protected by those rights defy resolution. Each category is seen to protect an absolute value. As a result, it is exceedingly difficult to establish in principle how, and in what form, different kinds of individual and collective rights might be ranked. Of course, in conflicts between rights, some degree of priority can be set. This is precisely what the Royal Commission recommends when it suggests that the individual rights upheld by the Charter should be subject to the interpretive provisions of section 25, which, the commission adds, are cultural and collective in their intent. Nevertheless, the fact that choices must be made at the fundamental level of first principles remains unchanged. When conflict between individual and collective rights ensues, difficult choices still need to be made between which is the more important claim.

Second, and perhaps more importantly, framing conflicts within Aboriginal communities in terms of individual versus collective rights puts emphasis in the wrong place where many Aboriginal identity-related claims are concerned. As the analysis of this chapter has demonstrated, a good number of Aboriginal women and youth are critical of current expressions of Aboriginal identity on the ground that these expressions are too often the products of colonial oppression. Hence, Aboriginal women and youth argue that it is imperative they assume greater control over these expressions to be able to transform them. However, this interest in identity transformation is seldom framed in competitive rights talk. Instead, I believe that, for a significant portion of witnesses appearing before RCAP, their interest in cultural autonomy and individual freedom is subservient to a greater value: the Aboriginal right to self-definition.

No doubt, for some, this process of identity transformation is framed in the absolute terms of individual versus collective rights. The Quebec Native Women's Association, for example, argued before RCAP that collective rights should not take priority: "To speak the truth ... means combating the lies suggesting that only collective rights are important and reducing individual rights – which are often fundamental human rights – to an infectious illness transmitted by whites of European origin."[64] The National Action Committee on the Status of Women framed its arguments in similar terms. It also insisted that it may be foolhardy to allow Aboriginal traditions of government to prevail over the equality rights of the Charter because "not all the traditions [are] worth reviving in the context of the twentieth century."[65]

However, the vast majority of witnesses who addressed the question of individual and collective rights did so in terms of having greater decision-making authority at the levels of both individual and community. In the words of Peter Apikan, speaking for the Native Council of Canada,[66] "If we only look at individual rights, or only collective rights, we may be missing something that has eluded us for at least a century."[67] Generally, Aboriginal witnesses did not trade in the language of normative absolutes; few insisted that cultural autonomy and individual freedom are mutually exclusive. From this perspective, Aboriginal rights are better thought of as instruments to protect the collective capacity of Aboriginal communities to exercise decision-making authority. One might add, moreover, that decision-making authority itself is only rendered meaningful if all eligible and interested members of the community are allowed to participate. Consequently, what I conclude from the statements of women and youth before RCAP is that most see individual freedom and community development as part of the same process; one cannot occur in the absence of the other.

My claim here, in other words, is that the nature of the conflict that Aboriginal women and youth take up within their communities is often misunderstood by non-Aboriginal people: what they claim to detect is defined more by the "individual versus collective rights" perspective that they bring to their analyses of the conflict than by the character of the conflict itself. The problem stems from the propensity of both individualist and communitarian approaches to oversimplify the complex ways in which Aboriginal individuals can belong to their ethnic communities.

To explain the process of Aboriginal identity formation and the conflict generated by it, individualist approaches usually focus on the importance of voluntary aspects of Aboriginal association with their ethnic communities, while communitarian approaches usually focus on nonvoluntary aspects. In my view, neither is correct, though an approach that combines the two without indulging in the excesses of either is considerably closer to the mark.

Liberal theory embodies a philosophical anthropology in which ethnic identity is seen as a chosen lifestyle. Naturally, the theory embodies an acceptance of the idea that individuals have no choice about the ethnic groups into which they are born and that ethnic groups often provide individuals with important contexts for the acceptance and development of personal values. But liberalism's overriding commitment to individual autonomy means that ethnic identities should always be viewed as a matter of choice, something that individuals can take up and shed like membership in a voluntary association. The logic of the position is straightforward: when ethnic communities are viewed as voluntary associations, this view preserves the individual's right to adopt community values and assume community obligations if the individual is convinced that he or she will be well served by them. Conversely, if the values and obligations come to be viewed as oppressive, the fact that they are voluntarily assumed means they can also be discarded at will. Individual autonomy is thus preserved. Individuals are free to pursue other life plans and take up new obligations in either their own or alternative communities, remaining free to change these commitments should new plans and obligations appear to be more fulfilling in the future. The individual rights perspective champions precisely this kind of approach to individual freedom.

This liberal approach to ethnic identity formation has received its fair share of criticism. While criticism varies, most is directed at the purportedly inaccurate characterization of the kinds of ties between individuals and their ethnic groups. For example, John Gray argues that, "In the real world of human history, ... cultural identities are not constituted, voluntaristically, by acts of choice; they arise by inheritance, and by recognition. They are fates rather than choices."[68] In a similar vein, Iris Marion Young argues that the liberal approach fails to take seriously the deeper existential sources of ethnic and cultural life forms or the fact that ethnic groups are not defined by individual interests but by a "sense of identity" that comes to people because they share origins, history, and common purposes. Young notes further that ethnic affiliation "has the character of what Martin Heidegger calls 'throwness': one finds oneself as a member of a group which one experiences as always having been."[69] The implication here is that, unlike voluntary associations in which individuals are integrated into group life in terms of a functional role, ethnic groups meet a deeply felt human need for integration on the basis of personal belonging.

Thus, for scholars such as Gray and Young, ethnic identities are what people acquire at birth; they are nonvoluntary because they are formed in settings over which the individual has little or no choice. Being Aboriginal is said to constitute precisely such a nonvoluntary affiliation. Aboriginal individuals can choose to cultivate their ethnic identities or distance themselves from them. What they cannot do, however, is choose their ethnic identities and then discard them at will.

An important political implication follows from this nonvoluntary understanding of ethnic identity. The relationship that Aboriginal individuals have with their communities is often seen to be one of deep and abiding significance for them. Aboriginal communities are regarded as places in which Aboriginal individuals enjoy the closeness of extended family relations, develop economic endeavours, contribute to social life, and participate in ceremonial rituals. As a result, when conflict ensues between individuals and their communities, collective rights should have ascendancy in most cases. The ongoing viability and integrity of the cultural context in which Aboriginal individuals live and from which they gain personal meaning depend on it.

In my view, both voluntary and nonvoluntary approaches to ethnic identity formation identify important features that tie Aboriginal individuals to their communities. On one level, a self-governing Aboriginal community derives its moral justification from its shared bonds of ancestry, history, and common life. Being Aboriginal therefore has an important nonvoluntary component.

At the same time, however, Aboriginal identities are not culturally determined. While individuals are born to Aboriginal parents through no choice of their own, how they decide to give expression to their Aboriginal identity is often a matter of choice. Being Aboriginal therefore also has an important voluntary component. One consequence of Aboriginal immersion in an increasingly integrated global environment, for example, is that new ways of life have become available to Aboriginal individuals that were simply unavailable in the traditional order – ways of life based on intensive agriculture, trades, and professions, to name but a few. Other institutions, such as the capitalist economy, Christian churches, and formal education, further expanded choices, as did the option of living in urban centres away from tribal settings. Taken together, these choices have made it possible for Aboriginal individuals to adapt their self-definitions as Aboriginal peoples to their surroundings; they now have opportunities to reflect on their Aboriginal identities and make decisions about what it means to be Aboriginal in today's world.

The real challenge facing Aboriginal communities is thus to avoid subjecting Aboriginal individuals to the demands of community-sanctioned cultural and national images of identity. Aboriginal persons are not Aboriginal only when they are able to reflect normative standards of traditional objective culture. Rather, ties of ancestry, history, and traditional culture need to be creatively adapted and applied to the needs of the present so that Aboriginal individuals can develop their communities together as a collective people. The issue, then, is not one of traditional cultural integrity versus the individual right to dissent. Rather, in most cases, the object of individual political action should be understood in terms of attempts by individuals to transform relations of power within communities to expand participatory rights and thus make them more inclusive places to live. It is dimensions of this struggle that I believe are reflected in much of the testimony of Aboriginal women and youth before RCAP.

CONCLUSION

I have explored in this chapter how some of the representatives of Aboriginal women and youth described the features of their political identities within RCAP's public hearings. Clear from the preceding analysis is that Aboriginal political identity is not a coherent whole, capable of being described in a crisp formula as a collectively shared thick cultural identity.

Rather, Aboriginal political identity can better be understood as "a cluster of interrelated and relatively open-ended tendencies and impulses pulling in different directions ... capable of being developed and balanced in different ways."[70] As historically marginalized persons, Aboriginal women and youth should be understood as engaged in a political struggle to secure recognition for those images of identity that they say will further their capacity to flourish within their communities as well as the broader Canadian setting.

The strength of individualist pluralism also contributes to its essential weakness. The approach teaches us that Aboriginal individuals need freedom of choice to be able to develop and balance their identities in different ways. Yet it also takes the principle of freedom of choice and then juxtaposes it against cultural aspects of identity taken to be all-encompassing, deterministic, and thus potentially oppressive. The result is that the individualist approach often defines relationships between individual and communal aspects of Aboriginal identity in terms that are unduly antagonistic.

In diagnosing Aboriginal people's marginalization and in formulating solutions, the communitarian and individualist faces of pluralism pay insufficient attention to the empirical reality of Aboriginal diversity, by which I mean the shifting communal boundaries and changing individual identities of Aboriginal life. The relational face of pluralism more adequately confronts this reality. This approach dissolves the dichotomy between individualist and communitarian approaches because it constructs the relationship between individual and community in another way. A relational diagnosis is based on the premise that arguments about Aboriginal self-government should be understood as a problem of power differences within Aboriginal communities and between Aboriginal and Canadian governments. Less conspicuous in this line of reasoning is a commitment to preserve cultural differences, the autonomy of nations, or the right to individual choice, on the purported premise that these are goods in and of themselves. Exploring the implications of this approach is what constitutes the analyses of the next two chapters.

CHAPTER 5

ABORIGINAL BOUNDARIES AND THE DEMAND FOR EXTERNAL EQUALITY

I have shown that arguments both for and against greater Aboriginal self-government that are based on communitarian and individualist pluralism share a measure of incompleteness. In the name of freedom, equality, and self-definition, individualist pluralism advances a political morality of ethnic association that is voluntary, chosen, and strategic, while communitarian pluralism advances a political morality based on preserving common understandings, shared cultural values, and national structures. The perspectives diverge on where to locate the principal object of political attention: in the body of the free individual or in the character of the constitutive community. But, once Aboriginal identities and relations are defined, both develop similar strategies to analyze Aboriginal political activity: relations are described in terms of binary or oppositional encounters between Canadian state and Aboriginal nations or between Aboriginal nations and Aboriginal individuals.

This and the next chapter aim to provide a different justification for an Aboriginal right to self-government, one that relies on the relational face of pluralism. To advance my argument, I return one last time to the public hearings of RCAP. Here I document the remarkable consistency with which Aboriginal witnesses ground their claims to self-government in principles of equality. I then turn to the assumptions of relational pluralism. I examine how a relational perspective leads me to discuss the political principle of equality not in terms of membership in social and political structures but in terms of relationships and the formative role that individual power and group power have on Aboriginal identity. In this chapter, I discuss the implications of this view for relations between Aboriginal communities and Canadian governments, while in the next I apply these implications to relations within Aboriginal communities.

EQUALITY OF PEOPLES

The Hearings

Testimony before RCAP affords an unparallelled view into the diversity of the modern Aboriginal experience in Canada as described by Aboriginal persons themselves. Naturally, the sheer volume and scope of the testimony mean that it defies easy categorization. In Chapter 3, however, I pointed out that a number of key themes can be distilled from the testimony. Numerous Aboriginal witnesses repeatedly link in one way or another the significance of one or more of the following themes to their own experience: the tragic and heroic dimensions of the Aboriginal past, the devastating impact of exploitation meted out at the hands of Canadian governments, and the corresponding intent to resist the forces of colonialism and to heal communities and individuals, to resuscitate traditional culture and rekindle spiritual connections to ancestral territory, and to rebuild nations on the firm foundation of an adequate land and resource base.

Although not always consciously articulated or explicitly developed, there is a general theme to the public comments of many Aboriginal witnesses that I infer. Whether male or female, status or nonstatus, reserve or urban dweller, many demand resources so that they can construct identities according to their own designs. Indeed, the arguments of witnesses often read as a normative imperative: current imbalances in power at all levels must be equalized if Aboriginal persons are to enjoy a full measure of freedom and dignity within Canada. I conclude, therefore, that on closer inspection, the demand for Aboriginal rights by witnesses can be read as a demand for equal treatment. Moreover, this recurring demand for equal treatment appears to constitute one of the main themes that links a major part of the testimony of Aboriginal witnesses.

The prominence of this theme of equality operates on two closely related levels: some witnesses define equality as a formal relationship that ought to exist between Aboriginal communities (usually First Nations) and Canadian governments, while others are more preoccupied with attaining equality of political status between Aboriginal persons within Aboriginal communities. While the distinction here is important, both arguments can be seen as addressing current imbalances in relations of power. In the remainder of this section, I visit the testimony of Aboriginal witnesses again, this time in the hope of identifying explicitly the ways in which witnesses express the interlocking nature of these claims to equal relations. Throughout this chapter, I will address the issue of equality as a function of intergovernmental relations, leaving the matter of how Aboriginal witnesses address the question of political equality between Aboriginal persons within local communities for the next chapter.

Some witnesses identify the nation-based expression of political identity as central to Aboriginal existence, so what they demand is equal standing and recognition as peoples within Canada. In this form, claims to equal standing as peoples are regularly justified in terms of one or more of the following three explanations.

First, common in testimonials is the claim that Aboriginal peoples should be recognized as the original occupants of Canada: "We are the original inhabitants of this country now called Canada, and as First Nations peoples we never gave up our right to sovereignty. We are the First Peoples and we are a Nation with the inherent right to create and maintain our own identities and cultures, languages, values, practices, to govern ourselves and to govern our relations with other governments as distinct entities."[1] One can readily see the significant assertion to political power that flows from this construction of events. The right to self-government is generally held to be inherent and thus cannot be given or taken away by the Canadian federal government or the Constitution. This purported original status as sovereign nations is then used by witnesses to justify their normative claims to restitution in the form of restoring historical equivalency between Aboriginal and non-Aboriginal governments. Most often this restoration process is described in terms of recognizing the entitlement of Aboriginal communities to a nation-to-nation relationship with the Canadian state: "the spirit and intent of the treaty relationship is based on nation to nation relationships between First Nations and the government of Canada ... there must be a form of pluralism in Canada that allows Aboriginal laws, traditions and customs to flourish."[2]

Second, some witnesses make the case that, while Aboriginal peoples now live under the Crown's protection, doing so does not in any way diminish their historical right to govern their internal affairs. One witness noted that "We do not want a form of self-government that is subject to all the existing laws and policies of the federal and provincial governments, but one that co-exists equally and recognizes our needs. Self-government must be more than just self-administration but must encompass our form of laws and policies based on our culture and way of life."[3]

While the idea of self-government is clearly intended to sustain a claim to autonomy and equality, few witnesses go on to argue that the right is unlimited. Indeed, witnesses seldom put self-government forward as an end in itself. Rather, in keeping with the preceding statement, what most witnesses appear to be saying is that self-government is a tool to enable Aboriginal communities to exercise greater control over matters critical to the development of their individual and collective identities. I believe that, when Aboriginal witnesses use the language of equality, it should be seen as contributing to this objective. Witnesses generally seem to use the concept to refer to a relationship between nations who, because they share historical status as politically self-governing entities, ought to recognize and respect the right of each to develop and express their respective collective identities free from interference by the other.

And third, Aboriginal witnesses consistently describe relations between Aboriginal and Canadian governments in terms of treaty making. These witnesses seem to view treaties as formalized relations of reciprocity and consent: "what is needed is not a new relationship, but a return to the original agreement based on co-existence that [our] ancestors and non-Aboriginal peoples entered into in the pre-Confederation treaties ... Aboriginal and non-Aboriginal Canadians should sign a national treaty of renewal that recognizes Aboriginal culture, language, and treaty rights as well as the right of Aboriginal peoples to self-determination and to co-exist with other Canadians."[4]

The treaty issue that Aboriginal witnesses address most often concerns their desire to restore governmental relations of peace, friendship, and reciprocal obligations that they say flow from their treaty rights with the

Canadian Crown. In many instances, Aboriginal witnesses describe how treaty rights have been ignored, unfulfilled, or diminished by federal and provincial laws. Yet many of these witnesses say that the original treaty principles have survived to this day. What some then propose is a "bilateral process between treaty nations and the Crown to interpret, define and implement treaties based on their original spirit and intent."[5] "Before we can proceed, the relationship with the federal and provincial governments must be corrected as based on our Treaty. The Treaty must be implemented in the spirit in which it was made from the viewpoint of our people. Our elders tell us that the agreement was to share the land with the newcomers, not to surrender it for a handful of beads and a few scraps of land."[6]

Many witnesses thus reclaim what they see as original relations of symmetry between settler and Aboriginal nations and then draw that model forward as the political and legal norm for the present. In my view, these claims can be seen as containing an important conception of equality. Because Aboriginal nations are political communities whose members are both original occupants of Canada and in many cases possess treaty entitlements, these nations are said to be entitled to equality of status in their relationships with Canadian governments. Patrick Macklem frames this relationship in terms of "formal equality." He says that the fact of their prior sovereignty places Aboriginal nations in a legal position of formal equals with Canadian governments.[7] What necessarily follows from this line of reasoning is an important conception of justice for many Aboriginal witnesses: as equals among the peoples who make up Canada, Aboriginal nations are fully within their rights to exercise independent power over the form, expression, and development of their distinct individual and communal identities.

Implications and Analysis

Most Aboriginal witnesses who testified before RCAP insisted on the intrinsic value of their Aboriginal identity and, perhaps more importantly, on their right to maintain and develop historically and communally structured forms of Aboriginal life. There are Canadians who possess Aboriginal ancestry (some 375,000 as identified by RCAP) but have no identification with that ancestry or, if they do, little or no feeling of membership in a local Aboriginal community. Given the centrality of communities to pluralism, it is to persons for whom their Aboriginal affiliation draws them into community that I direct my attention.

Furthermore, one distinct feature of Aboriginal political rhetoric is that it has generated a picture of Aboriginal communities as nations. This political form of shared community is viewed by many witnesses to carry the weight of tradition and the prerogative of history; the role is intended to validate Aboriginal communities' claim to formal equality of status in their relations with the settler state. This category of Aboriginal community I take to be crucial. In my view, First Nations are meaningful entities from the perspective of pluralism because, to this point, they are the only feasible vehicles for Aboriginal self-government – from the standpoint of public policy, little else comes as close in practice. I believe that there is much to be gained by situating this political rhetoric of Aboriginal nationhood within, first, the identification approach to ethnic identity and, second, a relational theory of pluralism.

First, an identification approach suggests that national identities be understood as the expressions of choices made by Aboriginal individuals in community. From this perspective, there is an important distinction to be made between the sources of Aboriginal identity and its aspects. The abiding source of Aboriginal identity is identified as consisting in a shared ancestry and a shared historical experience of belonging to one another over time. These sources are further identified as having been profoundly shaped by the historical experience of suffering as a result of colonialism; it is this experience that in large part is said to lend to Aboriginal identity its Aboriginal character.

Hence, shared ancestry and shared historical experiences are what frame the context for the further development of Aboriginal identity. Cultural and national elements of identity are then characterized in the identification approach as the manifestation of this development. They are regarded as elements called into being and given political and other forms of expression in response to the relations that Aboriginal peoples either choose or are forced to take up with others. Thus, while the identification approach highlights that cultural and national manifestations of Aboriginal identity are genuine, they are simultaneously identified as particular historical expressions of identity, stimulated into existence by the specific and contingent conditions surrounding Aboriginal communities. As a result, just as the processes of individual self-definition are defined as inherently dynamic and susceptible to change, so too are the structures through which Aboriginal persons give expression to political association.

As the analysis of Chapter 3 demonstrated, the conventional approach to Aboriginal self-government emphasizes the importance of Aboriginal nations because nations are said to preserve culture, which is taken as that which makes Aboriginal communities distinctive. I also demonstrated, however, that, when cultural difference is made the basis for arguments supporting Aboriginal rights, doing so can not only undermine the justification for those rights but also promote unduly antagonistic relations between Aboriginal and Canadian governments. This antagonism occurs as the result of a threefold process. First, cultural elements of Aboriginal identity are taken as fundamental markers of Aboriginal community identity. Second, Aboriginal rights are tied to only those elements of practices, customs, and traditions said to be integral to distinctive Aboriginal culture. Consequently, when those elements change (through contact or assimilation), the Aboriginal right associated with their protection is also understood to disappear. Third, Aboriginal communities are forced to preserve the distinctive elements of their cultures from the encroaching influences of non-Aboriginal society because, if they do not, they may lose their rights and, by extension, their community identities. Consequently, what results is a competitive claims-based relationship between Aboriginal and Canadian governments motivated by Aboriginals' concern to protect their essential identity-conferring attributes. The question is whether Aboriginal and Canadian governments are well served by the use of categories that construct their relationship in terms of cultural competition. In my view, the relationship would be far better served by a different set of categories, one that promotes cooperative governmental relations based on a more complex, layered, and overlapping understanding of Aboriginal community identity.

If the ongoing viability of Aboriginal nations is to be protected, then it is important from the identification perspective not to equate cultural and political aspects of Aboriginal identity with their sources. To do so draws us into the dangerous terrain of assuming that, when a particular aspect of Aboriginal identity is transformed into another form, the experience of Aboriginality itself is, for all intents and purposes, over rather than merely changed. It is far better, therefore, to lodge Aboriginal identity within its source: that is, within ancestry, history, location, and the abiding ties of loyalty and affinity that these connections generate, since the source lends to Aboriginal community identity a more permanent foundation. From the identification perspective, these connections are of intrinsic importance where the identity of what are now commonly referred to as First Nations is concerned.

Second, in Chapter 1, I established that relational pluralism is a normative theory that upholds certain standards of equality within and between groups. From a relational perspective, equality within groups is important because human subjectivity is regarded as the outcome of the relations that we keep, and healthy individual development thus depends on having power to shape the course of those relations. But equality between groups is also important because individual self-development is dependent on the capacity of groups to develop. Consequently, groups are also said to need power. The idea here is that group members should be able to construct protective boundaries around themselves so that they can decide on and express their group identities free from external domination. On both individual and communal levels, the evaluative standard of justice is relational: equality is understood to be about relationships that empower individuals and their communities to exercise control over the directions of their individual and communal lives.

What are the implications of this view for the politics of Aboriginal self-government? Rather than stress distinctive cultural elements or the preservation of nations as central to Aboriginal identity, a relational pluralist stresses that a healthy Aboriginal identity is the outcome of Aboriginal communities and the members within them having control over their lives in ways consistent with their own aspirations. While these aspirations may include expressions of distinctive culture and nationhood, they may include other expressions as well. According to this approach, then, key from the point of view of justice is that Aboriginal communities possess the right to develop and give expression to any element of communal identity, whether culturally distinctive or otherwise. The central issue is not one of culture- or nation-based preservation, in other words, but more broadly the Aboriginal right to be self-defining within Canada.

With both the identification perspective on Aboriginal identity and the relational theory of pluralism in hand, I can now take the next step in the argument of this chapter. What happens if we take the identification perspective on Aboriginal identity as opposed to a "cultural" or "national" one and if we link it to a relational theory of pluralism as opposed to a communitarian or individualist one? Are there particular political problems associated with Aboriginal self-government that currently defy resolution that could be better handled within this framework? Of course, Aboriginal communities are not homogeneous entities, nor can one distill from Aboriginal discourse a single perspective on Aboriginal governance issues. Confronting the challenge of Aboriginal self-government, in other words, is both multifaceted and highly complex. In the remainder of this chapter, I articulate one view on what Aboriginal self-government might involve. This view, informed by relational pluralism, relies less on elements of cultural and political structures as the reference point for Aboriginal community equality and more on relationships and the Aboriginal right to equality and freedom from domination in those relationships.[8]

Finally, to raise the standard of power and its just distribution necessarily requires that I also address the question of what is possible given the reality of power relations and their associated limitations in Canada. Changing one's categories of analysis in the way proposed is intended to shed greater light on what is involved in the challenge of Aboriginal self-government in Canada. But this approach does not do away with the fact that many Aboriginal persons and communities face serious and ongoing constraints on their freedom. The aspirations of some, for example, may be constrained by what they see as the structural limitations attached to the practice of Canadian federalism, while others may regard the treaty process under way in parts of Canada, such as in British Columbia, to demand an extraordinarily high level of compromise. There are thus clear structural limitations to what Aboriginal communities can achieve, some associated with the natural limitations of the Canadian political system itself and others with the tendency of the Canadian state to refuse to break fundamentally with assumptions of colonial dominance.

My point is not to ignore these real constraints but to think about the relationships that stand behind them in a different way. By stressing the importance of Aboriginal community identity as complex, evolving, and situational, relational pluralism highlights not only the degree to which different kinds of political choices can be made by Aboriginal communities but also that those choices may be legitimate from the perspective of promoting genuine Aboriginal freedom. I believe that acceptance of this central pluralist insight preserves an avenue for not only softening cultural and political confrontation between Aboriginal and Canadian governments but also generating genuine political relationships of interdependency and cooperation. Precisely what this might involve is a matter that I turn to next.

COLONIALISM AND EQUALITY

The importance of freedom from domination is reinforced by the pluralist commitment to equality between groups, no small challenge in the context of an environment in which Aboriginal peoples have suffered oppression associated with colonial domination and control. In the colonial setting, the relationship was unabashedly hierarchical, one in which non-Aboriginal people regarded themselves as primary and independent and Aboriginal peoples as lesser and dependent. Such colonial attitudes are what lent purported legitimacy to the Crown's right to claim political control over Aboriginal nations and underlying title to Aboriginal lands. Put simply, a pluralist framework accentuates the importance of a politics that redresses injustices done to Aboriginal nations flowing from this hierarchical relationship. A just settlement of Aboriginal grievances requires that these colonial relations be understood for what they are and that the oppression generated by those relations be stopped and repaired.

As the testimony before RCAP illustrates, the experience of colonialism translates into an overall Aboriginal perception that Aboriginal people are disadvantaged and oppressed not only as individuals but also as communities. Thus, while social justice refers to granting Aboriginal individuals "the socially supported substantive opportunity ... to develop and exercise their capacities and realize their choices," this in and of itself is not enough.[9] As Iris Marion Young has shown, oppression is a collective phenomenon in which groups become hostage to standards imposed on them by the external world.[10]

So, insofar as a pluralist framework addresses unequal distributions of power, it also compels us to consider Aboriginal communal affiliations as a legitimate form of political mobilization. One can conclude from the general thrust of the testimony by Aboriginal witnesses that they want to strengthen sources of communal power to ameliorate conditions of social and economic disadvantage and to shatter stigmatizing images and stereotypes that have rendered their own community-generated experiences and identities as inferior. Many point to the structures of Aboriginal nationhood as the boundary markers behind which they wish to take up community rehabilitation. Consequently, if Canada is not to remain an alienating environment for Aboriginal persons, it seems that, among other things, a positive culture of equality is needed in which equality is understood to entail a public affirmation and recognition of the specific experiences, identities, and social contributions that Aboriginal persons have as members of nations.

Macklem suggests that this Aboriginal concern for equality should be understood in terms of both "formal" and "substantive" objectives.[11] He argues that, by virtue of their original occupancy and inherent sovereignty, Aboriginal peoples constitute nations and are thus formally entitled to a just distribution of political power with their Canadian governmental counterparts (formal equality), a condition clearly denied to them during the colonial period. But Macklem also insists that equality requires a distribution of power so as to address substantive ends: "Aboriginal communities have been and continue to be oppressed by various social and economic forces which have had a profound effect on their social and economic status." Consequently, what Aboriginal peoples both need and are entitled to is equality of resources to "remedy the oppression that [they] experience in their daily lives" and thus be in a position "to obtain greater control over their individual and collective identities."[12] In either case, the bottom line here is self-government: Aboriginal witnesses consistently argue in one fashion or another that what they need is the framework provided by self-rule so that their communities can have political boundaries behind which to make independent decisions. These decisions include the right to decide land ownership and occupancy issues in traditional territories, to create social and economic policies, to develop or rebuild political institutions, and to nurture distinctive cultural and religious practices.[13]

To date, defining self-government has been notoriously difficult, in no small measure because Aboriginal communities are far "too diverse to operate under a single set of rules."[14] However, obsessive concern about pinning down the substantive meaning of self-government as a prerequisite to exercising the right itself is to miss the point that many witnesses before RCAP make. While the substantive content of the right is important, most witnesses seem to be far more interested in using the claim to self-government to put an end to governmental paternalism. Of first importance, in other words, is "Aboriginal rather than external authority over jurisdictions and institutions of relevance to Aboriginal peoples."[15] As Patricia Monture-Angus argues, it is about rejecting what was imposed without Aboriginal consent and is thus "a call for the opportunity to remedy the consequences of colonialism and the corresponding oppression we carry as individuals and collectively."[16]

This strikes me as language consistent with the normative thrust of relational pluralism. What I infer from comments like those of Monture-Angus is that most Aboriginal leaders do not seek self-government as an instrument to secure their separation from Canada or as a way to exercise absolute and unconstrained powers within Canada. Rather, self-government constitutes an attempt by Aboriginal leaders to establish flexible political relationships with Canadian governments based on mutually agreeable patterns of divided and shared power over lands, resources, and people. This sentiment is regularly expressed in the scholarship of James Tully. He argues that key to the relationship are ideals such as reciprocity, coexistence, and consent: Aboriginal governments must be equal partners in the political discourse that they take up with Canadian governments if the specific evolving and changing needs and circumstances of their communities are to be met.[17]

What direction this relational discourse takes would necessarily be up to the Canadian and Aboriginal governments themselves. My point is simply that there need be no rigid list of jurisdictions and powers that Aboriginal governments must exercise if they are to function as communities of self-definition for their members. In practice, rather, one would expect to find that different kinds of political choices would be made by Aboriginal leaders about the range of self-governing powers that they may wish to exercise: some will be modest, while others will be more wide-ranging, perhaps reflecting in part those currently exercised by federal and provincial governments. Framed in this way, Aboriginal self-government is primarily about trying to find ways to integrate Canada politically based on the idea of coordinating rather than subordinating Aboriginal communities and their governments. Beyond this basic commitment of relational respect for governmental coexistence, self-governing structures are to "evolve over time in accordance with local needs and regional aspirations."[18] As noted by Radha Jhappan, these local needs and aspirations would be shaped by (among other things) whether the particular Aboriginal community "has a land base under the reserve system and Indian Act, whether it is rural or urban, and whether it has a substantial population and resource base."[19]

Now one could argue with justification that, with respect to external relations between Aboriginal communities and the Canadian state, a pluralist commitment to equality and freedom from domination at the level of politics is hardly a novel position. Recent work by nationalist and liberal scholars,[20] for example, as well as the primary policy thrust of RCAP's report,[21] offer justifications similar to those of relational pluralism for group-based Aboriginal emancipation. However, in this literature, the kind of power that Aboriginal communities aspire to is usually discussed as a problem of federalism or, more specifically, treaty federalism.[22] While Aboriginal communities are generally considered too small and, in the main, uninterested in the idea of functioning as independent states, they are nevertheless understood to be interested in political and administrative power sharing with Canada. Treaty federalism is not only the proposed institutional solution but also often put forward as the only just solution because through it Aboriginal governments could enjoy continued affiliation with the Canadian state while still realizing the objective of local control through constitutional guarantees of partial autonomy.[23]

Within the Canadian political setting, federalism can be conceived of as a political device built simultaneously on two main pillars: shared rule and self-rule. In theory, neither pillar should take precedence over the other; if one does, then this action will jeopardize the entire federal system. In the Canadian case, the shared rule criteria are met in the form of formal, structured representations for both pan-Canadian and regional interests within central governmental institutions (e.g., Parliament and the Supreme Court), while the self-rule criteria are met in the form of constitutionally divided power between the federal government and provincial governments.[24] The important principle that federalism is said to uphold is that of equitable (if not equal) territorial representation via the parliamentary branch of government and that of governmental independence. Central to the practice of Canadian federalism, in other words, is partnership: its constant challenge is often said to involve striking an institutional equilibrium between the forces of centralization and decentralization or, if one prefers, between unity and diversity.

Aboriginal political integration into the Canadian federal system in this way is the solution preferred by RCAP. For it, the chief virtue of federalism is that it can accommodate the cultural differences of Aboriginal peoples by affording their communities control over governmental structures that, for certain purposes, would be largely autonomous. RCAP argues that the Aboriginal right to self-determination gives Aboriginal peoples governmental options that could involve a "high degree of sovereignty," but it also insists that those options must be exercised "within Canada."[25] For RCAP, enactment of section 35 of the Constitution Act, 1982, "confirmed the status of Aboriginal peoples as partners in the complex federal arrangements that make up Canada."[26] Federalism is regarded positively because it provides "the basis for recognizing Aboriginal governments as one of three distinct orders of government in Canada." The hallmark of Canadian federalism, argues RCAP, is a commitment to shared sovereignty, which means that, in "the three-cornered relations" that link Aboriginal, provincial, and federal governments, all three "are sovereign within their respective spheres and hold their powers by virtue of their constitutional status rather than by delegation."[27]

In practical terms, RCAP recommends that this federal arrangement include two measures: the creation of an Aboriginal parliament leading eventually to a House of First Peoples (shared rule), and the development of an organic form of Aboriginal self-government (self-rule). The recommendation concerning an Aboriginal parliament and House of First Peoples was offered to stimulate greater direct participation by Aboriginal people "in the decision-making processes of Canadian institutions of government."[28] Yet, as Alan Cairns notes, this shared rule pillar of federalist practice received minimal attention.[29] It has also generated little interest among Aboriginal and non-Aboriginal leaders alike and, of all RCAP's many recommendations, was one of the first to be dismissed.

On the "self-rule" side of federal practice, however, RCAP had much more to contribute. In this sense, when RCAP refers to federalism as a solution for Aboriginal community revitalization, it does so almost entirely with reference to only one of its two pillars. RCAP argues that shared sovereignty is the feature of Canadian federalism that holds the greatest promise for Aboriginal emancipation because through it Aboriginal people could exercise the independent power that they need to rebuild their communities and nations. RCAP thus clearly subordinates the federal idea of shared rule to that of self-rule. For it, shared rule may be an attractive ideal but will amount to little if lacking political foundation in viable and self-sufficient Aboriginal communities.

As defined by RCAP, Aboriginal nations would have "an *actual* right to exercise jurisdiction over certain core subject-matters ... of vital concern to the life and welfare of the community" as well as "a *potential* right to deal with a wider range of matters that lie beyond the core area and extend to the outer periphery of potential Aboriginal jurisdiction."[30] The criteria for determining the difference between *core* and *peripheral* authority as well as areas that lie outside Aboriginal jurisdiction relate to Aboriginal community identity and interest. Core areas refer to those legislative responsibilities of government in which Aboriginal communities should have jurisdiction if they are to be self-defining. These would include areas such as citizenship; lands and resources; social, educational, and health services; economic development; language and culture; and various aspects of the criminal justice system. Peripheral areas refer to those responsibilities in which Aboriginal governments may have an interest but that also have "a major impact on adjacent jurisdictions or attract transcendent federal or provincial concern."[31] These areas (among them, criminal justice) require a substantial degree of coordination between Aboriginal, federal, and provincial governments, so RCAP concluded that Aboriginal governments cannot legislate in these areas "until agreements have been concluded with federal and provincial governments."[32] Areas that lie outside Aboriginal jurisdiction include national defence, international trade, banking and currency, bankruptcy and insolvency, navigation and shipping, postal service, and so on. These are areas in which the federal government currently has law-making authority and that are said to involve matters that can continue to be best handled at the national level.

For a relational pluralist, federalist solutions to the Aboriginal demand for self-government such as those proposed by RCAP are meaningful only when nested in a relational dynamic. Herein, I would argue, lies the principal contribution that relational pluralism can make to the debate about how to deepen external relations of cooperation, negotiation, and dialogue between Aboriginal and Canadian governments. For relational pluralists, federalism refers to a relationship of political equality between two orders of government. Of critical importance to this relationship from a pluralist point of view is a decentralization of power from the government of Canada to Aboriginal communities. Less conspicuous in this line of reasoning are demands for formal constitutional relations between Aboriginal, federal, and provincial governments of a kind that one finds in the scholarship of Henderson, Macklem, and Tully, for example, or for formal structured representation for Aboriginal political leaders in the institutions of the federal government – in short, arrangements that might be characterized as more typically federalist. One way to accentuate what this relational contribution involves is to contrast it with federalist approaches to self-rule that link Aboriginal identity to structural attributes of difference.

Under the difference model, Aboriginal political identity is taken to be equivalent to nationhood. Nations are then regarded as of intrinsic importance because they are seen to be, by definition, the source of Aboriginal political identity. What this model promotes is a structuralist approach to Aboriginal-Canadian state relations: the integrity of Aboriginal political identity is said to rely specifically on the structural integrity of the political institutions of Aboriginal nations. Federalist solutions developed in this vein, therefore, seek to empower and rebuild the structural capacity of Aboriginal nations as an end in itself. Here federalism is framed in terms of the need to manage relations between coexisting political entities; Aboriginal and non-Aboriginal peoples are each said to be entitled to exercise political authority because they are structurally separate and independent.

Furthermore, the language associated with this structuralist model often carries the assumption that relations between Aboriginal and Canadian governments are inevitably oppositional or at least associated with asserting cultural difference. The cultural strain of the argument suggests that, if Aboriginal peoples are to survive as communities, they must preserve their cultural uniqueness. The justification for Aboriginal self-government is thus seen to rest specifically on this desire to preserve culture: nations are said to be particularly well suited structurally to preserve and promote the distinct cultural elements of Aboriginal ways of life. It is this justification that one finds, for example, at the heart of RCAP's report. As Cairns argues, "The Commission's decision to opt for 'nation' as the Report's key organizing concept sprang from the priority it attached to the goal of cultural survival and the nation's right of self-determination to achieve it."[33]

The more nationalist strain, meanwhile, accedes to the political vocabulary of sovereignty in which the sovereignty of Aboriginal nations is regularly juxtaposed with that of the Canadian state. In this version, Aboriginal nations are viewed as partners among the nationalities that constitute the Canadian federation. Here Aboriginal self-government is justified on restorative grounds: a history of colonial relations has denied Aboriginal nations their sovereign right to exercise the political autonomy to which they remain entitled. The image presented here is often one of centralized and unified sovereign powers engaged in adversarial relations of political competition over power, land, and resources. As P.G. McHugh phrases it, the "approach supposes two closed political systems in competition, the state asserting its domination and paramountcy with Aboriginal peoples counter-asserting a self-contained independence."[34]

A relational pluralist analysis of self-government avoids associating the Aboriginal right to jurisdiction over its own collective life with the qualification of cultural uniqueness or political competitiveness and, for this reason, is considerably more realistic. No doubt intergovernmental relations between Aboriginal and non-Aboriginal people can result in political conflict, opposition, and the assertion of cultural difference, and this outcome can be advantageous when it serves to fulfill the Aboriginal need for political power and resources necessary to rebuild Aboriginal communities. Yet a relational approach promotes less disputatious and adversarial orientations between Canadian and Aboriginal governments on the ground that this approach is far better given the inevitable permanency of their political relationship. Peaceful coexistence, in other words, is far more likely when political agreement, cooperation, and mutual cultural influence are featured as central to the relationship rather than cultural and political incompatibilities. It is my view that relational pluralism takes this latter possibility more readily into account.

From a relational pluralist point of view, management of relations between Canadian and Aboriginal governments is seen to lie more in tripartite processes that ensure a cooperative and participatory political relationship than in the delivery of particular cultural and political structures as ends in themselves. Here the Aboriginal right to self-government is seen as the outcome of a process in which Canadian governments recognize their federal obligation to create political space for Aboriginal communities so that they can develop and express their communal identities in freedom. In this sense, self-government serves as the legal and normative foundation for Aboriginal governments to establish their authority across a range of jurisdictions, cultural, political, or otherwise. Naturally, Canadian governments remain the more powerful collectivity in the relationship with Aboriginal governments; this fact is not in question. What is questioned, however, is the federal government's presumed right to arbitrarily set limits on Aboriginal power and to unilaterally determine the range of powers that Aboriginal communities may exercise under self-government. Under the terms of relational pluralism, when Canadian and Aboriginal governments relate, they should do so as equals so that Aboriginal communities possess the freedom to decide what is in their best interests.

As for the source of the Aboriginal right to self-government, there is no presumption within relational pluralism that it must originate from practices associated with Aboriginal cultural difference or precolonial political sovereignty. The source, rather, would need to be more relational in origin – that is, in keeping with the kinds of obligations assumed by colonial representatives of the Crown and later by Canadian governments on initial contact with Aboriginal communities. Here two relational elements seem to be important. The first is that of original occupancy: the Aboriginal right to self-government originates from an Aboriginal status as organized political communities, rooted in territory, with an independent existence prior to the creation of the new state now called Canada. The second is that of community: the Aboriginal right to self-government is activated by the collective Aboriginal desire to have the political, social, and economic instruments to guarantee the development of their communities. When I refer to federalism as a solution, I do so in this relational sense.

The strength of the relational pluralist tradition thus lies in its attention to the question of whether political relations (as opposed to structures) contribute to genuine equality and freedom from domination between Aboriginal and Canadian governments. A number of distinct, though rarely recognized, implications relating to Aboriginal community boundaries and power, and the proper and improper limits on Aboriginal claims, follow from this central insight.

BOUNDARIES, INTERDEPENDENCE, AND ABORIGINAL POWER

First, self-government implies an Aboriginal right to protection against intrusion by external authority into Aboriginal social and political structures. This right requires of non-Aboriginal governments a duty of noninterference so that Aboriginal communities can engage in their own processes of self-definition.

A helpful metaphor here is that of boundaries. Justice for pluralists is captured by the idea of egalitarian relationships. What is important, therefore, is not using the power of self-government to maintain cultural and political differences between Aboriginal and non-Aboriginal communities but using that power to maintain boundaries — and boundaries not for their own sake but for the sake of extending to Aboriginal communities a protected sphere in which to build lives that correspond to their own priorities. This emphasis on a boundary and the need to protect it can simultaneously separate and relate Aboriginal nations and the Canadian polity. It recognizes that, while some aspects of identity might be different on either side of the boundary, these aspects themselves do not define difference. The difference, rather, is defined by each Aboriginal community's entitlement to decide what kind of political organization is in its best interests, whether and to what degree it wants to be integrated into the broader society, and which kinds of political, economic, and social relations it wants to establish with other groups in Canada. The character of the relationship between Aboriginal and non-Aboriginal governments should thus be determined not by the substance of their cultural and political differences but by the style of relations between them. Boundaries are thus the antidote to colonialism. Furthermore, the capacity to be self-defining is the central element in just relations.

The related implication is that Aboriginal self-government is most fundamentally about the capacity to exercise political authority at the local level. Wayne Warry describes the kind of political dynamic that I have in mind here: self-government "is what happens 'on the ground' ... It is about increasing self-sufficiency and the process of capacity-building whereby communities can identify their needs, exercise their ability to address these needs, and evaluate approaches so as to ensure that human and financial resources are allocated effectively and efficiently."[35] Framed in this way, self-government constitutes a process by which Aboriginal communities build institutions to respond to local conditions. Boundaries of noninterference are important because they afford Aboriginal governments the political authority they need to map out areas of local jurisdiction in their relations with the Canadian state.

Second, self-government implies an Aboriginal right to an equal share of power with non-Aboriginal governments when they define the ground rules for their relationship with one another. This right requires of Canadian governments a commitment to reciprocity so that Aboriginal governments can develop relations of interdependence with their Canadian counterparts in ways that derive from joint deliberation and mutually acceptable compromise.

The assertion that Aboriginals are sovereign peoples in need of a nation-to-nation relationship with the Canadian government could be equated with a separatist sentiment and an Aboriginal rejection of Canadian society. This assumption harmonizes well with the literature on nationalism that generally assumes ethnic ideologies become nationalist the moment they demand a state on behalf of an ethnic group.[36] Construed in this way, nationalism possesses the character of a zero sum game: whatever Aboriginal peoples gain in self-government powers is necessarily a direct loss in powers for the Canadian state.

However, while the idea that every nation must have its own state is common, there is no necessary connection between the two. Indeed, this proposition is borne out by the empirical evidence in the Aboriginal context. Aboriginal leaders in Canada have not made the acquisition of a state for their nations a political priority, nor is their claim to self-government intended as a threat to the territorial integrity or the sovereignty of the Canadian state. As Gerald Alfred points out, there are different forms of nationalism in the world today. He defines Aboriginal nationalism as a community-based ethnic nationalism best understood as a reaction to Western political and cultural hegemony.[37] Its objective is "to achieve self-determination not through the creation of a new state, but through the achieve-ment of a cultural sovereignty and a political relationship based on group autonomy and reflected in formal self-government arrangements in coop-eration with existing state institutions."[38] The objectives of the state-based and community-based nationalist movements are thus essentially different: "Where the state-based nationalist project is geared toward displacing the existing state in the creation of a new one, community sovereignty nation-alism accepts the state's present existence and attempts an accommodation that preserves the integrity of both the challenging ethnic group and the state itself."[39]

A relational pluralist perspective on self-government can facilitate how we might think about this accommodation. Under the pluralist model, Aboriginal self-government aims to find the means for a deeper political integration into the Canadian state based on the idea that integration is a result of the coordination and mutually acceptable interdependence rather than subordination of Aboriginal communities.

Communitarian pluralists such as Will Kymlicka and Charles Taylor argue that this kind of accommodation can be facilitated only if non-Aboriginal Canadians accept what they call a theory of "deep diversity."[40] For them, Aboriginal people's sense of political integration into Canada depends on their Canadian identity "passing through" their more funda-mental identity as members of Aboriginal nations. This understanding of identity leads Kymlicka to argue that for Aboriginal groups Canada is wor-thy of their allegiance only if it conducts itself as "a federation of national groups which respect each other's right to be a distinct societal culture within Canada."[41] Taylor also accepts that community identity can be ex-pressed through language and culture, but he argues that, with respect to Quebec at least, its allegiance to Canada rests more broadly on the degree to which Canada contributes to the survival and furtherance of the Québécois nation.[42] One can safely assume that for Taylor the situation of Quebec and that of Aboriginal nations is roughly analogous. He argues that, by virtue of their prior occupancy as functioning societies on the ter-ritory now called Canada, Aboriginal peoples constitute nations with the right to self-rule.[43] Thus, as with nationalists in Quebec, Taylor would undoubtedly also say that many Aboriginal persons also believe that Canada is worthy of their allegiance only to the degree that it provides their

communities with the political autonomy they need to defend and promote those attributes they take to be central to their identities.

Tully's strategy for accommodating Aboriginal self-government is more
consistent with relational pluralism. This is evident, for example, in the priority that Tully places on the need to establish normative ground rules for
a just relationship between Aboriginal and non-Aboriginal peoples in
Canada. He believes that Aboriginal peoples can flourish within Canada
only when "Aboriginal peoples and Canadians recognize and relate to each
other as equal, coexisting, and self-governing peoples throughout their
many relations together."[44] A just form of associating together, in other
words, must be built on the foundation of equality. Tully then proceeds to
employ a series of relational concepts to illustrate what an equitable association between self-governing peoples would involve in practice. These concepts include dialogues of intercultural negotiations; commitments to
mutual understanding, respect, and sharing; and acts of responsibility for
one another that would result in uncoerced agreements and relations of
cooperation over time.[45]

It is also clear, however, that Tully's use of relational concepts is harnessed
to explicitly cultural concerns. For Tully, the aim of reaching agreements on
self-government is to generate a form of "intercultural" understanding that
would allow both Aboriginal and non-Aboriginal peoples to "govern
themselves and their lands by their own laws and cultures."[46] Tully is sensitive to the fact that over 300 years of interacting mean that Aboriginal and
non-Aboriginal peoples now share a lot of common cultural ground.
Nevertheless, he insists that the aim of their partnership must not be "to reduce one partner to the image of the other" but "to show respect for each
other – for their languages, cultures, laws, and governments –" in a way that
allows each to maintain its differences.[47] One can conclude, therefore, that
for Tully relational pluralism functions at bottom as an instrument to secure
the greater good of Aboriginal cultural integrity.

In my view, Taylor's, Kymlicka's, and Tully's understandings of what
motivates the interest of multinational entities also dictate the political accommodation that these entities require: if Aboriginal interest is defined in
terms of belonging to a constituent national element of Canada, then accommodation necessarily requires a degree of cultural separation (Kymlicka),
and/or political autonomy (Taylor), and/or dialogue respectful of cultural

difference (Tully). But what if one looks at the relationship between Aboriginal and non-Aboriginal governments from the more elemental perspective of equal power and reciprocity in the relations that distribute political power? Would it not make a difference to the debate about Aboriginal accommodation if the idea of "deep diversity" is thought of less in terms of difference (as Taylor puts it) and more in terms of empowering the marginalized voices of Aboriginal individuals and communities in their multiple and ever-shifting relations with the Canadian state?

Proponents of relational pluralism concern themselves with the presence of systemic political inequality between societal groups. They seek to address cases where concentration of power has led to the sustained inability of marginalized individuals and groups to exercise power and control over their own lives. In the case of Aboriginal peoples, loss of power and control came at the hands of Europeans who committed gross injustices against them in the settlement of North America. These injustices, therefore, are of first concern.

What implications follow from this view? While Aboriginal identification with Canada may continue to "pass through" Aboriginal communities, there is no requirement that Aboriginal self-development depends on degrees of cultural or political independence from Canada. Instead, what self-development depends on is consent. It is the Aboriginal ability to make choices in freedom at both individual and community levels that is important.[48] This position, it seems to me, corresponds closely to Macklem's notion of equality.[49] While Aboriginal communities may need status as formal equals to Canadian governments to gain political leverage in their dealings with those governments, key from the perspective of justice is substantive equality. Justice requires that Aboriginal communities possess power commensurate with their need to overcome their position of social and economic disadvantage and with their right to be self-defining within Canada at both individual and community levels. Seen in this light, any arrangement with the Canadian polity that satisfies the aspirations of Aboriginal communities can be viewed as an exercise in self-government.

Where these choices take Aboriginal and Canadian governments is naturally an open question. But the point is that nothing should in principle preclude the possibility of their developing deeper relations of cooperation and interdependence with one another. All that is required is that those

relations be processes in which Aboriginal peoples, through their governments, enjoy full participation. In addition, the negotiated outcomes of
those relations should be ones to which Aboriginal peoples offer their full
consent. It seems to me that thinking about "deep diversity" in this way,
while still not guaranteeing a deepened sense of political integration of
Aboriginal and non-Aboriginal peoples, at least allows the door to swing
more widely open on this possibility.

Significantly, some of the judicial interpretations of Aboriginal rights
under section 35(1) of the Constitution Act, 1982, impose legal and political duties on Canadian governments that follow, in part, the lines advanced
by the two principles of internal noninterference and external reciprocity
in governmental relations as defined above. Since the 1980s, the Supreme
Court has defined the federal government's constitutional role to "Indians
and Lands reserved for the Indians" (section 91 [24]) as fiduciary or trustlike. One of the most important decisions on Aboriginal rights in this respect was rendered in 1990 by the Supreme Court of Canada in *R. v.
Sparrow*.

The court ruled that the "existing rights" in section 35 are those that
Aboriginal people possessed prior to the assertion of Crown sovereignty
and that continue to exist because they were not explicitly extinguished
prior to the enactment of section 35.[50] Furthermore, by virtue of the constitutional protection afforded to Aboriginal rights in the post-1982 era,
those rights are not only now insulated against extinguishment but also
must be interpreted in a "generous and liberal" manner.[51] The court did
qualify its ruling by saying that Aboriginal rights are not absolute and that
they can be regulated by federal legislation, but it also insisted that such legislation must be justified according to a test that imposes as little hardship
as possible on the Aboriginal persons affected. Federal legislation with respect to Aboriginal rights, in other words, must be reconciled with what
the court terms its fiduciary obligations.

Furthermore, with respect to the interpretation of section 35(1) more
generally, the Supreme Court insisted that Canadian governments act in a
way that promotes Aboriginal interests and encourages trustlike rather than
adversarial relations. The court's emphasis on the necessity of generous and
liberal interpretations of Aboriginal rights and the importance of trustlike
relations establishes an important constitutional framework for Aboriginal

self-government negotiations. Indeed, RCAP itself relies heavily in places on principles such as these in its approach to Aboriginal self-government.[52] One can readily see, then, how words such as "generous" and "liberal" and "trustlike" connote types of relationship building that might well include duties of noninterference in the internal affairs of Aboriginal communities and commitments to cooperative agreement between Aboriginal and non-Aboriginal governments about the form that their relations of interdependence will take.

The Supreme Court has further urged that reconciliation of Aboriginal rights with the assertion of Crown sovereignty should be resolved through negotiations. The question is whether the emerging understandings of Aboriginal self-government reflected in negotiations undertaken to date establish a framework for coexistence that is adequate by the standards of relational pluralism. The Nisga'a treaty is the first negotiated settlement of Aboriginal land and resource rights and self-government powers in British Columbia. Moreover, some have suggested that the Nisga'a have won "the most comprehensive treaty ever"[53] negotiated in Canada and therefore have established a new standard for other treaty negotiations. Given that the governments of Canada and British Columbia will likely sign more than fifty additional treaties with Aboriginal communities in the province in the coming years, the Nisga'a treaty may have considerable precedent-setting value. But how does the treaty measure up to relational principles that uphold duties of internal noninterference and commitments to equal external relations? While it is clear that the self-government provisions are by no means a perfect reflection of these principles, they do go much further along the path of meeting them than most self-government arrangements to date.

THE NISGA'A TREATY

The Nisga'a treaty provides for areas of exclusive and paramount Nisga'a self-governing authority over Nisga'a citizens and lands. Taken together, these areas can be seen as providing the Nisga'a with a significant sphere of noninterference over their internal affairs. The terms of the treaty set out the definition of basic Nisga'a institutions and regulations of governance as well as rules of citizenship. It recognizes the Nisga'a nation as a self-governing entity and establishes two levels of Nisga'a government, the Nisga'a Lisims Government and Nisga'a village governments.[54] The treaty also provides the Nisga'a nation with ownership in fee simple of both the surface and the subsurface rights of 1,992 square kilometres of land and resources and provides the Nisga'a government with authority to set conditions on any new interests in their lands independent of federal or provincial consent.[55] Ownership rights extend to all forest resources on Nisga'a lands as well as to a guaranteed annual allocation of salmon, comprising about 26 percent of the Nass River allowable catch. As for legislative powers, the Nisga'a government can enact laws in areas such as Nisga'a public institutions; citizenship; language and culture; property in Nisga'a lands; Nisga'a assets; public order, peace, and safety; employment; traffic and transportation; marriages and families; social and health services; child custody and adoption; and education. While the Nisga'a do not exercise exclusive powers in these areas, in a number of them they do possess paramountcy in the sense that their laws will prevail in the case of a direct conflict with federal and provincial laws.[56]

Other features of the Nisga'a treaty reflect areas in which the Canadian, British Columbian, and Nisga'a governments have agreed to weave closer ties of interdependence. For example, the cash settlement of the treaty will involve a capital transfer of $190 million from primarily the federal government to be paid out over fifteen years. Nisga'a negotiators describe this cash settlement as a form of compensation for the historical use of their traditional lands and resources by non-Aboriginal peoples without Nisga'a consent. Five-year financing agreements will also be negotiated so as to ensure that the Nisga'a government can provide services and programs at levels reasonably comparable to those delivered to non-Aboriginal persons in northern British Columbia.[57] This commitment reflects the well-established national equalization program designed to support the programming responsibilities of provincial governments in poorer parts of Canada. Nisga'a persons will be required to pay federal and provincial sales taxes in eight years and income tax in twelve years. However, the Nisga'a government will acquire jurisdiction over the direct taxation of Nisga'a citizens on Nisga'a lands.

The treaty also makes numerous provisions for resource management agreements that link federal, provincial, and Nisga'a governmental standards of protection and enhancement. In all cases, however, Nisga'a rules for management must meet or exceed provincial and/or federal standards. Here the treaty authorizes the Nisga'a government to exercise management and conservation leadership over proposed projects on their lands and over the use of forests, fish, wildlife, and water.[58] Finally, the agreement enjoys constitutional protection as a section 35 treaty and land claims agreement under the Constitution Act, 1982.[59] While it is not clear that such protection elevates the status of the Nisga'a government to that of a co-equal with federal and provincial governments (the language of the treaty generally suggests not), it does guarantee that the treaty itself cannot be unilaterally changed by one without the other two lending their consent. Furthermore, the self-government provisions of the agreement, as a section 35 treaty, enjoy constitutional protection, a development that distinguishes it from all other prior treaties.

The Nisga'a treaty is complex, but its essential elements are straightforward. Moreover, by the standards of relational pluralism, three observations can be made. First, the Nisga'a powers of self-government are both modest and appropriate. The balance struck between paramount and subservient powers seems to meet the desire of the Nisga'a people for local control over their political, economic, social, and cultural development. As Douglas Sanders points out, the Nisga'a government constitutes "a new order of government" because, "with its constitutional basis in s.35, [it] has a sphere of legislative jurisdiction that can prevail against federal and provincial laws."[60] In this sense, the standard of internal noninterference in areas regarded by the Nisga'a as integral to their capacity to be self-defining seems to have been met.

Second, the areas of Nisga'a jurisdiction are not narrowly confined to those expressions of identity linked to cultural difference. Culture, language, education, spirituality, and control over artistic treasures are certainly included as areas of Nisga'a interest, but so too are areas associated with the Nisga'a interest in political, economic, environmental, and social participation and control. In this sense, the treaty addresses the Aboriginal right to be self-defining in a way that does not limit those rights to Aboriginal practices that are culturally "distinctive."

Third, the treaty weaves closer ties of interdependence between federal, provincial, and Nisga'a governments in ways that mark a clear departure from the paternalism of the past. Nisga'a lands no longer fall under federal jurisdiction, nor do Nisga'a citizens fall under the terms of the Indian Act.[61] Nisga'a governments will share in the fiscal resources of equalization much like the provinces and will participate in some of the managerial duties associated with resource conservation where federal, provincial, and Nisga'a governments share an interest. The Nisga'a government is also recognized and integrated into the constitutional system of Canada. In this sense, the treaty promotes recognition of Aboriginal governments as permanent partners in a constitutional design that has traditionally been understood to include only federal and provincial governments.

Naturally, the Nisga'a treaty represents only one negotiated settlement, tailored to the specific needs and aspirations of the Nisga'a people.[62] As the 1995 federal policy statement on Aboriginal self-government states, "Indian, Inuit, and Métis peoples have different needs, circumstances, aspirations, and [will] want to exercise their inherent rights in different ways."[63] No negotiated self-government agreement, in other words, can be cut from the same cloth, nor should one model be imposed on all Aboriginal communities. Indeed, to do so would be to violate a fundamental tenet of democracy: namely, that the structure and jurisdictional competence of local Aboriginal governments should be negotiated on a case-by-case basis in keeping with the aspirations of those specific Aboriginal communities.

But here again the principles of relational pluralism can lend clarity to what is central to the idea of Aboriginal self-government. What relational pluralism draws into focus is that the integrity of the political relationship between Aboriginal and Canadian governments does not lie in the capacity to deliver prototypical political structures consistent with the needs of relatively sizable national Aboriginal communities such as the Nisga'a. Indeed, this would be unrealistic given that many Aboriginal persons identify with relatively small Aboriginal communities and that a majority now live off reserve. In such settings, for example, negotiated forms of self-government might take on far more modest proportions, possibly in terms of designing, delivering, and monitoring specific economic, social, educational, or cultural programs and services. Moreover, while treaties might be the instrument through which some of these agreements could be given effect, others could be realized through federal legislation, contracts, or even memoranda of understanding.

Scholars such as James Youngblood Henderson, Patrick Macklem, and James Tully argue that justice between Aboriginal and non-Aboriginal peoples requires treaty federalism.[64] My notion of relational pluralism is compatible with this view if treaty federalism is understood to be a formal constitutional arrangement in which legal and political powers are shared between Aboriginal and Canadian governments in ways compatible with the aspirations of each and according to agreements that cannot be unilaterally changed by one or the other partner. What does not follow in my view, however, is that all Aboriginal self-government arrangements must possess the status of treaties in order for the demands of justice to be met. All that is essential from a relational point of view is that the mechanisms used to give effect to Aboriginal self-government be the product of genuinely equitable dialogue and agreement between Aboriginal and Canadian governments. Treaties, therefore, constitute one among a range of political options that Aboriginal communities may wish to pursue. Framed in this way, the particular mechanism that an Aboriginal community may select, whether treaty, federal legislation, interim agreement, contract, or memorandum of understanding, can be regarded not as a contradiction of its right to self-government but as a facilitative instrument for its expression.

Despite differences, then, what seems to be universal in Canada is the Aboriginal desire for a measure of local control and influence over the political, economic, and social processes that shape Aboriginal lives. By utilizing a relational pluralist perspective on Aboriginal-state relations, we see that it is the exercise of free choice by Aboriginal persons in developing self-governing arrangements for their communities that is important. The structural outcome of self-government arrangements can be either modest or extensive depending on the specific needs of the Aboriginal community in question. Actual structural outcomes are, in this sense, secondary from the point of view of justice. What is paramount are the actual relationships between Aboriginal and Canadian governments; they should be built on duties of internal noninterference and commitments to equality in areas of mutually agreed on external interdependence. Put differently, where understandings negotiated between Aboriginal governments and the Canadian state are based on the full participation and consent of both parties, we can say that the Aboriginal right to self-government is being realized.

CONFLICTING ABORIGINAL ASPIRATIONS

The Nisga'a treaty constitutes an important expression of what the Canadian government and the government of British Columbia regard as an acceptable form of Aboriginal self-government. But what if the choices made by the Nisga'a in the self-government portions of their treaty fall short by the standards of others? Will other Aboriginal communities be able to secure more jurisdictional power and greater independence from the federal and provincial governments if their members perceive it critical to their communal sense of self-definition that they do so? The Union of British Columbia Indian Chiefs (UBCIC), for example, in speaking on behalf of a number of Aboriginal communities in the interior of British Columbia, has refused to participate in provincial treaty negotiations. Its refusal is based on the conviction that treaties should be negotiated on a nation-to-nation basis between Canadian and Aboriginal governments. In its view, therefore, the provincial government should have no role in the treaty process since it is not a nation.

Other Aboriginal nations and organizations, while accepting the legitimacy of the BC treaty process, have been hostile to some of the terms of the Nisga'a treaty. The Assembly of First Nations (AFN) falls into this camp. While the AFN supported the treaty because it was what the Nisga'a wanted, it also qualified its support because, in its view, the treaty elevated the constitutional role of the provincial government in ways that it believed gave the province too much control over Aboriginal nations and because it granted little more than what it termed "municipal-like" powers to the Nisga'a.[65] Others go further, suggesting that treaty making such as that undertaken by the Nisga'a constitutes a form of co-optation because through it Aboriginal peoples surrender their traditional territories and accept the extension of Canadian sovereignty over them.[66] This reality, say some, is demonstrated by the fact that the Nisga'a obtained title to only 8 percent of the land in their original claim and by the fact that their political autonomy is constrained by the Charter and by federal and provincial laws of general application.

Such objections are difficult to respond to in a satisfactory way. Self-government negotiations that may lead to mutually acceptable compromise by the standards of some Aboriginal communities may constitute a violation of justice by the standards of others. The problem with the Nisga'a treaty, as suggested by the AFN, is one of standards: Aboriginal communities with more comprehensive demands may find their range of options foreclosed by the purported limitations imposed on the negotiation process by Aboriginal communities such as the Nisga'a, who were willing to settle for something less.

I believe that there is simply no way around this difficulty except to defer to the objectives for self-government set by the members of Aboriginal communities for themselves. They are the most directly affected, after all, by the settlements that their leaders negotiate on their behalf. Moreover, while organizations such as the AFN and UBCIC can play a significant role in shaping federal and provincial Aboriginal policies, it is Aboriginal nations that possess statutory political authority to act independently and exercise self-government at the local level. For this reason, I conclude that individual negotiated settlements should be seen as just to the degree that they establish a jurisdictional framework for Aboriginal communities to develop a communal sense of self-definition that is satisfying by their own standards.

But the challenge is not to let one self-government settlement affect others in a negative way. This is why I believe that the language of the "template" so often associated with the Nisga'a treaty needs to be avoided. Templates serve as rigid guides for all treaty negotiations to follow. But because Aboriginal self-government aspirations range from local endeavours to comprehensive demands, the language of templates has little meaning. Rather, insofar as the Nisga'a treaty has set a new precedent, it should be seen in relational terms. For the Nisga'a, their treaty constitutes the end of paternalistic relations and the terms by which they wish to come fully into Canada. It is this "relational" test, in my view, that other self-government negotiations in Canada should strive to meet.

I want to consider a final, closely related question. Some argue that, "when Aboriginal claims are dealt with on their own merits ... Aboriginal peoples are muscled into agreements that leave colonialism very much in place."[67] The argument here is that Canadian governments are favourable to Aboriginal claims only when dealing with them gives Canadians firmer control over the lands, resources, and lives of Aboriginal persons. Free choice for Aboriginal communities in self-government negotiations is thus

seen by some to be extremely limited. Aboriginal scholars such as
Monture-Angus and Alfred, for example, argue that Canadian governments
only accept solutions that hold no cost to them and that do "not disturb
existing power relationships between the Crown and the Indians."[68] In
short, they argue that what passes for a progressive framework, such as the
BC treaty process, is in fact "an advanced form of control, manipulation,
and assimilation."[69] Two recent developments that have been the subject of
this kind of stinging criticism are the 1995 federal policy guide on Aboriginal
self-government and the 1998 Supreme Court decision in *Delgamuukw v.
British Columbia*.

The 1995 federal policy guide stated the government of Canada's willingness to recognize the inherent right to self-government as an existing
Aboriginal right under section 35 of the Constitution Act, 1982. This recognition of inherency followed on the heels of a similar declaration of recognition under the terms of the 1992 Charlottetown Accord. Although the
accord was never ratified, it, together with the declaration of recognition
under the 1995 federal policy statement, seems to constitute an unprecedented event in Canadian state-Aboriginal relations. Never before had a
Canadian government been willing to accept that Aboriginal political powers might be inherent.

Yet some Aboriginal leaders were quick to denounce the policy statement. In their view, it constituted a hollow victory because what was extended in symbolic recognition carried few of the substantive sovereign
political powers that they argued followed from the idea of inherency. They
pointed out that the policy simply asserts that the Charter of Rights and
Freedoms and the Criminal Code would apply to Aboriginal governments,[70] that "laws of overriding federal and provincial importance" would
prevail over Aboriginal laws,[71] and that the exercise of the inherent right
would be restricted to matters "internal to the group, integral to its distinct
culture, and essential to its operation as a government or an institution."[72]
Dan Russell argues that negotiations conducted under these terms can result only in a limited form of municipal-like self-governance for Aboriginal
communities.[73] For this reason, among others, the AFN called the policy
"demeaning and paternalistic."[74]

The 1998 Supreme Court decision in *Delgamuukw v. British Columbia*
ruled that Aboriginal title constitutes a legal Aboriginal right to exclusive

use and occupation of lands that Aboriginal peoples have occupied consistently and exclusively since the assertion of European sovereignty. In addition, unless explicitly surrendered through treaty, or alienated by some other means to the Crown, Aboriginal title to traditional territories remains intact. The court further ruled that, where title infringement does occur, the Aboriginal people in question have a protected right to be both consulted and appropriately compensated. On these grounds alone, the Delgamuukw decision is generally seen to be a progressive expansion of the definition of Aboriginal title, yet it too is not immune from criticism. Aboriginal scholars, among others, have noted, for example, that, while the court now recognizes that Aboriginal people have a right *in* as opposed to *on* (i.e., personal and usufructuary rights) the land, it also insists that the range of uses to which those lands can be put must be consistent with the definition of the cultural bond that exists between the Aboriginal group and the land. But who gets to define the nature of the bond and the limitations of land use that flow from it? If it is to be the federal government, argues Monture-Angus, then the Aboriginal right to self-government will only be further compromised.[75]

Undoubtedly, structural limitations to Aboriginal aspirations of the kind associated with the 1995 federal policy, Delgamuukw, and the Nisga'a treaty are both real and dehabilitating from the perspective of some. It is not my intention to challenge those who hold this position. My interest, rather, lies in deciding how one might respond to such criticism from the perspective of relational pluralism.

One response would be to frame this criticism in terms of what J. Rick Ponting calls symbolic politics.[76] According to Ponting, in the absence of substantial power, some Aboriginal leaders use political metaphors, symbols, and images as a strategy to apply countervailing pressure against the pressure that they say is being applied against Aboriginal communal boundaries. Defining the contemporary relationship between Aboriginal and non-Aboriginal peoples in Canada in colonial terms is thus regarded as one such symbolic representation. The point is not to suggest that, when Aboriginal scholars and political leaders construe contemporary relations in colonial terms, this is a fabrication. Rather, Aboriginal leaders choose symbols based on their experiences (in this case, colonialism) to advance their preferred definition of Aboriginal status and rights within Canada. To the degree that the symbols are effective, they are said to act as potent power resources for offsetting "the otherwise substantial power differences between the government and the First Nations."[77]

What one can reasonably conclude is that Aboriginal scholarship and political advocacy are multifaceted and that each, in its own way, has the potential to contribute to the larger goal of Aboriginal emancipation within Canada. Naturally, some of this scholarship and political advocacy represents a radical view, while some is more modest in scope. How extensive the range of choice that Aboriginal communities actually enjoy as a result of these efforts clearly remains one of perspective. Yet here too progress can be measured in the terms provided by relational pluralism. Aboriginal leaders, particularly at the local level, have generally conducted self-government negotiations with a resolve to gain local control over the political, economic, social, and cultural areas that they determine to be central to their communal existence. Canadian governments, meanwhile, have become more willing to meet Aboriginal aspirations, possibly as a result of experience gained in previous negotiations and possibly because of legal principles established in the developing jurisprudence on Aboriginal rights. What we see, in other words, is development that is beginning to feature duties of internal noninterference and obligations of cooperative coexistence as significant elements in the relations that Aboriginal and Canadian governments take up with one another.

Where are the visible manifestations of this relational development? Here one must take a historical perspective by recognizing that movement toward a more relational approach has been the result of hard work over time. To take but one example, until the late 1980s, the federal government resisted connecting the resolution of land claims to self-government as demanded by Aboriginal leaders.[78] Yet, by the late 1990s, the federal government had embraced not only the idea that self-government agreements could be linked to land claims but also the idea that the two sets of negotiations could be constitutionally protected as treaty rights under section 35 of the Constitution Act, 1982. To date, this shift in federal policy is represented most fully by the Nisga'a treaty.[79] For other Aboriginal communities already under treaty, the federal government has also signalled its willingness to negotiate self-government arrangements that would become treaty rights under section 35.[80] This measure would not only exempt the agreements from the provisions of the Indian Act but also insulate them from the possibility of unilateral amendment by the federal government. In my view, such developments suggest a new approach to self-government negotiations and agreements that, while perhaps not entirely postcolonial, are nevertheless moving in a more relational pluralist direction.

CONCLUSION

Many Aboriginal witnesses who addressed RCAP in its public hearings made Aboriginal self-government one of their central demands. I believe that these demands can be read as containing an important conception of equality. The many witnesses who raised the issue did so by linking their interest in self-government to their membership in nations, communities that many say are entitled to equality of status in their relations with Canadian governments because they are the bearers of Aboriginal and treaty rights. What follows from this view is a particular conception of self-government: many witnesses consistently associate it with the right of Aboriginal communities to tend to their own affairs.

This chapter has demonstrated that an understanding of Aboriginal self-government can be considerably enriched when framed within the normative language of relational pluralism. This approach moves the discussion of self-government away from radical assertions about the incompatibility of Western and Aboriginal ways of life and the often associated unilateral claims to political power. Instead, a relational pluralist analysis recasts claims to self-government in the normative language of equality and freedom from domination. What is important here is that the issue of self-government be tackled in ways that build relationships of peaceable coexistence and mutual interdependence between Aboriginal and Canadian governments. It is precisely this kind of language that one regularly finds in presentations on Aboriginal self-government made to RCAP. One can reasonably conclude that, for at least some Aboriginal persons, the perspective presented in these pages is not foreign. My point throughout has been that the principles used to assess the justice of self-government initiatives in Canada ought to be more explicitly pluralist.

CHAPTER 6

ABORIGINAL IDENTITY AND THE DESIRE FOR INTERNAL EQUALITY

As the analysis of Chapter 4 demonstrated, when Aboriginal communal identity is equated with elements of cultural nationalism, conflict within Aboriginal communities is often framed in terms of the collective right of Aboriginal nations to cultural autonomy versus the individual right of Aboriginal persons to freedom. I also demonstrated, however, that, when conflict is framed in this way, it puts emphasis in the wrong place where many Aboriginal identity-related claims are concerned. In my view, the purported Aboriginal interests in cultural autonomy and individual freedom are better understood as manifestations of a larger Aboriginal desire to be self-defining: that is, Aboriginal persons should be seen to want greater decision-making authority and local control over their lives at both individual and communal levels.

Relational pluralists analyze group relations in terms of two evaluative standards: groups must be able to declare who they are from their own rather than a more powerful group's standpoint, and group members must be able to contribute to their group identity free from domination by other group members. Equality of relations and freedom from domination both between and within groups are thus the key normative aspects of this theory. In this chapter, I focus on the second set of relations: namely, those within Aboriginal communities. I address the problem of individual political power, influence, and rights to inclusion from the perspective of the

Aboriginal individual. To advance my argument, I link the assumptions of relational pluralism to ideas about individual political equality and the structural means for its realization as expressed in testimony by some Aboriginal individuals in RCAP's hearings.

EQUALITY OF PERSONS

The Hearings

A central message that I take from the testimony before RCAP is that many Aboriginal witnesses wish to enhance their communities' capacity for self-government. Yet witnesses address the challenge of self-government in diverse ways that often raise significant points of contention between them. Some see self-government as an institutional form of equal relations that ought to exist between Aboriginal and Canadian governments. Testimony in this vein typically addresses normative questions about the justification for Aboriginal governmental power (rooted, for example, in arguments about original occupancy, inherent political rights, and treaty recognition) and institutional questions about the kinds of political jurisdiction that Aboriginal governments ought to have if they are to restore to their communities a measure of autonomy within Canada.

For others, self-government is less about external equality between Aboriginal and Canadian governments and more about equality of relations between individuals within Aboriginal communities. Testimony in this vein typically addresses questions about empowering individuals within Aboriginal communities so that self-government is a process built locally, involving all members. Put another way, what I detect in some of the testimony is a general fear that, if Aboriginal leaders press ahead in complex self-government negotiations with Canadian governments, they may neglect to build models that are sufficiently consultative and thus consistent with local wishes. For example, as I demonstrated in Chapter 4, a good number of Aboriginal women and youth pinned the future success of self-government on the ability of their communities to recapture traditional models of gender equality and make them relevant for the present, to address outstanding equality issues left over from Bill C-31, to confront questions about political accountability among the Aboriginal leadership, to address violence and the importance of healing at individual and community levels, and to develop modes of community political participation that accept the legitimacy of bicultural Aboriginal identities.

One of the most important questions for non-Aboriginal Canadians is how to respond to these demands and associated differences in emphasis. For example, should the differences in demands be analyzed as confrontations between rights to collective cultural and political security versus rights to individual freedom? Or should these differences be understood in terms of something else? I believe that, among the divisions that run through Aboriginal communities, there is historically a common ground where factors such as poverty, loss of self-determination, and communal accountability networks have broken down. I believe that this common experience of marginalization and the concurrent demand for greater power at both individual and community levels should be the focus of attention, not purported conflicts between individual and collective rights.

Moreover, Aboriginal witnesses frequently move back and forth in their talk about individual and community power in ways that suggest they regard both as part of the same dynamic. While some Aboriginal witnesses point out that a fairer distribution of power is needed between Aboriginal and Canadian governments, they also say that this distribution needs to be built on a fairer distribution of power within Aboriginal communities. Self-government is thus seen to have both an internal and an external dimension: it involves a commitment to shared decision making and political participation at the local level that in turn is said to provide the foundation for autonomous decision making and independent political representation in community relations with the Canadian state. Again, as I suggested in the previous chapter, though not always consciously articulated or explicitly developed, the general theme that I infer from the public comments of a number of Aboriginal women, youth, and urban dwellers is that their political concerns can be read as a demand for equal treatment.

Where lack of power and influence is said to be felt by Aboriginal women, youth, and urban dwellers, their demands for equality can be understood with respect to two key themes: (1) overcoming community-based disadvantages that act to suppress the expression of individual identity, and (2) acquiring power sufficient to attain standing and recognition as full participants in the Aboriginal self-governing process. What follows examines each theme in turn.

First, in the testimony of some Aboriginal women, youth, and urban dwellers, there are frequent references to having experienced domination at the hands of political leaders and other members of their communities. Some attribute the origins of this domination to forms of political representation imposed on Aboriginal communities by the Indian Act – band councils and elections. Witnesses note that band councils often constitute small political elites, sometimes made up of one or more family factions, who often fall to the temptation of using power for their own or their extended family's benefit (e.g., with respect to housing, land entitlement, or band employment). It is not surprising, then, that one finds in the testimony of witnesses regular accusations that the band council system of governance on reserves is not representative of the wishes of the larger community. Some women, for example, state repeatedly that the current system of governance favours elected chiefs and councillors, most of whom are male: "Aboriginal self-government means male power, male domination, and the silencing of the lambs."[1] Some youth also emphasize that "they feel their concerns are not taken seriously by their leaders and communities. When they speak out, their voices go unheard."[2] A number of urban Aboriginal witnesses, meanwhile, regularly draw attention to the fact that, relative to their reserve-based counterparts, their people and organizations lack a satisfactory level of political standing and influence in Canada. In a similar vein, RCAP notes that, although Aboriginal people living in urban areas "now account for more than half of Canada's Aboriginal population," they "feel excluded from Aboriginal political organizations" and inequitably treated "in terms of services or entitlements provided by the federal government."[3]

One can reasonably infer from these statements that a number of Aboriginal persons are concerned that the power to define what self-determination means has been usurped by a minority within Aboriginal communities. Some women, youth, and urban dwellers are convinced that they experience unique circumstances of oppression. They say that they suffer not only because they are part of a colonized minority within Canada but also because they have been forced into inequitable relations with the Aboriginal men, adults, or reserve-based dwellers to whom they are related. The following statement illustrates this reading of the situation: "We must never stop demonstrating forcefully our solidarity with the major Aboriginal demands which, fundamentally, concern the right to life and to dignity. But at the same time, we must not confuse solidarity with a false superficial unanimity that excludes all thinking and debate. On the contrary, it is important to stimulate thinking and discussion if we, as women and men on an equal footing, are to succeed in defining our future together. This is the best demonstration of solidarity that we can give."[4]

Second, to militate against what might be termed their conditions of double disadvantage, some witnesses also employ language associated with equality. In particular, witnesses make frequent appeals to the need for a more balanced relationship between all Aboriginal persons, a condition that they say is possible only through a genuine sharing of power.

This demand for power sharing is expressed differently by the witnesses. For the most part, the women who address this issue say that they want greater involvement in the local governing structures of their communities.[5] As one woman noted, "I would just like to say that for our men that we don't want to walk behind you. We want to walk beside you. We want to heal with you and we want to help you make those decisions that are needing to be made for the future of our people and that we walk together."[6] Youth similarly demand involvement in band councils and in decisions affecting their rights. For example, some view their relationship in terms of "a tradition of providing ideas, creativity, energy, and the moral judgement to question our leaders."[7] It thus seems reasonable to conclude that, for a number of women and youth, self-government initiatives can be authentic only when the processes by which they are established are inclusive and reflect the aspirations of all sectors of Aboriginal communities.

Urban Aboriginal witnesses, meanwhile, draw two themes into focus. First, some say that they moved to cities because of lack of jobs, educational institutions, and housing on reserves. Second, though, most of those who moved to urban settings do not wish to sever ties to their nations of origin or abandon their Aboriginal identity more generally. Urban Aboriginal witnesses, therefore, tend to view the present challenge as finding ways to remain fully Aboriginal community members and city residents at the same time. To this end, some urban witnesses say that urban dwellers who maintain strong ties to their nations of origin should be entitled to participate in the development of their nation's self-governing arrangements. They also say that these participatory arrangements should be reciprocal. These urban witnesses conclude that it is not unreasonable to expect that their nations take some responsibility for their needs and well-being while living off reserve.[8]

It is clear from the evidence provided by RCAP's hearings that, on the whole, Aboriginal witnesses are not happy with the power that Canadian governments exercise over their communities, nor are they always happy with the power that their leadership exercises over them as individuals. Is there an end, then, toward which the aspirations of Aboriginal witnesses could be said to converge? Do they possess a commonality of purpose? My reading of the testimony suggests that a major part of this commonality of purpose is captured in the concept of equality. Intrinsic to the idea of self-government is the individual right to inclusion in community political decision making. In aggregate, then, the testimony by Aboriginal witnesses before RCAP suggests that the most important criterion for evaluating political relations is the contribution of those relations to equality. Yet the same testimony illustrates that the dimensions of Aboriginal equality are many and cannot be easily reconciled with one another.

Implications and Analysis

Again, I want to suggest that much can be gained if this political rhetoric of individual Aboriginal equality is situated within the identification approach to ethnic identity and a relational theory of pluralism.

The identification approach suggests that individual Aboriginal identity should not be regarded in a deterministic fashion, originating from traditional cultural or political attributes. Rather, Aboriginal identity is more properly understood as a relational phenomenon; one acquires it by virtue of one's connection to others through ancestry, shared historical memories and territories, and shared commitment to one another in community over time. This approach, in other words, lends flexibility to Aboriginal identity; it can be shaped to meet challenges posed by new circumstances without necessarily jeopardizing the integrity of Aboriginal identity itself.

Put another way, Aboriginal identity is seen to contain both nonvoluntary and voluntary elements. On one level, being Aboriginal is nonvoluntary. Persons are Aboriginal because they are part of interlocking communal networks that are the result of shared bonds of ancestry and history. But on another level, being Aboriginal has important voluntary elements. As the

analyses of previous chapters demonstrate, Aboriginal identity is differentiated by nation, culture, history, age, gender, and other attributes, any one or
more of which can become important depending on how Aboriginal individuals in community choose to express themselves in given contexts.

A key element in the identification approach is that collective solidarity
in Aboriginal communities is identified as originating from the desire of
Aboriginal persons to be members of self-defining communities, a process
also seen as invariably facilitated by the selective use of shared elements of
ancestry, history, territory, and culture. As a result, if Aboriginal persons are
primarily interested in the right to be self-defining both as individuals and
as members of Aboriginal communities, it becomes critical from this perspective that they are able to adapt their self-definitions and make decisions
about what it means to be Aboriginal in today's world.

As the analysis of Chapter 4 demonstrated, some tend to identify conflict within Aboriginal communities in terms of basic struggles over individual and collective rights. Aboriginal nations are regarded as being
preoccupied with preserving traditional cultural differences and political
autonomy, while Aboriginal women, youth, and urban dwellers are regarded as wanting to break free of some of these traditional cultural and political structures. I also demonstrated, however, that, when conflict within
Aboriginal communities is framed in this way, it tends to misrepresent the
nature of the political claims that a number of Aboriginal witnesses appear
to be making.

I believe that Aboriginal women, youth, and urban dwellers are often
critical of what passes for current expressions of Aboriginal identity because
they regard them as products of colonial relations. On balance, therefore,
public comments seem to be more focused on the desire to acquire greater
personal power so that individuals can contribute to the transformation of
community identity expressions that they now regard as demeaning and
paternalistic. This interpretation leads me to conclude on closer inspection
that what is often referred to as a competition between individual and collective rights can be read as a demand for individual political inclusion at
the Aboriginal community level. The categories of relational pluralism clarify, in part, what is involved in addressing this challenge.

From a relational pluralist perspective, rights to community inclusion
are important because healthy individual identity is understood to be the

outcome of individuals possessing power to influence the course of relations that they consider integral to their self-image. By extension, rather
than suppress internal Aboriginal expressions of identity, a relational pluralist approach accentuates the importance of addressing relations of power
within Aboriginal communities. That is, relational pluralism highlights the
importance of granting multiple expressions of individual Aboriginal identity equality of status and influence in the actual development of Aboriginal
communal identity.[9]

There is, of course, no guarantee that such multiple individual expressions will be granted such equality. To expose an injustice is not necessarily
to create a constituency with sufficient power to eradicate it. Entrenched
Aboriginal leaders, for example, who insist that Aboriginal individuals
comply with their particular images of cultural and national identity may,
in some cases, be exceedingly difficult to dislodge. My point is simply that
entrenched power relations of this kind only lend more urgency to the
need to talk about Aboriginal identity in the more expansive terms that relational pluralism invites. What follows addresses several implications that
flow from such a commitment.

ANCESTRY VERSUS IDENTITY

The Royal Commission notes that, while one million people in Canada
possess Aboriginal ancestry, only 626,000 actually identify themselves as
Aboriginal.[10] This leaves some 375,000 people for whom their ancestry has
a negligible impact on their identity.[11] While the Royal Commission holds
out hope that these 375,000 may eventually return to the Aboriginal identity fold, for now the statistics point to quite a different reality: 375,000 persons no longer possess any meaningful identification with the Aboriginal
people of their birth.

This distinction between "ancestry" and "identity" can be attributed in
part to the manner in which Parliament has exercised jurisdiction over
"Indians and lands reserved for Indians" under section 91(24) of the
Constitution Act, 1867. The "Indians" referred to in section 91(24) are those
registered or entitled to be registered as Indians under the Indian Act.
Indians with status are those registered as Indians under section 2(1) of the
Indian Act. Registered (or status) Indians can also be treaty Indians if they

have special rights that flow from the treaties that their communities of origin signed with the Crown. An important implication follows from this Canadian practice of Indian policy and law. As P.G. McHugh observes, while treaties were negotiated with tribal or band leaders, and while status is conferred through ancestry from originally registered band members, the rights associated with each "were and remain individual in orientation."[12] Some Indian persons may therefore have entitlements under the Indian Act or under treaty but lack membership in a First Nations community and have no desire to participate in a community-based Aboriginal way of life. Individuals may thus possess ancestry, and some may even possess treaty and other rights, but they may have ceased, for all intents and purposes, to be Aboriginal.

While Canadian Indian policy may allow for an individualized element to Indian and treaty rights, relational pluralists focus on communities and groups as essential to the development of a good society and thus make Aboriginal communities (among others) the fundamental unit of their concern. But they also allow for change in identity and recognize that individuals can and often do change affiliation. For this reason, relational pluralists also acknowledge that persons of Aboriginal ancestry need not take on Aboriginal identity. Aboriginal ancestry is entirely unchosen (one is either born to parents of Aboriginal ancestry or one is not), but such individuals retain an important element of choice concerning what to do with that ancestry. A person of Aboriginal descent can choose, for instance, to make affiliation with an Aboriginal community an important element of personal identity or not. The strength and significance of Aboriginal identity naturally vary between individuals; some have a powerful sense of identification with their Aboriginality, while others do not. Aboriginality is thus a subjective phenomenon associated with community affiliation even though it also refers to "objective" elements such as ancestry, history, culture, and territory. The premium that relational pluralism places on individual self-definition means that no individual among the 375,000 should be required to acquire an Aboriginal identity if perceived not to be in his or her interest to do so. However, while persons of Aboriginal ancestry may choose not to establish ties of affiliation with an Aboriginal community, they may nevertheless be able to claim some rights and/or benefits from the federal government. Until the Indian Act is amended or repealed and treaties changed, this is an inevitable consequence of federal policy that, to date, defines its responsibility to Indian persons, in part, through Indian status and treaty entitlements.

Perhaps more pertinently, for those possessing identity and wishing to reestablish community affiliation, no communal roadblocks should be placed in their way, since these individuals often did not lose those affiliations through any choice of their own. As testimony before RCAP demonstrates, some of the politics of Aboriginal women and youth is devoted to removing precisely such roadblocks. Some identify these roadblocks as existing at the level of their reserve-based communities. These complaints are most often registered by current band members who may possess Indian status and live either off or on reserve. Here witnesses identify community power as a jealously guarded resource that, because it is often monopolized by a tiny, largely male, Aboriginal elite, is said to leave many Aboriginal women and youth powerless to imprint community life with identity images of their choosing.

Other witnesses say that the federal government's Indian Act is responsible for their loss of community affiliation. These witnesses do say on occasion that Bill C-31 has rectified the matter of lost rights for some by restoring to them full status and the associated benefits of Indian registration and band membership. Many others, however, point out the significant pitfalls associated with tying Aboriginal identity and entitlement to community membership to the presence or absence of legal status. For example, reinstated Indians spoke to RCAP about how they are regularly referred to in pejorative terms by members of their communities as "Bill C-31ers." The connotation here is that to have lost status and then regained it is somehow to be less than a full Indian.

In addition, "Bill C-31ers" sometimes spoke about their unique experiences of the legal hierarchy set in motion by the welter of new registration categories associated with descent rules of Bill C-31. Indians who had status before 17 April 1985, then lost it through the discriminatory sections of the Indian Act and applied for reinstatement, were most typically reassigned status under the act's subsection 6(1).[13] Those with one Indian parent entitled to registration under 6(1) and one non-Indian parent who applied for reinstatement were assigned Indian status under subsection 6(2).[14] The consequences of falling under subsection 6(2) are enormous for those who later choose to marry non-Indians: according to the new rules, their children will be ineligible for Indian status. Stewart Clatworthy and Anthony Smith conclude that, given the high rates of intermarriage (62 percent for the off-reserve population and 34 percent for the on-reserve population), and the fact that the inheritance of Indian status and membership in many bands is now dependent on "in marriage" criteria as of 1985, Indian status for many will be extinguished after two successive generations (or fifty years).[15]

Furthermore, and perhaps more seriously, bands experiencing high rates of "out-marriages" and employing the membership eligibility rules of the Indian Act (63 percent of bands), or community codes that rely on two Indian parents (9 percent of bands) or blood quantum rules (9 percent of bands), may also, with time, cease to exist.[16] What has resulted, therefore, is not only the introduction of a descending scale of legal identity security, as noted in the comments of some witnesses (from full, to half-, to non-Indian, as Clatworthy and Smith put it),[17] but also the prospect of losing entire First Nation communities.

From the perspective of relational pluralism, RCAP's policy recommendations go some distance in meeting the challenges associated with the disproportionate power differentials between Aboriginal men and women and the potential round of stigmatizing labels as well as loss of status set in motion by the new rules of the Indian Act. RCAP can meet these challenges because it places the Aboriginal right to self-definition at the normative heart of many of its recommendations. RCAP emphasizes Aboriginal people's right to define themselves, both with respect to individual self-identification and community identification of members.

With respect to the issue of community power, RCAP argues that Aboriginal identity is the outcome of an evolutionary collective process in which "history, ancestry, culture, values, traditions and ties to the land" all play a part.[18] As the identity of modern Aboriginal nations lies in their collective community life, it is simply inconceivable from the perspective of RCAP that anyone with a legitimate stake in that collective life be barred from participating. To this end, RCAP insists that Aboriginal women be provided with full and fair opportunities to participate in Aboriginal governments, including all aspects of nation building.[19] Indeed, in its view, section 35(4) of the Constitution Act, 1982, which guarantees Aboriginal and treaty rights equally to male and female persons, requires such inclusion.[20]

As for legal status, RCAP develops a model that would see Aboriginal individuals rely on their nations for political identity rather than on the legal categories of the federal government's Indian Act. RCAP argues that Aboriginal nations have "the right to determine which individuals belong to the nation as members and citizens."[21] The commission also insists that the Aboriginal right to determine citizenship should not be unqualified. It should meet strict constitutional standards both to get around the kind of hierarchy created by the Indian Act's post-1985 rules and to ensure that no one is unfairly excluded from enjoying the collective right to self-government. To that end, RCAP insists that membership rules and processes must not discriminate against individuals on the ground of sex or specify "that a certain degree of Aboriginal blood ... is a general prerequisite for citizenship."[22] Instead, rules of ancestry such as having one parent belonging to the community should be used in combination with other criteria such as "birth in the community, long-time residency, group acceptance and so on."[23]

OPEN DIALOGUE

A pluralist framework accentuates the idea that it is up to Aboriginal individuals to choose whether to define themselves within or outside the communities of their ancestry. Having made the choice to define themselves within their communities, however, a second implication follows. As argued, Aboriginal communal identity is fluid and changes over time; hence, as concrete decisions about identity are made, Aboriginal persons' perception of what it means to be Aboriginal may gradually shift. One example here that plays heavily in RCAP's analysis will suffice. Think of the difference in political self-perception that accompanies a communal identity associated with the concept of "nation" as opposed to "band." The former carries an association of communal autonomy and political self-determination, while the latter carries an association of communal dependency and political reliance on the Canadian state.

When fundamental shifts in communal identity occur in this way, it is imperative that all Aboriginal persons with an interest in the matter have access to relatively equal amounts of power so that they can influence the process that leads to a new community identity outcome. Naturally, the capacity for equal influence and power, coupled with the inevitability of different choice making that flows from different perspectives, may well fuel social conflict of various kinds. Such conflict is to be expected given that individuals typically participate in a number of community social settings simultaneously, each of which may contribute in greater or lesser degree to dimensions of an individual's sense of self.

As this study has shown, conflict over communal identity is evident in precisely this way in numerous Aboriginal communities. In the RCAP hearings, many Aboriginal women stressed, first, that their identities are constituted by a plural combination of ascriptive characteristics (they are both female and Aboriginal); second, that these characteristics sometimes cut through and across one another and so are not always easily reconciled (one's emancipatory interests as a woman and as a person of Aboriginal identity may conflict); and third, that projected strategies of emancipatory fulfillment that focus on only one feature of identity will more than likely be politically constricting (one who is given room to flourish as an Aboriginal person by the standards of some may still find herself marginalized as a woman). From a pluralist perspective, paramount is that the Aboriginal communal attempt to resolve conflicting positions and so arrive at consensus should never come at the cost of extinguishing pluralism within the community itself. There are defensible and indefensible versions of Aboriginal communal identity, in other words, and according to the pluralist position those that are indefensible are the ones dictatorially imposed.

We can see, then, how a pluralist can never, as a matter of principle, offer a blanket endorsement of any and all expressions of community identity. One might, for example, assess Aboriginal communal identity on the basis of what that identity presently consists in and consider that the end of the matter. Here all forms of Aboriginal cultural nationalism could be endorsed on the ground that, because many Aboriginal leaders say that these are the most fundamental manifestations of Aboriginal political difference, they are therefore legitimate expressions of community identity. According to this line of reasoning, because Aboriginal communities are collective in nature, the interests of Aboriginal individuals must share a singleness of purpose, and their communities must in some sense be characterized by cultural uniformity.

In my view, however, this image does not do justice to the complex commitments held by many Aboriginal persons. As my discussion of RCAP's hearings demonstrates, Aboriginal persons regularly disagree with one another about what makes for an Aboriginal way of life. Cultural and political images of community identity are regularly contested, often in the name of the values of equality and freedom from domination that relational pluralism champions. It is unfair, therefore, that certain Aboriginal persons should be allowed to impose their preferred view of an Aboriginal way of life on those who may disagree with it simply in the name of a cultural survival based on the purported moral superiority of traditional cultural principles and values.

A relational pluralist framework is founded on a commitment to the integrity of the individual and the importance of political participation. The framework fits well with many of the individual equality arguments made by Aboriginal participants in RCAP's public hearings. Its standard of defensibility flows from an assessment of the process that brings expressions of Aboriginal identity into being. What matters here is not so much the character of the outcome as the fact that all points of view should be represented through an open dialogue in the arrival of that outcome. Mediating the important commitment to communal self-definition, in other words, is the pluralist's commitment to equal power for community members. For Aboriginal persons to be free, each must have a guaranteed voice in the community and an equal opportunity to be heard so that each can play a part in community decision-making processes.

Following this line of reasoning, one might argue that an expression of Aboriginal communal identity is authentic when the process of identity formation encourages input from all sectors of the community in such a way that each can successfully imprint the communal identity with some feature of its own image. Of course, no Aboriginal communal identity will ever be perfectly representative of all competing viewpoints. In political settings of equality of opportunity, one must be prepared to lose some of the time provided that one can reasonably expect to win at other times in future exchanges. Nevertheless, there is a large difference between a communal identity developed through a broadly participatory process and one developed mainly through external or internal political imposition. Relational pluralism provides a useful normative guideline for distinguishing this difference.[24]

By these criteria, the real challenge facing Aboriginal communities is not to be obsessive about preserving specific traditions and expressions of nationhood as an end in itself. As suggested by the testimony summarized in this and previous chapters, Aboriginal women and youth do not always agree with the decisions on self-government taken by their community leaders. Some witnesses in both categories point to their desire for a self-definition process that includes a reconstruction of Aboriginal community life based on healing of domestic abuse, the acquisition of skills and knowledge by women and youth so that they can self-sufficiently contribute to their own communities and the larger Canadian society, and the development of Aboriginal identity models that would allow women and youth to integrate and express both traditional and modern elements of who they perceive themselves to be.

By many accounts, the currently entrenched elite of largely male chiefs and councils is often hostile to the ideas of women and youth and is thus often unwilling to relinquish the power that both need to pursue their ideas. Yet some women and youth also persist in claiming that they too offer elements of a vision for communal development that are appropriate for their communities. One sees here an internal struggle for influence by various persons within Aboriginal communities at the deepest political level of communal self-definition and self-government. My point is simply that, by the standards of relational pluralism, no cultural or political vision can by definition possess "objective" authority as "true" against which all other visions can be judged.

There is no escape from the realities of social power. Aboriginal individuals are just as capable as anyone else of using power in ways that others might consider self-serving. The crucial point, then, is that the question of whose vision for individual and community health may be right should be decided against a full recognition and acceptance of social pluralism. There is, after all, only one route that Aboriginal communities can follow to build lives that meet overall priorities: they must extend to their members the same power and influence of self-definition that they demand for their communities more generally within Canada. Aboriginal women and youth must have grounds for identifying with their Aboriginal communities if those communities are to survive. If they do not, then their communities will be condemned to marginality and sterility.

BICULTURAL ENGAGEMENT

Those who employ a relational pluralist framework do not just assess justice within Aboriginal communities in terms of the presence or absence of individual participation and consent in public discussions leading to the development of community identity. The framework also provides the means for Aboriginal individuals to analyze critically their communal relationships in light of the associational ties that they develop with individuals and groups outside their communities.

In a large, complex, and highly differentiated society such as Canada, the vast majority of Aboriginal communities are neither internally insular nor culturally homogeneous "but mirror in their own differentiations many of the other groups in the wider society."[25] Aboriginal communities are not closed, in other words; as Alan Cairns puts it, they are "massively penetrated by external forces."[26] During their long histories of cultural, economic, and political exchanges, Aboriginal and non-Aboriginal communities have unavoidably influenced and shaped one another. This process of mutual influence manifests itself in the obvious fact that each community shares similar social divisions based on age, gender, culture, language, religion, and nation. But mutual influence over a long period also results in the blurring of cultural boundaries between communities. Aboriginal individuals inevitably participate to greater or lesser degrees in Canadian society, where there is an interspersion of peoples, a constant exchange of ideas, and an interdependency of action. From the viewpoint of John Borrows, the narrative of "exclusive citizenship" and "measured separatism" that Aboriginal nationalism represents, "however appropriate and helpful, is not rich enough to encompass the range of relationships we need to negotiate the diversity, displacement, and positive potential that our widening circles represent."[27]

It is perhaps an obvious point that in precontact times Aboriginal and non-Aboriginal peoples lived in worlds that were starkly divided, so Aboriginal people would have had little choice about their identities, since they would have been deeply intertwined with those of their Aboriginal nations.[28] In a postcontact society, however, Aboriginal individuals can make choices about how to express their identities, and they can make connections with others based on a whole range of interests. Some of this interaction may result in Aboriginal and non-Aboriginal persons accentuating

the cultural differences between their communities. But community interaction can also lead to the sharing of experiences, culture, and values.
Indeed, Aboriginal persons may perceive themselves to be very different
from non-Aboriginal persons in one setting but similar to them in another
setting. So an Aboriginal person may want to identify with her Aboriginal
community and thus make it an integral component of her identity, but she
may also want to go to a mainstream Canadian university and achieve an
adequate standard of living by participating in the economy of the dominant society. For certain portions of her life, then, the cultural boundaries
between her and her non-Aboriginal counterparts become murky; she essentially takes on a bicultural identity. In light of such realities, Borrows argues that Aboriginal persons simply must develop a "more fluid notion of
what it means to be Aboriginal" in order to incorporate the developing reality of "intercultural education, urbanization, politics, and intermarriage."[29]
Failure to do so, says Borrows, would essentially marginalize Aboriginal
persons for whom their Aboriginal community membership includes participation in Canadian affairs.

But how can an Aboriginal person retain an Aboriginal identity when
she is so deeply implicated within the structures of the non-Aboriginal
world? Won't such Aboriginal persons break down under the strain of having to live between two cultures, and won't their sense of Aboriginal identity eventually fade under the weight of assimilationist pressures? While
incoherence, confusion, and assimilation are always possibilities, a pluralist
perspective on the world demonstrates that it is also possible to look at this
situation more positively.

Numerous Aboriginal individuals testifying before RCAP said that allegiance to their communities does not imply cultural and political subordination. Indeed, many witnesses seemed to accept the idea that community
allegiance need not be a one-dimensional, all-encompassing affair. Human
subjectivity is complex, in other words, so, while fragmentation "can and
does cause problems for all of us at particular times," we also recognize "the
way in which we can hold multiple commitments, relationships, views,
desires and roles together" without total disintegration.[30] I am convinced
that this sentiment is being expressed by Aboriginal witnesses who refuse
to accept the idea that traditional and modern ways of Aboriginal life cannot be reconciled. Aboriginal identity should not be viewed in terms of

categorical cultural opposition, nor need it be sustained by political separatism to survive. All it needs are Aboriginal individuals committed to its
development. Aboriginal identity can change without disappearing; it can
blend modern Western values and practices with values and practices that
symbolize Aboriginal community differences. What a relational pluralist
perspective on human personality accentuates is that one can be fully
Aboriginal while still participating in the multiple social and political settings of Canadian society.

Some pluralist scholars have also shown that these kinds of multiple
commitments can be put to good political use. For instance, Avigail
Eisenberg and others have demonstrated that the capacity to draw from
one's experiences in a diversity of group situations can promote multidimensional personal development.[31] While one's affiliation with (in this case)
one's Aboriginal community may be firm, Eisenberg points out that freedom of movement can encourage individuals to develop new critical perspectives. These perspectives enable individuals to regularly reevaluate the
activities that they take up in their communities of primary affiliation by
the criteria that they develop in others.[32] The point that some pluralists
wish to reinforce is that, if individuals are constituted too much by single
sets of traditions and values, they may have limited resources for self-
development. The virtue of relational pluralism is that it highlights the degree to which a plurality of affiliations and perspectives can help individuals
to identify and subsequently liberate themselves from group practices that
they may now find to be oppressive.[33]

A telling illustration of the multifaceted nature of Aboriginal identity is
revealed in the testimony of Aboriginal women. Some have joined their
voices with those of the larger feminist movement's repudiation of sexist
practices that inhibit women from assuming positions of social and political power.[34] These Aboriginal women locate the sources of their oppression
in the sexist policies of the Canadian government's Indian Act and among
leaders of their communities who, in many instances, are reluctant to relinquish the power that they now hold by virtue of the Indian Act's provisions.
In response, these Aboriginal women seek to transform the structured patterns of gender inequality so that they can function as full participants and
equal citizens within their communities.

A relational pluralist framework reinforces that, in their struggle to transform their oppressive situation, the objectives of Aboriginal women are considerably enhanced because they can draw on the resources of multiple perspectives. The testimony itself reveals a number of these resources. Some Aboriginal women delve deeply into their own histories, drawing forward old, more equitable, relationships between men and women as normative models for modern conduct. Some also highlight modern progressive resources within their own and other Aboriginal cultures that they say have yet to be tapped. Finally, some Aboriginal women draw on the resources available to them outside their communities, the kinds of resources contained within the non-Aboriginal feminist movement. Here, for example, Aboriginal women often applaud the Canadian feminist movement's successful acquisition of sexual equality rights in sections 15 and 28 of the Charter. These rights are often noted because they were also the critical legal leverage that Aboriginal women needed to get the federal government to address the sexual biases contained in the pre-1985 version of the Indian Act. A pluralist framework highlights that this kind of intercultural dialogue ought to be encouraged for the sake of justice. In this case, insights gained into the possibilities for human development as promoted by the Charter acted as important critical levers for identifying and thus addressing destructive tendencies within Aboriginal communities.

THE CHARTER AS A TOOL FOR POLITICAL INCLUSION

A key element associated with relational pluralism is that, where Aboriginal community identities are concerned, they have to be worked out creatively; they have to be adapted from time to time if persons who want to live together are to do so successfully. But how is this adaptation to be achieved? What remedies exist if what some term "the entrenched male leadership" simply refuses to adapt or change cultural and political images of community identity that others say marginalize them?

In my view, substantive remedies at the level of politics are exceedingly difficult to find. One cannot, for example, simply legislate changes in attitude, nor can one easily dislodge long-standing patterns of institutionalized political and legal power. Yet the question remains: what political instruments might facilitate a process of greater inclusion where Aboriginal community self-definition is concerned?

One route, albeit limited, may be the Charter. The 1995 federal policy statement on self-government stated that the Charter must apply to Aboriginal governments under the terms of any agreement negotiated between Aboriginal and federal governments.[35] The federal policy guide also states that the protective shield of section 25 means that the Charter will be interpreted "in a manner that respects Aboriginal and treaty rights, which would include, under the federal approach, the inherent right" to self-government. In this sense, the Charter is designed to protect Aboriginal and treaty rights from the Charter itself, and presumably this protection cannot be removed or reduced by any treaty, legislation, or other agreement. In the words of the federal policy guide, "the Charter is thus designed to ensure a sensitive balance between individual rights and freedoms, and the unique values and traditions of Aboriginal peoples in Canada."[36]

It is not clear from the federal policy guide how the Charter will impact on the practice of Aboriginal self-government. However, one potentially profitable impact, likely consistent with Aboriginal and treaty rights, may lie in its upholding Aboriginal governments to the standard of political inclusion. This standard not only follows logically from the equality provisions of the Charter's section 15 but is also entirely consistent with the normative thrust of relational pluralism and with what a number of Aboriginal women, youth, and urban dwellers were advocating before RCAP.

From the perspective of relational pluralism, if the collective Aboriginal right to self-definition is exercised in a manner that does not protect the participatory rights of individual Aboriginal persons such as women, youth, and urban dwellers, the justification for protecting the collective right is itself questionable. Seen in this light, the Charter's equality rights are not in the first instance about assuring individual Aboriginal persons the right to decide on, revise, and pursue their own distinct conceptions of the good from the cultural mainstream in Aboriginal communities, although on occasion this may be their intent if the context demands it. Rather, the equality rights can also be seen as a tool to safeguard the rights of Aboriginal women, youth, and urban dwellers to participate in the communal process of building Aboriginal lives that correspond to their own priorities.

This understanding of the Charter is, in my view, far more consistent with the actual political discourse of a number of those who claim to represent the concerns of Aboriginal women, youth, and urban dwellers. Aboriginal self-government is a claim to acquire control over resources and to make communal choices free from overbearing and insensitive interference by non-Aboriginal society. The testimony of a number of Aboriginal women, youth, and urban dwellers establishes that, while Aboriginal governments may be assuming greater power, these governments often deny them the power that they need to participate to their satisfaction in the process of self-governing. To fight the status imposed on them by their communities, some women, youth, and urban dwellers demand equality rights. Such rights are defined as membership rights; they are tools to acquire and safeguard what some say is their entitlement to full membership within their own communities.

Some organizations representing Aboriginal women in particular establish a close link between Aboriginal membership rights and the legal guarantees of the Charter. While most organizations support the collective rights of Aboriginal communities, they view the Charter as an important device to guarantee women their "right to define their own place within the group."[37] The Charter could thus be regarded as a fighting tool that Aboriginal women can use against their governments to keep them accountable.[38]

One recent Supreme Court of Canada decision is worthy of note here because it marks a serious attempt by the court to justify the Aboriginal desire for political inclusion on the legal grounds provided by the Charter. In *Corbiere v. Canada* (1999),[39] the Supreme Court considered whether band members who live off reserve are unjustly discriminated against by section 77(1) of the Indian Act, which allows only members "ordinarily resident on a reserve" to vote in band elections. The off-reserve members in this case argued that this section of the Indian Act violated their equality rights under section 15(1) of the Charter. The Supreme Court agreed, arguing that section 77(1) constitutes discrimination because it treats off-reserve members in a stereotypical way. In the court's view, the section treats them as less worthy and as unentitled to political participation simply on the presumption that "they are not interested in maintaining meaningful participation in the band or in preserving their cultural identity."[40] For the court, this presumption perpetuates the historical disadvantage experienced by off-reserve residents because it denies them political control, through elections, over their ongoing interests in band assets and lands of which they remain co-owners. As a result, the court's remedy was to strike out the words "and is ordinarily resident on the reserve" from the Indian Act. Nonetheless, the court did accept that some electoral distinction may be justified to protect the legitimate and possibly unique interests of band members on reserve. So, while extending the franchise to off-reserve members, the court also urged that electoral processes be developed to appropriately balance the rights of off-reserve and on-reserve members.

I believe that the Corbiere decision has implications that may well extend beyond the matter of the consistency of section 77(1) of the Indian Act with the Charter. The Supreme Court has served notice that it will not tolerate instances in which Aboriginal communities exclude members from political participation on the basis of what the court terms personal characteristics that are "immutable or unchangeable only at unacceptable cost to personal identity."[41] Clearly, being female and/or young is an immutable feature of personal identity, while being an urban dweller is, for many Aboriginal persons, changeable only at unacceptable personal cost. Consequently, it seems that, when Aboriginal women, youth, or urban dwellers are excluded from the political proceedings of their Aboriginal communities due to factors relating to gender, age, or residence, they may be able to enlist the Canadian court system as a ready ally.

Yet the Charter's equality provisions are completely ineffectual in ameliorating many of the problems that numerous Aboriginal witnesses named before RCAP as foremost among their concerns, such as discrimination, dominance, and the violence that they suffer within their personal relationships in their communities. Charter rights offer little if any help, for example, to individuals caught up in domestic abuse and violence. Moreover, even with respect to unequal treatment and abuse at the political level, which the Charter explicitly addresses, remedies may be limited. It is not clear how external pressure on Aboriginal governments by the Charter would actually curb the exercise of power by Aboriginal male elites perceived as being little concerned with the interests of Aboriginal women, youth, and urban dwellers. Nevertheless, and despite these limitations, without the external protection of the Charter, some organizations (women's in particular) express little confidence that Aboriginal women will have a chance to share power more equally with men and thus be in a position to set priorities for the development of Aboriginal communal existence. One witness mentioned that "We want to voice our opinions and ensure that our rights will be protected, especially in the area of Aboriginal self-government. We believe that we have the inherent right to self-government, but we also recognize that since European contact, our leaders have mainly been men, men who are the by-products of colonization ... We, therefore, want the Charter of Rights and Freedoms enforced in Aboriginal self-government until such time as our own Bill of Rights is developed that will protect women and children."[42]

A relational pluralist perspective on Aboriginal self-government thus provides an important context for understanding the relationship between Charter rights and affective Aboriginal communal bonds. In many cases (as in Corbiere), to invoke the individual rights of the Charter is simultaneously to invoke the claims of community. From this perspective, the tough mesh of Charter equality rights can be seen as a safety net should relationships in community go awry or leaders become exclusionary. In either case, the point of Charter rights remains the same: at the least, they give Aboriginal individuals the conceptual and legal tools to criticize those in authority who refuse to share power. More positively, when Charter rights are called upon, they can also serve to equalize the distribution of community power so that those who have an entitlement to determine how community resources are to be used in the present and the future can do so with impunity. Community and individual liberty should thus be seen as irrevocably linked; individual freedom of choice within community is what makes it possible for members to carry on in their common project of developing community.

CONCLUSION

Relational pluralism accentuates the degree to which the organized political forms of Aboriginal communities are aspects of a communal self-definition process. Individuals necessarily constitute the origin of the political and cultural structures of Aboriginal nations, meaning that it is individuals who give those structures their character and form. In addition, as the relationships of individuals to their structures develop, so too can the structures themselves. Aboriginal structures should, therefore, be viewed not as ends in themselves, cast in a single cultural or political mould, but as aspects of community identity in process, the result of ongoing choices made by their individual participants. For this reason, the multiple expressions of individual Aboriginal identity should be given equality of status and influence in the actual development of Aboriginal structures. What matters from the point of view of justice is not what the substantive character of a particular Aboriginal community identity amounts to but that the process by which the outcome was derived was a fully participatory one.

I began with a criticism of the idea that much of Aboriginal politics in Canada can be explained in terms of fundamental conflicts between individual and collective rights. When we use the language of communitarianism and individualism, we tend to adopt ideas of uniformity, implicitly assuming that Aboriginal communities possess a singleness of cultural identity and political purpose against which some of their members struggle. It should be clear by now how the framework of relational pluralism goes beyond this interpretation to provide context and perspective. The core of an Aboriginal community is not to be found in its cultural or national identity but in the commitment of its members to remain together, as a community, over time. What matters here is the specific character of the relationship that individual members take up with one another – a relationship based on the idea that all members possess participatory rights to shape the present and future identity of their community. A relational pluralist perspective thus shifts the focus of analysis from cultural preservation to the question of power and its equitable distribution. Naturally, resolving problems associated with power differences within Aboriginal communities is seldom easy, but at least conceptualizing problems in terms of power differences can clarify where and how we might more profitably direct our attention. As demonstrated, it is rights to inclusion and participatory status, not rights against the imposition of specific cultural and political images, that I would suggest are often of greatest importance to most Aboriginal individuals who struggle within their communities.

An effective foundation for Aboriginal self-government should thus have the following characteristics. First, the dominant Canadian governments must relinquish their hegemony over Aboriginal governments by ceding to them power of increased autonomy so that they can control their processes of collective self-definition. Solutions here must seek to empower Aboriginal communities as a whole, not just the individual members of Aboriginal communities. Second, an Aboriginal way of life pursued by a First Nation is simply what Aboriginal persons in that nation define it to be; there are no cultural or political criteria outside their choices that can be imposed on Aboriginal persons on the purported ground that those expressions more authentically represent Aboriginal identity. Third, in return for increased autonomy, Aboriginal governments must provide assurances that the victimization and oppression experienced by their internal minorities will be addressed. Aboriginal individuals in all their diversity must be given freedom to develop and contribute to community life without undue interference from their governing structures.

These characteristics together place a normative limitation on the exercise of the right to self-government that ought to be reinforced. Aboriginal political practices and processes are legitimate only to the degree that a community's members willingly accede to them. So long as community members feel part of their community because they contribute to it and believe that its political constraints are acceptable, to that degree the processes and practices are legitimate. The limitation on community power here hinges on the matter of individual choice. Aboriginal political choices need to be creatively developed and adapted, sometimes in the form of compromise between Aboriginal persons, if those who want to live together in Aboriginal communities are to do so successfully.

ABORIGINAL SELF-GOVERNMENT AND THE POLITICS OF PLURALISM

In this book, I presented three sets of questions as central to my analysis. The first set concerned Aboriginal political identity. Here I asked whether Aboriginal political identity should be thought of in cultural terms, national terms, or broader terms. I also asked if conceptualizing this question in terms other than those traditionally understood might make a difference in the way that we think about the Aboriginal right to self-government.

The second set concerned justification and intent. Here I asked whether the Aboriginal right to self-government is justified because it sustains an Aboriginal interest in preserving cultural difference and/or historical nationhood. I then asked whether culture- and nation-based justifications for self-government are adequate or whether justification might be better framed in terms of the need to address deficits in Aboriginal community power and imbalances in relations between Aboriginal and Canadian governments.

The third set addressed the issue of limitations on Aboriginal self-governing power. I asked which principles ought to be employed when setting limits on the political power that Aboriginal governments exercise over their community members. Should the primary principle be individual freedom of choice? Or does this principle put emphasis in the wrong place concerning many individual Aboriginal identity claims against their communities?

In the preceding six chapters, I set out some procedural and substantive ideas that can be used in responding to each set of questions. I dealt with each set in two ways: using an existing and recognized approach of analysis, and using one that I have developed myself. The existing approaches that I used are the difference approach to ethnic identity and communitarian and individualist approaches to pluralism. I demonstrated that the use of each was less than fully helpful in dealing with the relevant aspects of my subject matter. In this concluding chapter, I use the approach that I have developed to demonstrate some of the major ways in which it can stimulate a deeper understanding of Aboriginal identity politics.

Concerning the first set of questions, I showed in Chapter 1 that the most commonly held assumption among social scientists is that Aboriginal political identity arises out of the unique cultural and political attributes associated with Aboriginal community life. I referred to this manner of analysis as the difference approach. It proceeds from the assumption that the well-being of Aboriginal individual identity is tied directly to the strength and vitality of those community practices linked to distinctive artistic endeavours, economic pursuits, political organizations, and social arrangements. It is these expressions of difference that are seen to validate Aboriginal individuals and communities as Aboriginal. The politics of Aboriginal self-government is then understood to be about the desire of Aboriginal communities to preserve these distinct cultural and political attributes from the homogenizing influences of non-Aboriginal Canadian society. Indeed, failure to do so, from this perspective, jeopardizes Aboriginal community identity itself. The status of Aboriginal communities as nations within Canada is thus identified as crucial. Nations are seen as uniquely suited structurally to preserve Aboriginal culture. As nations, for example, Aboriginal communities are bearers of Aboriginal rights, including a land base and self-government that, when taken together, are understood to be essential elements for the cultural survival of those communities as distinct societies.

However, as I have tried to show throughout, the difference approach to Aboriginal identity is misguided. The problem is not that it mistakenly identifies Aboriginal communities as culturally and politically distinct; indeed, as RCAP's public hearings show, many Aboriginal witnesses clearly hold this view about both themselves and their communities. The problem, rather, is that the approach is simply incomplete. It is doubtful whether the majority of Aboriginal individuals within First Nations see the security of their Aboriginal identities as tied solely to the preservation and enhancement of objective traits of cultural and political difference. For many, Aboriginal identity is much more comprehensive, and, from the point of view that I developed, the route to its security lies elsewhere.

What I conclude from my reading of the RCAP testimony is that for most witnesses Aboriginal identity originates simply from personal identification with, and ongoing commitment to, the Aboriginal community in which they are (or see themselves to be) members. I used the identification perspective to demonstrate how this approach to Aboriginal identity might be understood. From this perspective, the key element that shapes Aboriginal identity is a sense of relatedness, whether based on real or assumed bonds of kinship, shared historical memories, elements of common culture, ties to specific territory, and/or a sense of solidarity among community members. Here, in other words, there is no one-to-one correspondence between Aboriginal identity and the communal and individual expression of distinctive cultural and political attributes. Instead, Aboriginal identity is seen to flow much more broadly from the sense of personal belonging to an Aboriginal community over time.

An important implication follows for the politics of Aboriginal self-government. From an identification perspective, the politics of self-government is understood to be about the Aboriginal desire to establish balanced relationships between Aboriginal and Canadian governments so that the former can govern their communities free from external interference by the latter. This position strikes me as not only more realistic than the difference approach but also as in keeping with much of the testimony by Aboriginal witnesses.

Testimony recounting the tragic and heroic dimensions of the Aboriginal past, experiences of personal and community exploitation at the hands of the Canadian state and the corresponding presence of resistance and healing, and the persistence of Aboriginal cultural and political differences from the Canadian mainstream can, on one level, all be interpreted in light of the same reality: for many Aboriginal persons, identification with their communities of origin remains strong. Seen in this way, testimony about self-government is understood to be fundamentally about the expression of an Aboriginal desire for local control over internal affairs. This approach suggests, therefore, that Aboriginal community survival depends not on the protection of cultural and political differences per se but on boundaries that establish a degree of separation between Aboriginal communities and the Canadian state. Aboriginal rights to land, resources, and self-government, in other words, are what maintain community boundaries. It is boundaries and not difference that are of first concern; they are what place Aboriginal persons in a position of security to define personal and community identities in ways consistent with their own aspirations.

In addressing the second set of questions, I suggested that there are merits to evaluating justifications for and the intent of Aboriginal self-government from the perspective of pluralism. However, pluralism is a diverse tradition, so I discussed the strengths and weaknesses of what I called, for heuristic purposes, its communitarian, individualistic, and relational faces. The pluralism tradition itself is held together by the idea that group diversity is a permanent feature of most societies, so the tensions and conflicts generated by group encounters must be framed within public arrangements that uphold standards of group recognition and affirmation. The meanings given to pluralism by its users, in other words, address the matter of political power. Pluralists assert that, provided no particular group captures a monopoly of political power within a state, the balancing of competing group interests that follows from the use of power can, and often does, represent a just accommodation. With respect to Aboriginal self-government in Canada, however, I argued that, while the communitarian and individualist faces of pluralism are valuable, they rely too heavily on an understanding in which Aboriginal identity is equated with specific cultural and national traits. Here the resulting political accommodations with the Canadian state are evaluated and then justified either in terms of the ability of Aboriginal communities to protect their cultural differences from the homogenizing influences of Canadian society or in terms of the ability of Aboriginal individuals to escape from their cultural institutions if and when they see them as oppressive.

In the third chapter, I demonstrated that communitarian pluralism provides an incomplete answer to the question of what justifies Aboriginal self-government. Those who employ this approach simply assume that the chief purpose of Aboriginal self-government is to preserve common cultural understandings and shared norms that differentiate Aboriginal communities from others in Canada. Communitarians claim, in other words, that group diversity exists because life has an inescapably cultural dimension; they make cultural difference the basis of community identity because they understand individuals to be formed in substantive measure by the cultural attributes of the communities in which they enjoy membership. Political conflict between Aboriginal and Canadian governments is thus construed in cultural terms: if Aboriginal individuals are to enjoy the "authentic" sources of their Aboriginal identity, then they must maintain the cultural originality of their communities at all costs. Here Aboriginal self-government is justified because it is said to put Aboriginal communities in a position of political strength to protect their cultural characteristics from the pressures applied against them by the surrounding, more powerful, Canadian polity.

However, the communitarian response is misguided. The problem, as I have shown, is not that it is too focused on Aboriginal community. Many of the issues addressed in the preceding chapters are indeed about the capacity of Aboriginal persons to rebuild and reclaim their communities and to develop strategies necessary to take up the responsibilities of self-government. Instead, in my view, the problem is that the communitarian community focus is too narrow.

In the fifth chapter, I used the perspective of relational pluralism to illuminate how I came to this conclusion. The relational face of pluralism approaches the question of what justifies Aboriginal self-government less in terms of community cultural preservation than in terms of the political relations that establish Aboriginal community identity and, more pertinently, in terms of who wields power in the political processes that define those relations. As a normative theory, relational pluralism shifts the object of our reflection about self-government to the more complex and ubiquitous question of Aboriginal community power. For relational pluralists, one judges the justice of the Canadian political system in part by the degree of independence and self-direction permitted to Aboriginal governments in their relations with the Canadian state. The standard of justice in this scheme is relational rather than cultural. Here real pluralism is marked by the capacity of Canadian governments to leave to Aboriginal communities the power to change and grow on their own terms, free of Canadian governmental domination. Naturally, what Aboriginal communities require to be free of domination will vary depending on the priorities that each community sets for its own jurisdictional independence. More broadly, however, the essential point that relational pluralists make is that Aboriginal self-government is justified not because it protects an Aboriginal right to cultural difference but because it promotes the Aboriginal right to use community resources of ancestry, history, shared commitment, culture, land, and politics to build communities that correspond to their own priorities, whether culturally distinct or otherwise.

Relational pluralism also promotes a more pragmatic view of Aboriginal self-government. Self-government is fundamentally about Aboriginal communities gradually building capacity to exercise control at a local level over a range of jurisdictions that they consider essential to their community identities. Viewed thus, self-government is a relational process with long-term implications for the transfer of power from Canadian to Aboriginal governments. The relational dimensions of this process are revealed in the steady but often slow movement that accompanies Aboriginal nations' work to resolve how powers and jurisdictions will be divided and/or shared between federal, provincial, and Aboriginal governments. The Nisga'a treaty provides one example of how complex and lengthy this process can be. Clearly, considerable work remains to be done as other Aboriginal communities across Canada carry on in their quests for greater self-government powers. Yet it is precisely here that the central insights of relational pluralism can be put to both pragmatic and profitable use. When Aboriginal self-government is framed in relational terms, the goal of equality in relations between Aboriginal and Canadian governments is more open to cultural and political coexistence, solidarity, and interdependency.

In answering the third set of questions, I used the testimony of Aboriginal women and youth before RCAP to gain insight into the issue of Aboriginal governmental power and the proper limitations of its use over Aboriginal citizens. I showed in the fourth chapter how individualist pluralism runs into insurmountable obstacles when addressing this question, because it frames its answer in ways informed by the difference approach to Aboriginal identity.

Many liberals now accept the idea that, if a liberal theory of justice is not to be condemned to irrelevance, its proponents must come to terms with the rights of minorities (including those of indigenous peoples) that arise out of the new politics of cultural difference. Liberals, in other words, are increasingly of the view that individual identity necessarily arises out of the cultural characteristics that one shares with others in community. Consequently, to preserve the settings in which individual identity acquisition takes place, some vulnerable cultural minorities may need special protection.

But these liberals are also quick to stress the importance of placing limits on cultural rights. In particular, they fear that, if communities are empowered against the state to uphold their distinct cultural ways of life, there must also be guarantees that individuals not be totally engulfed by the cultural demands of their communities. Here a premium is placed on individual choice. The thrust of individualist pluralism is that, where Aboriginal self-government is concerned, Aboriginal individuals must be free to dissent from and/or propose alternative cultural images of identity and not be penalized by their communities for doing so.

While framing the question of limitations in this way makes some sense, it fails to address what I take to be the major concern of many Aboriginal women and youth. My reading of the testimony before RCAP leads me to conclude that most Aboriginal women and youth do not fear cultural oppression in their communities as much as exclusion from the political decision-making processes of their communities. As I showed in Chapter 6, the relational face of pluralism provides resources that more adequately allow us to confront questions of justice that arise out of this concern.

Relational pluralism directs its evaluative focus on political relations and on the appropriate use of governmental power within Aboriginal communities. While some Aboriginal women and youth within Aboriginal communities may express a range of interests that compete with those held by community leaders, this fact should not constitute the ground for their exclusion from the political process. For relational pluralists, acceptable forms of Aboriginal self-government enable Aboriginal individuals to believe that they can contribute to the political process and motivate elected political leaders to respond according to members' expectations. Evaluating Aboriginal self-government initiatives in terms of this criterion, it seems to me, is much more in keeping with the primary political concerns of Aboriginal women and youth.

My conclusion is that key tools in answering the three sets of questions are better drawn from a political theory that starts out from an identification approach to ethnic identity and that gives central place to a theory of pluralism in which interaction between Aboriginal and Canadian governments is analyzed in relational terms. I do not suggest that the use of such a political theory will resolve every issue arising from the questions. Aboriginal politics in Canada is far too complex for that. Rather, my point is that employing an identification approach together with relational pluralism can appreciably deepen insight into and understanding about the Aboriginal self-government question in Canada.

Relational pluralism emphasizes a set of principles that can make a difference to the way that we think about a wide range of issues associated with Aboriginal politics in Canada – self-government, individual and community identities, the Charter, and federalism, to name just those that I have examined. Yet in the attempt to evaluate Aboriginal politics by using these principles, one cannot immunize oneself against the risk of misidentifying power relations. Unfortunately and unavoidably, this risk accompanies political life – and political analysis – especially when, as in Canada today, much is subject to flux and change. As Michael Walzer notes in another context, wherever relationships are involved, "we never know exactly where to put the fences ... boundaries ... are vulnerable to shifts in social meaning, and we have no choice but to live with the continual probes and incursions through which these shifts are worked out."[1]

Still, a political system must be equipped with receptors sensitive to political change that arises out of complex processes of interaction whether they be the interplay between Aboriginal and Canadian governments, the development of diverse Aboriginal self-governing structures, or the movement of Aboriginal individuals within these structures. The central insights of the identification approach to ethnic identity and of relational pluralism not only make this change more tangible and explicit but also give us useful normative guidelines about how to respond to the political challenges contained within that change.

NOTES

INTRODUCTION

1 For example, the Aboriginal right to self-government formed one of the central and most important constitutional innovations of the 1992 Charlottetown Accord. Although the accord failed, the Aboriginal right to self-government later formed one of the central planks of federal Aboriginal policy. See Government of Canada, Federal Policy Guide, *Aboriginal Self-Government: The Government of Canada's Approach to Implementation of the Inherent Right and Negotiation of Aboriginal Self-Government* (Ottawa: Minister of Public Works and Government Services Canada, 1995). Governmental recognition of the Aboriginal right to self-government was further endorsed and extended in its official response to the five-volume report of the Royal Commission on Aboriginal Peoples. See Government of Canada, *Gathering Strength: Canada's Aboriginal Action Plan* (Ottawa: Minister of Public Works and Government Services Canada, 1997).
2 The following figures are taken from the Royal Commission on Aboriginal Peoples (hereafter RCAP), *Report, Volume 1: Looking Forward, Looking Back* (Ottawa: Minister of Supply and Services, Canada, 1996), 15-19.

CHAPTER 1: IDENTITY POLITICS AND PLURALIST THEORY

1 Jean L. Cohen, "Democracy, Difference, and the Right of Privacy," in Seyla Benhabib, ed., *Democracy and Difference: Contesting the Boundaries of the Political* (Princeton: Princeton University Press, 1996), 188.
2 Will Kymlicka, *Multicultural Citizenship: A Liberal Theory of Minority Rights* (Oxford: Clarendon Press, 1995), 11.
3 Ibid.
4 Bhikhu Parekh, "Discourses on National Identity," *Political Studies* 42 (1994): 503.
5 See P.G. McHugh, "Aboriginal Identity and Relations in North America and Australasia," in Ken S. Coates and P.G. McHugh, eds., *Living Relationships (Kokiri ngatahi): The Treaty of Waitangi in the New Millennium* (Wellington: Victoria University Press, 1998), 145, 149.

6 See Kymlicka, *Multicultural Citizenship*; Patrick Macklem, *Indigenous Difference and the Constitution of Canada* (Toronto: University of Toronto Press, 2001); Charles Taylor, *Reconciling the Solitudes: Essays on Canadian Federalism and Nationalism* (Montreal: McGill-Queen's University Press, 1993); and James Tully, "A Just Relationship between Aboriginal and Non-Aboriginal Peoples in Canada," in Curtis Cook and Juan D. Landau, eds., *Aboriginal Rights and Self-Government: The Canadian and Mexican Experience in North American Perspective* (Montreal: McGill-Queen's University Press, 2000), and *Strange Multiplicity: Constitutionalism in an Age of Diversity* (Cambridge, UK: Cambridge University Press, 1995).

7 Taylor, *Reconciling the Solitudes*, 45.

8 Stephen Cornell, "The Variable Ties that Bind: Content and Circumstance in Ethnic Processes," *Ethnic and Racial Studies* 19, 2 (1996): 271. See also Arden R. King, "A Stratification of Labyrinths: The Acquisition and Retention of Cultural Identity in Modern Culture," in Thomas K. Fitzgerald, ed., *Social and Cultural Identity: Problems of Persistence and Change* (Athens: Southern Anthropological Society, 1974), 106.

9 Kymlicka, *Multicultural Citizenship*, 76. Kymlicka's understanding of culture as all-encompassing is reflected in both earlier and other contemporary studies as well. See, for example, Cynthia H. Enloe, *Ethnic Conflict and Political Development* (Boston: Little, Brown, 1973), 15; Michael Novak, "Pluralism: A Humanist Perspective," written for the Stephen A. Thernstrom edition of the *Harvard Encyclopedia of American Ethnic Groups* (Cambridge, MA: Harvard University Press, 1980), 773; Nitya Duclos, "Lessons of Difference: Feminist Theory on Cultural Diversity," *Buffalo Law Review* 38, 2 (1990): 330; Avishai Margalit and Moshe Halbertal, "Liberalism and the Right to Culture," *Social Research* 61, 3 (1994): 497-98; and Denise G. Reaume, "Justice between Cultures: Autonomy and Protection of Cultural Affiliation," *U.B.C. Law Review* 29, 1 (1995): 120.

10 Margalit and Halbertal, "Liberalism and the Right to Culture," 505.

11 Cornell, "The Variable Ties that Bind," 271.

12 Jeremy Webber, "Individuality, Equality, and Difference: Justifications for a Parallel System of Aboriginal Justice," in Royal Commission on Aboriginal Peoples, *Aboriginal Peoples and the Justice System: Report of the National Round Table on Aboriginal Justice Issues* (Ottawa: Minister of Supply and Services Canada, 1993), 137.

13 Macklem, *Indigenous Difference and the Constitution of Canada*, 56.

14 Tully, *Strange Multiplicity*, 10.

15 Webber, "Individuality, Equality, and Difference," 137.

16 See Patrick Macklem, "Distributing Sovereignty: Indian Nations and Equality of Peoples," *Stanford Law Review* 45 (1993): 1356; Kymlicka, *Multicultural Citizenship*, 11; and Tully, *Strange Multiplicity*, 4, 6.

17 See Benjamin Akzin, *State and Nation* (London: Hutchinson University Library, 1964), 33; Gerald R. Alfred, *Heeding the Voices of Our Ancestors: Kahnawake Mohawk Politics and the Rise of Native Nationalism* (Toronto: Oxford University Press, 1995), 10; and John Rex, *Ethnic Minorities in the Modern Nation State: Working Papers in the Theory of Multiculturalism and Political Integration* (New York: St. Martin's Press, 1996), 85, 173.

18 George De Vos, "Ethnic Pluralism: Conflict and Accommodation," in George De Vos and Lola Romanucci-Ross, eds., *Ethnic Identity: Cultural Continuities and Change* (Palo Alto: Mayfield Publishing Company, 1975), 11. See also Alfred, *Heeding the Voices of Our Ancestors*, 10.

19 Paul R. Brass, *Ethnicity and Nationalism: Theory and Comparison* (New Delhi/Newbury Park, CA: Sage Publications, 1991), 20.

20 Tully, *Strange Multiplicity*, 4.

21 Taylor, *Reconciling the Solitudes*, 50.

22 Margalit and Halbertal, "Liberalism and the Right to Culture," 502.

23 David Mayberry-Lewis, *Indigenous Peoples, Ethnic Groups, and the State* (Boston: Allyn and Bacon, 1997), 60.

24 Thomas Hylland Eriksen, *Ethnicity and Nationalism: Anthropological Perspectives* (London: Pluto Press, 1993), 4. This and the following paragraph draw from McHugh's argument that the key element in ethnicity is that of self-definition. See McHugh, "Aboriginal Identity and Relations in North America and Australasia," 145, 149.

25 Anthony D. Smith, *National Identity* (Reno: University of Nevada Press, 1991), 21. Virtually identical understandings of ethnicity are employed by Harold J. Abramson in "Assimilation and Pluralism," in Thernstrom, ed., *The Harvard Encyclopedia of American Ethnic Groups*, 151; Baha Abu-Laban and Donald Mottershead, "Cultural Pluralism and Varieties of Ethnic Politics," *Canadian Ethnic Studies* 8, 3 (1981): 48-51; Adeno Addis, "Individualism, Communitarianism, and the Rights of Ethnic Minorities," *Notre Dame Law Review*, 66, 5 (1991): 1260; Brass, *Ethnicity and Nationalism*, 19; Leo Driedger, "Introduction: Ethnic Identity in the Canadian Mosaic," in Leo Driedger, ed., *The Canadian Ethnic Mosaic: A Quest for Identity* (Toronto: McClelland and Stewart, 1978), 15-19; and Enloe, *Ethnic Conflict and Political Development*, 17-18. In addition, similar understandings are employed by Patrick Macklem in his definition of "peoples" and by David Miller in his definition of "nations." See Macklem, "Distributing Sovereignty," 1356; and David Miller, *On Nationality* (Oxford: Clarendon Press, 1995), 22-27.

26 Smith, *National Identity*, 25.

27 Cornell, "The Variable Ties that Bind," 268. See also Alfred, *Heeding the Voices of Our Ancestors*, 14; Brass, *Ethnicity and Nationalism*, 19; and Smith, *National Identity*, 22.

28 Smith, *National Identity*, 22.

29 Eriksen, *Ethnicity and Nationalism*, 34.

30 Numerous anthropologists have demonstrated that ethnic identity is far more resilient than this. In particular, see the important study by Eriksen, *Ethnicity and Nationalism*.

31 Macklem, *Indigenous Difference and the Constitution of Canada*, 53. Tully makes virtually the same point concerning the elasticity of culture in *Strange Multiplicity*, 7-14.

32 Macklem, *Indigenous Difference and the Constitution of Canada*, 54, 53.

33 Here see Fredrik Barth, ed., *Ethnic Groups and Boundaries: The Social Organization of Cultural Difference* (Boston: Little, Brown, 1969); Brass, *Ethnicity and Nationalism*; Eriksen, *Ethnicity and Nationalism*; Adam Kuper, ed., *Conceptualizing Society* (London: Routledge, 1992); Rex, *Ethnic Minorities in the Modern Nation State*; Richard A. Wilson, ed., *Human Rights, Culture, and Context: Anthropological Perspectives* (London: Pluto Press, 1997).

34 As cited in Eriksen, *Ethnicity and Nationalism*, 37.

35 Ibid.

36 Brass, *Ethnicity and Nationalism*, 19.

37 Eriksen, *Ethnicity and Nationalism*, 38.

38 Cornell, "The Variable Ties that Bind," 269.

39 Ibid., 266. See also 269.

40 Eriksen, *Ethnicity and Nationalism*, 68.

41 On this point, see Daniel Salee, "Identities in Conflict: The Aboriginal Question and the Politics of Recognition in Quebec," *Ethnic and Racial Studies* 18, 2 (1995): 281.

42 Brian M. Bullivant, *Pluralism: Cultural Maintenance and Evolution* (Clevedon: Multilingual Matters, 1984), 1.

43 I am indebted to P.G. McHugh for this very helpful distinction. See McHugh, "Aboriginal Identity and Relations in North America and Australasia," 113.

44 Eriksen, *Ethnicity and Nationalism*, 117.

45 On the various kinds of pluralism, see Gregor McLennan, *Pluralism* (Minneapolis: University of Minnesota Press, 1995). On legal pluralism, see Sally Engle Merry, "Legal Pluralism," *Law and Society Review* 22, 5 (1988): 869-901; and Martha-Marie Kleinhans and Roderick A. Macdonald, "What Is a Critical Legal Pluralism?," *Canadian Journal of Law and Society* 12 (1997): 25-46.

46 Chantal Mouffe, "Democracy, Power, and the 'Political,'" in Benhabib, ed., *Democracy and Difference*, 246.

47 Danielle Juteau, "Multicultural Citizenship: The Challenge of Pluralism in Canada," in Veit Bader, ed., *Citizenship and Exclusion* (Basingstoke: MacMillan Press, 1997), 97.

48 Iris Marion Young, *Justice and the Politics of Difference* (Princeton: Princeton University Press, 1990), 188.

49 Taylor, *Reconciling the Solitudes*, 183.

50 Macklem, *Indigenous Difference and the Constitution of Canada*, 4.

51 Tully, "A Just Relationship between Aboriginal and Non-Aboriginal Peoples of Canada," 43.

52 Charles Taylor, *Multiculturalism and "The Politics of Recognition,"* ed. Amy Gutmann (Princeton: Princeton University Press, 1992).

53 On this point, see Brass, *Ethnicity and Nationalism*, 50-63.

54 The texts most commonly cited here include Michael Sandel, *Liberalism and the Limits of Justice* (Cambridge, UK: Cambridge University Press, 1982); Alasdair MacIntyre, *After Virtue: A Study in Moral Theory* (Notre Dame: University of Notre Dame Press, 1984), and *Whose Justice? Which Rationality?* (Notre Dame: University of Notre Dame Press, 1988); Charles Taylor, *Sources of the Self: The Making of Modern Identity* (Cambridge, MA: Harvard University Press, 1989); Michael Walzer, *Spheres of Justice: A Defense of Pluralism and Equality* (New York: Basic Books, 1983); Will Kymlicka, *Liberalism, Community, and Culture* (Oxford: Clarendon Press, 1991), and *Multicultural Citizenship*; and James Tully, *Strange Multiplicity*. Tully explicitly rejects a political theory of constitutionalism based on an implicit and substantive conception of the good, a position that he attributes as central to the communitarian ideal. In this sense, his position constitutes an important departure from what might be termed communitarian orthodoxy. Yet Tully attributes an irreducible role to culture in community identity formation, a position that he shares with scholars such as Taylor and Kymlicka. For this reason, I place Tully within the communitarian tradition. On this point, see Tully, *Strange Multiplicity*, 62, 64.

55 It could also be argued that Taylor's extensive treatment of Quebec nationalism is analogous. Alan Cairns, however, begs to differ given that the relatively small nature of most Aboriginal communities makes it virtually impossible for them to build societal cultures in a manner within the reach of francophone Quebeckers. See Alan Cairns, "Finding Our Way: Rethinking Ethnocultural Relations in Canada" [book review], *Canadian Journal of Political Science* 32, 2 (1999): 369-71. Taylor's treatment of Aboriginal issues in

Canada is sparse. Taylor does address, albeit briefly, some of the problems that he believes many Canadians mistakenly attribute to the kinds of relations the Nisga'a treaty promotes between the Nisga'a people and other Canadians. See Charles Taylor, "On the Nisga'a Treaty," *BC Studies* 120 (1998-99): 37-40.

56 Tully, *Strange Multiplicity*, 1-6.

57 Markate Daly, "Introduction," in Markate Daly, ed., *Communitarianism: A New Public Ethics* (Belmont: Wadsworth Publishing Company, 1994), xvii.

58 Taylor, *Multiculturalism and "The Politics of Recognition,"* 27-28.

59 Ibid., 42, 66.

60 Kymlicka, *Multicultural Citizenship*, 35-44, 108-15.

61 This figure comes from the Royal Commission on Aboriginal Peoples, *Report, Volume 1: Looking Forward, Looking Back* (Ottawa: Minister of Supply and Services Canada, 1996), 15.

62 Kymlicka, "Liberalism, Individualism, and Minority Rights," in Allan C. Hutchinson and Leslie J.M. Green, eds., *Law and Community: The End of Individualism?* (Toronto: Carswell, 1989), 198.

63 Tully, "A Just Relationship between Aboriginal and Non-Aboriginal Peoples of Canada," 68.

64 Ibid.

65 Ibid., 68-69.

66 Ibid., 67.

67 Jeremy Webber, *Reimagining Canada: Language, Culture, Community, and the Canadian Constitution* (Montreal: McGill-Queen's University Press, 1994), 236.

68 Claude Denis, *We Are Not You: First Nations and Canadian Modernity* (Peterborough: Broadview Press, 1997), 73.

69 Tom Flanagan, *First Nations? Second Thoughts* (Montreal: McGill-Queen's University Press, 2000).

70 Ibid., 9.

71 Ibid., see Chapters 2, 3, 4, and 5.

72 Ibid., see Chapters 6, 7, 8, and 9.

73 Ibid., 9, 195-96.

74 Daly, "Introduction," xiv.

75 Kymlicka, *Liberalism, Community, and Culture*, 13.

76 Ronald Dworkin, "Liberalism," in his *A Matter of Principle* (Cambridge, MA: Harvard University Press, 1985), 181-204.

77 On these points, see Daly, "Introduction," xvi.

78 Here see Arthur Bentley, *The Process of Government: A Study of Social Pressures* (Chicago: University of Chicago Press, 1908); David Truman, *The Governmental Process* (New York: Alfred A. Knopf, 1951); and Robert A. Dahl, *Democracy in the United States: Promise and Performance*, 2nd ed. (Chicago: Rand McNally, 1972). An important analysis of this tradition's contribution to the development of pluralist theory is provided by Avigail Eisenberg in *Reconstructing Political Pluralism* (Albany: State University of New York, 1995), Chapters 4 and 5.

79 Rand Dyck, *Canadian Politics: Critical Approaches*, 2nd ed. (Scarborough: Nelson Canada, 1996), 11.

80 See John Rawls, *A Theory of Justice* (Cambridge, MA: Harvard University Press, 1971), 62.

81 Daly, "Introduction," xiii.
82 On this point, see John Gray, *Post-Liberalism: Studies in Political Thought* (New York: Routledge, 1993), 298.
83 Daly, "Introduction," xix.
84 Ibid., xviii-xix.
85 Kymlicka, *Multicultural Citizenship*, 37.
86 Webber, *Reimagining Canada*, 247.
87 The analysis to follow does not start with a blank sheet. Rather, it draws from the work of several scholars, most of whom are associated in one way or another with the tradition of pluralism. Principal authors here include Addis, "Individualism, Communitarianism, and the Right of Ethnic Minorities," 1219-80; Denis, *We Are Not You*; Eisenberg, *Reconstructing Political Pluralism*; Milton Fisk, "Community and Morality," *Review of Politics* 55, 4 (1993): 593-616; Kleinhans and Macdonald, "What Is a Critical Legal Pluralism?"; Elizabeth Frazer and Nicola Lacey, *The Politics of Community: A Feminist Critique of the Liberal-Communitarian Debate* (New York: Harvester Wheatsheaf, 1993); Carol Gould, *Rethinking Democracy: Freedom and Social Cooperation in Politics, Economy, and Society* (Cambridge, UK: Cambridge University Press, 1988); McHugh, "Aboriginal Identity and Relations in North America and Australasia," 112; Merry, "Legal Pluralism"; Webber, *Reimagining Canada*; and Young, *Justice and the Politics of Difference*.
88 Frazer and Lacey, *The Politics of Community*, 173.
89 The following draws in part from Gould, *Rethinking Democracy*, 105-7; and Young, *Justice and the Politics of Difference*, 43-47. See also Kleinhans and Macdonald, "What Is a Critical Legal Pluralism?," 43.
90 Gould, *Rethinking Democracy*, 106.
91 Kleinhans and Macdonald, "What Is a Critical Legal Pluralism?," 38.
92 Young, *Justice and the Politics of Difference*, 43.
93 Frazer and Lacey, *The Politics of Community*, 191.
94 The implications of the legal subject participating in law not just by submitting to it but also by "inventing" it are examined in Kleinhans and Macdonald, "What Is a Critical Legal Pluralism?" 38-43.
95 Young, *Justice and the Politics of Difference*, 173.
96 Ibid., 174.
97 Michael Rustin, *For a Pluralist Socialism* (London: Verso, 1985), 36.
98 Walzer, *Spheres of Justice*, xiii.
99 Juteau, "Multicultural Citizenship," 108.
100 Merry, "Legal Pluralism," 883.

CHAPTER 2: APPROACHES TO ABORIGINAL IDENTITY
1 The examples here are numerous and varied. For a small sample, see Gerald R. Alfred, *Heeding the Voices of Our Ancestors: Kahnawake Mohawk Politics and the Rise of Native Nationalism* (Toronto: Oxford University Press, 1995); Ward Churchill, "The Tragedy and Travesty: The Subversion of Indigenous Sovereignty in North America," *American Indian Culture and Research Journal* 22, 2 (1998): 1-69; Ovide Mercredi and Mary Ellen Turpel, *In the Rapids: Navigating the Future of First Nations* (Toronto: Penguin Books, 1994); and Boyce Richardson, ed., *Drum Beat: Anger and Renewal in Indian Country* (Toronto: Summerhill Press, 1990).

2 See Constitution Act, 1867, section 91(24).

3 Government of Canada, *Statement on Indian Policy* (Ottawa: Queen's Printer, 1969).

4 The analysis of this and subsequent paragraphs are inspired by P.G. McHugh's critical assessment of structuralist relations (as he puts it) between Aboriginal and non-Aboriginal peoples in North America. See McHugh, "Aboriginal Identity and Relations in North America and Australasia," in Ken S. Coates and P.G. McHugh, eds., *Living Relationships (Kokiri ngatahi): The Treaty of Waitangi in the New Millennium* (Wellington: Victoria University Press, 1998), 110-13.

5 Alfred, *Heeding the Voices of Our Ancestors*, 13.

6 On this point, see ibid., 6-7.

7 Patrick Macklem, "Ethnonationalism, Aboriginal Identities, and the Law," in Michael D. Levin, ed., *Ethnicity and Aboriginality: Case Studies in Ethnonationalism* (Toronto: University of Toronto Press, 1993), 9.

8 Jeremy Webber, *Reimagining Canada: Language, Culture, Community, and the Canadian Constitution* (Montreal and Kingston: McGill-Queen's University Press, 1994), 66.

9 Ibid., 68.

10 The identical point is made by Paul L.A.H. Chartrand in "The Aboriginal Peoples of Canada and Renewal of the Federation," in Karen Knop et al., eds., *Rethinking Federalism: Citizens, Markets, and Governments in a Changing World* (Vancouver: UBC Press, 1995), 123.

11 James Tully, *Strange Multiplicity: Constitutionalism in an Age of Diversity* (Cambridge, UK: Cambridge University Press, 1995), 10, 62.

12 Ibid., 118, 4.

13 Ibid., 6.

14 Ibid., 119.

15 Alfred, *Heeding the Voices of Our Ancestors*, 9.

16 Ibid., 10.

17 Ibid., 12.

18 Patrick Macklem, "Distributing Sovereignty: Indian Nations and Equality of Peoples," *Stanford Law Review* 45 (1993): 1312.

19 Patrick Macklem, *Indigenous Difference and the Constitution of Canada* (Toronto: University of Toronto Press, 2001), 287.

20 Ibid.

21 Ibid.

22 Ibid., 4.

23 For one characterization of this disagreement, see Tom Pocklington's discussion of legal, political-institutional, rights-based, and well-being justifications for an Aboriginal right to self-government in "Arguing for Aboriginal Self-Government," in Don Carmichael, Tom Pocklington, and Greg Pyrcz, eds., *Democracy, Rights, and Well-Being in Canada,* 2nd ed. (Toronto: Harcourt Brace and Company, Canada, 2000), 102-17.

24 What follows draws in large part on the limitations that P.G. McHugh associates with what he calls a claims-based model of government-Aboriginal relations. See McHugh, "Aboriginal Identity and Relations in North America and Australasia," 114-16.

25 Jane Jenson, "Understanding Politics: Contested Concepts in Political Science," in James P. Bickerton and Alain-G. Gagnon, eds., *Canadian Politics* 2 (Peterborough: Broadview Press, 1994), 61.

26 Paul Brass, "Ethnic Groups and the State," in Paul Brass, ed., *Ethnic Groups and the State* (London: Croom Helm, 1985), 15.

27 Claude Denis, *We Are Not You: First Nations and Canadian Modernity* (Peterborough: Broadview Press, 1997), 21.

28 Macklem, Tully, and Webber are not guilty of this charge, though it is unclear from their analysis what they see as the substantive core of Aboriginal identity. While they all regard culture as central to Aboriginal identity, they also recognize that cultures are dispersed and diluted through intercultural influences. My question then is, if this is so, where lies the difference?

29 Scholars who characterize the Aboriginal-Canadian state relationship in adversarial terms include Alfred, *Heeding the Voices of Our Ancestors*, 13; Denis, *We Are Not You*, 26; Augie Fleras and Jean Leonard Elliott, *The Nations Within: Aboriginal-State Relations in Canada, the United States, and New Zealand* (Toronto: Oxford University Press, 1992), 21–22; and Daniel Salee, "Identities in Conflict: The Aboriginal Question and the Politics of Recognition in Quebec," *Ethnic and Racial Studies* 18, 2 (1995): 285.

30 David Mayberry-Lewis, *Indigenous Peoples, Ethnic Groups, and the State* (Boston: Allyn and Bacon, 1997), 54.

31 Paul Tennant, "Aboriginal Peoples and Aboriginal Title in British Columbia Politics," in R.K. Carty, ed., *Politics, Policy, and Government in British Columbia* (Vancouver: UBC Press, 1996), 45.

32 Ibid.

33 On this point, see Mayberry-Lewis, *Indigenous Peoples, Ethnic Groups, and the State*, 7–12.

34 Devon A. Mihesuah, "American Indian Identities: Issues of Individual Choices and Development," *American Indian Culture and Research Journal* 22, 2 (1998): 195.

35 Mayberry-Lewis, *Indigenous Peoples, Ethnic Groups, and the State*, 8.

36 Will Kymlicka, *Multicultural Citizenship: A Liberal Theory of Minority Rights* (Oxford: Clarendon Press, 1995), 23. A similar repudiation of descent-based criteria is advanced in Michael Seymour, Jocelyne Couture, and Kai Neilsen's discussion of ethnic versus culturally based nationalist movements. For them, ethnic nationalism incorporates descent-based criteria, is exclusive, and is therefore illegitimate, while cultural nationalism incorporates cultural criteria, is inclusive, and is thus acceptable. See Michael Seymour, Jocelyne Couture, and Kai Neilsen, "Introduction: Questioning the Ethnic/Civic Dichotomy," *Canadian Journal of Philosophy* supplementary volume 22 (1996): 2–9.

37 See Stewart Clatworthy and Anthony Smith, *Population Implications of the 1985 Amendments to the Indian Act: Final Report* (Ottawa: Assembly of First Nations, 1992), 13–20.

38 *Hamlet of Baker Lake v. Minister of Indian Affairs* (1979) 107 D.L.R. (3d), 549.

39 On this point, see McHugh, "Aboriginal Identity and Relations in North America and Australasia," 149.

40 What follows draws in large part from correspondence received from Paul Tennant, June 2001.

41 Government of Canada, Federal Policy Guide, *Aboriginal Self-Government: The Government of Canada's Approach to the Implementation of the Inherent Right and the Negotiation of Aboriginal Self-Government* (Ottawa: Minister of Public Works and Government Services Canada, 1995).

42 See Churchill, "The Tragedy and the Travesty," 3–5; Jane Jenson, "Naming Nations:

Making Nationalist Claims in Canadian Public Discourse," *Canadian Review of Sociology and Anthropology* 30, 3 (1993): 345; Kymlicka, *Multicultural Citizenship*, 10–33; and Charles Taylor, *Reconciling the Solitudes: Essays on Canadian Federalism and Nationalism* (Montreal: McGill-Queen's University Press, 1993), 155–86.

43 Danielle Juteau, "Multicultural Citizenship: The Challenge of Pluralism in Canada," in Veit Bader, ed., *Citizenship and Exclusion* (Basingstoke: MacMillan Press, 1997), 108–9.

44 Kymlicka, *Multicultural Citizenship*, 11.

45 Juteau, "Multicultural Citizenship," 109.

46 Alfred, *Heeding the Voices of Our Ancestors*, 13.

47 On this point, see McHugh, "Aboriginal Identity and Relations in North America and Australasia," 120–21.

CHAPTER 3: ABORIGINAL CULTURE, NATION, AND THE POLITICS OF DIFFERENCE

1 For a list of the sixteen areas in which RCAP was instructed to make recommendations, see "Opening Statement by the Right Honourable Brian Dickson, Former Chief Justice of the Supreme Court of Canada," in *Opening Statements on the Occasion of the Launch of the Public Hearings of the Royal Commission on Aboriginal Peoples* (Ottawa: Minister of Supply and Services, 1992), 4–5.

2 Royal Commission on Aboriginal Peoples (hereafter RCAP), *Public Hearings, Toward Reconciliation: Overview of the Fourth Round* (Ottawa: Minister of Supply and Services Canada, 1994), vii.

3 Over twenty months, members of the Royal Commission "visited 96 communities across the country, heard more than 2000 intervenors, sat for a total of 172 hearing days, and travelled hundreds of thousands of kilometres during four rounds of hearings." In terms of balance between Aboriginal and non-Aboriginal participation, the commission heard a total of 1,623 Aboriginal intervenors, among them 1,032 Aboriginal groups, organizations, or governments, and 591 individuals. In addition, 444 non-Aboriginal intervenors appeared before the commission, 361 of whom were groups, organizations, or governments and 83 of whom were individuals. See RCAP, *Public Hearings, Toward Reconciliation*, vii–viii, 95–100.

4 Furthermore, to encourage Aboriginal witnesses to come forward, most hearings were held in the nonintimidating contexts of Aboriginal friendship centres, community halls, band council offices, traditional long houses, schools, penitentiaries, women's shelters, hockey rinks, and, only where necessary, hotels and conference centres. See RCAP, *Public Hearings, Discussion Paper 1: Framing the Issues* (Ottawa: Royal Commission on Aboriginal Peoples, 1992), 1.

5 Ibid.

6 On the transformative power of these symbols for both politics and the world of scholarship, see Edward M. Bruner, "Ethnology as Narrative," in Victor W. Turner and Edward M. Bruner, eds., *The Anthropology of Experience* (Urbana: University of Illinois Press, 1986), 139.

7 Peter Stevens, *RCAP Public Hearings*, Eskasoni, Nova Scotia, 6–7 May 1992.

8 Wallace Labillois, *RCAP Public Hearings*, Kingsclear, New Brunswick, 19 May 1992. The theme of governmental duplicity was ubiquitous throughout RCAP's public hearings. For numerous examples, consult the six summary papers of the hearings: RCAP, *Public Hearings: Overview of the First Round* (Ottawa: RCAP, 1992); *Public Hearings, Discussion*

Paper 1: Framing the Issues; Public Hearings: Overview of the Second Round (Ottawa: Minister of Supply and Services Canada, 1993); *Public Hearings, Discussion Paper 2: Focusing the Dialogue* (Ottawa: Minister of Supply and Services, 1993); *Public Hearings, Exploring the Options: Overview of the Third Round* (Ottawa: Minister of Supply and Services Canada, 1993); and *Public Hearings: Toward Reconciliation.*

9 Stevens, *RCAP Public Hearings.*

10 Labillois, *RCAP Public Hearings.*

11 Margaret Donovan, Vice-President, Gwich'in Tribal Council, *RCAP Public Hearings,* Inuvik, Northwest Territories, 5-6 May 1992.

12 Dawna LeBlanc, Nishnaabe Language Teachers Association, *RCAP Public Hearings,* Sault Ste. Marie, Ontario, 11 June 1992.

13 Chief Dorothy McDonald, Fort McKay Indian Band, *RCAP Public Hearings,* Fort McMurray, Alberta, 16 June 1992.

14 Terry Nelson of the Rouseau River First Nation describes this loss of land as follows: "Rouseau River had over 3,000 square miles in southern Manitoba. We now have 12 square miles left. We lost 96.6 per cent of our land. The situation is the same in Canada. Overall, the Canadian land mass is over 3.8 million square miles of land. The 2,200 pieces of land that is identified as Indian reservation land amounts to about 10,313 square miles. In effect, 99.73 per cent of the land in Canada is under non-Aboriginal control. The majority of our people are existing on one quarter of one per cent of what their land was at one time." Terry Nelson, Rouseau River First Nation, *RCAP Public Hearings,* Rouseau River, Manitoba, 8 December 1992.

15 Jack Blacksmith, Waswanipi Band Councillor, *RCAP Public Hearings,* Waswanipi, Quebec, 9 June 1992.

16 RCAP, *Aboriginal Peoples in Urban Centres: Report of the National Round Table on Aboriginal Urban Issues* (Ottawa: Minister of Supply and Services Canada, 1993), 36-37.

17 Charlie Cootes, Chief of the Uchucklesaht Tribe, *RCAP Public Hearings,* Port Alberni, British Columbia, 20 May 1992.

18 Mary Guilbeaut, Vice President, Indigenous Women's Collective, *RCAP Public Hearings,* Winnipeg, Manitoba, 21-23 April 1992.

19 The theme of family violence as articulated in the public hearings of RCAP is explored by Madeleine Dion Stout (with the assistance of Catherine R. Bruyere), "Stopping Family Violence: Aboriginal Communities Enspirited," in J. Rick Ponting, ed., *First Nations in Canada: Perspectives on Opportunity, Empowerment, and Self-Determination* (Toronto: McGraw-Hill Ryerson, 1997), 273-98.

20 RCAP, *Public Hearings, Discussion Paper 2,* 52.

21 RCAP, *Public Hearings, Discussion Paper 1,* 22.

22 Of course, the authority of the AFN among First Nations is by no means universal. However, its mandate is to represent the political interests of First Nations at the national level, and for many it does so adequately.

23 RCAP, *Public Hearings: Toward Reconciliation,* 61.

24 RCAP, *Public Hearings, Discussion Paper 2,* 53.

25 Elder Violet McGregor, Birch Island Reserve, *RCAP Public Hearings,* Ottawa, Ontario, November 1993.

26 See RCAP, *Treaty Making in the Spirit of Co-Existence: An Alternative to Extinguishment* (Ottawa: Minister of Supply and Services Canada, 1995), 1-14.

27 See also RCAP, *Public Hearings, Discussion Paper 2*, 28-29; and RCAP, *Public Hearings, Exploring the Options*, 50-51.

28 The rhetoric of "worldviews" is sometimes invoked to describe these cultural frames of reference. As Martin Benjamin defines it, "a world view is a complex, often unarticulated (and perhaps not fully articulable) set of deeply held and highly cherished beliefs about the nature of the universe and one's place in it. Normative as well as descriptive – comprising interlocking general beliefs about knowledge, reality, and values – a world view so pervades and conditions our thinking that it is largely unnoticed." Being both normative and descriptive, worldviews also provide a point of orientation for individual and communal action. Worldviews provide a focal point for community identity because they are rooted in a perception that community members view the world through similar normative categories and so will relate to the world and behave within it in a more or less similar fashion. See Martin Benjamin, *Splitting the Difference: Compromise and Integrity in Ethics and Politics* (Kansas: University Press of Kansas, 1990), 88.

29 J. Anthony Long and Katherine Beaty Chiste, "Indian Governments and the Canadian Charter of Rights and Freedoms," *American Indian Culture and Research Journal* 18, 2 (1994): 96-97.

30 Ovide Mercredi, Grand Chief of the Assembly of First Nations, *RCAP Public Hearings*, Toronto, Ontario, 26 June 1992.

31 Radha Jhappan, "Inherency, Three Nations, and Collective Rights: The Evolution of Aboriginal Constitutional Discourse from 1982 to the Charlottetown Accord," *International Journal of Canadian Studies* 7-8 (1993): 232.

32 Chief Harold Turner, Swampy Cree Tribal Council, *RCAP Public Hearings*, The Pas, Manitoba, 19-20 May 1992.

33 A list of the research studies prepared for the Royal Commission can be found in volume 5 of its report. See RCAP, *Report, Volume 5: Renewal: A Twenty-Year Commitment* (Ottawa: Minister of Supply and Services Canada, 1996), 306-24.

34 In the years since the report's release, it has become obvious that many of the recommendations will never be implemented. For example, the commission urged that, within six months of the release of its report, leaders of the national Aboriginal organizations and first ministers meet to review its principal recommendations. This meeting never occurred. Furthermore, the commission recommended that meetings commence immediately to begin drafting a new Royal Proclamation and to set up a framework agreement for the funding of Aboriginal governments. Again, no such meetings took place. Other recommendations with specific targeted times have come and gone. Among them were abolishing the Department of Indian Affairs and Northern Development and replacing it with two new departments, a Department of Aboriginal Relations and a Department of Indian and Inuit Affairs (process to begin within one year after the report's release); establishing an elected Aboriginal parliament with enumeration of Aboriginal voters to occur during the federal election of 1997; and establishing an Aboriginal Peoples' University by the year 2000.

35 For a discussion of these four stages, see RCAP, *Report, Volume 1: Looking Forward, Looking Back* (Ottawa: Minister of Supply and Services Canada, 1996).

36 RCAP, *Report, Volume 5*, 141.

37 Ibid., 155, 158.

38 RCAP, *Report, Volume 3: Gathering Strength* (Ottawa: Minister of Supply and Services Canada, 1996), 530.

39 RCAP, *Public Hearings, Discussion Paper 2*, 7.

40 Ibid., 8.

41 RCAP, *Report, Volume 2: Restructuring the Relationship—Parts One and Two* (Ottawa: Minister of Supply and Services, 1996).

42 David Miller, *On Nationality* (Oxford: Clarendon Press, 1995), 92.

43 See RCAP, *Report, Volume 5*, 221 (schools), 227 (residential colleges), 228 (Aboriginal Peoples' International University), 233-34 (language), 236 (literary, visual, and performing arts), 210 (healing centres and lodges), 238-39 (youth centres and camps), 232 (cultural artifacts and heritage sites), 209 (health science), 214 (education), 245 (environment), and 247-49 (social services).

44 RCAP, *Report, Volume 4: Perspectives and Realities* (Ottawa: Minister of Supply and Services, 1996), 248.

45 RCAP, *Report, Volume 2, Part Two*, 451. Three hundred and fifty pages of the report's second volume are devoted to the theme of land and resources, an indication of how central this issue was to the overall mandate of RCAP.

46 See RCAP, *Report, Volume 2, Part One*. Chapter 2 lays out in extensive detail RCAP's approach to reinvigorating the treaty relationship between Canada and Aboriginal nations.

47 Ibid., 237. See also 237-39, 251-53.

48 Ibid., 178.

49 RCAP, *Report, Volume 5*, 165.

50 Ibid., 165-66.

51 RCAP, *Report, Volume 2, Part Two*, Chapter 4.

52 RCAP, *Report, Volume 2, Part One*, 280-310.

53 J. Rick Ponting, "Self-Determination: Editor's Introduction to Part 4," in Ponting, ed., *First Nations in Canada*, 367.

54 RCAP, *Report, Volume 2, Part One*, 223.

55 Ibid., 219.

56 Anthony D. Smith, *National Identity* (Reno: University of Nevada Press, 1991), 74.

57 RCAP, *Report, Volume 3*, 529-30.

58 Elizabeth Frazer and Nicola Lacey, *The Politics of Community: A Feminist Critique of the Liberal-Communitarian Debate* (New York: Harvester Wheatsheaf, 1993), 152.

59 Katherine Fierlbeck, "The Ambivalent Potential of Cultural Identity," *Canadian Journal of Political Science* 29 (1996): 12.

60 RCAP, *Report, Volume 3*, 529.

61 Ibid., 561.

62 Ibid., 500-1.

63 Ibid., 562.

64 I say "inadvertently" because I am sure that this was not the commission's intent.

65 Patrick Macklem, "Distributing Sovereignty: Indian Nations and Equality of Peoples," *Stanford Law Review* 45 (1993): 1343-44.

66 Samuel V. LaSelva, *The Moral Foundations of Canadian Federalism: Paradoxes, Achievements, and Tragedies of Nationhood* (Montreal: McGill-Queen's University Press, 1996), 142.

67 Alan C. Cairns, *Reconfigurations: Canadian Citizenship and Constitutional Change*, in Douglas E. Williams, ed. (Toronto: McClelland and Stewart, 1995), 254-55.

68 Miller, *On Nationality*, 139.

69 Ibid.

70 Ibid., 140.

71 Volume 5 of RCAP's report bears this point out. The capital expenditures required by Canadian governments over the next twenty-year period and beyond to restore Aboriginal communities to health are formidable. While RCAP argues that the expenditures are owing given the history of abuse that Aboriginal peoples have suffered, it is hard to imagine that this level of expenditure could be maintained without some promotion of reciprocal obligations of citizenship between Aboriginal and non-Aboriginal people. See, especially, Chapter 3, "A Good Investment," in RCAP, *Report, Volume 5*, 55-89.

CHAPTER 4: ABORIGINAL WOMEN, YOUTH, AND THE PRIORITY OF INDIVIDUAL CHOICE

1 Other Aboriginal minorities participated in RCAP as well, among them elders, disabled people, and gays and lesbians. However, since RCAP chose to emphasize the particular perspectives and realities of women, youth, and urban dwellers, I will do so as well. Given the complexities of the three minority constituencies that I am dealing with, limits need to be placed on the forthcoming discussion. To this end, I will focus on Aboriginal women, to a lesser extent Aboriginal youth, and to still a lesser extent Aboriginal urban dwellers (recognizing, of course, that many Aboriginal women and youth are urban dwellers).

2 Royal Commission on Aboriginal Peoples (hereafter RCAP), *Report, Volume 4: Perspectives and Realities* (Ottawa: Minister of Supply and Services Canada, 1996), 8.

3 Ibid., 149-50. See also 602, 611.

4 RCAP, *Public Hearings, Discussion Paper 2: Focusing the Dialogue* (Ottawa: Minister of Supply and Services Canada, 1993), 34.

5 RCAP, *Report, Volume 4*, 2.

6 Cora J. Voyageur, "Contemporary Indian Women," in David Alan Long and Olive Patricia Dickason, eds., *Visions of the Heart: Canadian Aboriginal Issues* (Toronto: Harcourt Brace and Company, Canada, 1996), 106.

7 Catherine Brooks, Executive Director of Anduhyaun, *RCAP Public Hearings*, Toronto, Ontario, 25 June 1992.

8 Bertha Allen, Native Women's Association of the Northwest Territories, *RCAP Public Hearings*, Yellowknife, Northwest Territories, 7 December 1992.

9 RCAP, *Report, Volume 4*, 18.

10 RCAP, *Public Hearings: Overview of the First Round* (Ottawa: Royal Commission on Aboriginal Peoples, 1992), 27.

11 RCAP, *Report, Volume 4*, 79.

12 Rita Arey, President, Northwest Territories Status of Women, *RCAP Public Hearings*, Inuvik, Northwest Territories, 6 May 1992.

13 Discussion of the implications of Bill C-31 for reinstated persons is extensive in recent scholarship. See Katherine Beaty Chiste, "Aboriginal Women and Self-Government: Challenging Leviathan," *American Indian Culture and Research Journal* 18, 3 (1994): 21; Nitya Duclos, "Lessons of Difference: Feminist Theory on Cultural Diversity," *Buffalo Law Review* 38, 2 (1990): 364-66; Julia V. Emberley, *Thresholds of Difference: Feminist Critique, Native Women's Writings, Postcolonial Theory* (Toronto: University of Toronto Press, 1993), 87-91; Jo-Anne Fiske, "Political Status of Native Indian Women:

Contradictory Implications of Canadian State Policy," *American Indian Culture and Research Journal* 19, 2 (1995): 4-7, 16-22; Wendy Moss, "Indigenous Self-Government in Canada and Sexual Equality under the Indian Act: Resolving Conflicts between Collective and Individual Rights," *Queen's Law Journal* 15, 2 (1990): 279-305; Joyce Green, "Constitutionalising the Patriarchy: Aboriginal Women and Aboriginal Government," *Constitutional Forum* 4, 4 (1993): 113; Thomas Isaac and Mary Sue Maloughney, "Dually Disadvantaged and Historically Forgotten? Aboriginal Women and the Inherent Right of Aboriginal Self-Government," *Manitoba Law Journal* 21, 3 (1992): 459-63; and J. Rick Ponting, "Historical Overview and Background: Part II 1970-96," in J. Rick Ponting, *First Nations in Canada: Perspectives on Opportunity, Empowerment, and Self-Determination* (Toronto: McGraw-Hill Ryerson, 1997), 50-51.

14 This discriminatory treatment is a result of the amended Indian Act's section 6(2), the "second generation cut-off" or "half-descent" rule. As described by Wendy Moss, the section "terminates Indian status for persons with fewer than two 'Indian' grandparents – Indian meaning with legal status as an 'Indian' under the Indian Act. This rule applies to children born after, and children of women, but not men, who married out prior to 17 April 1985. In the case of descendants of Indian men who married out before 1985, a quarter-descent rule applies. For these children, Indian status may be granted even where they have only one 'Indian' grandparent." Moss, "Indigenous Self-Government in Canada and Sexual Equality under the Indian Act," 281. See also the Royal Commission's extensive treatment of this matter in RCAP, *Report, Volume 4*, 37-43.

15 Sharon McIvor, Executive Council Member, Native Women's Association of Canada, *RCAP Public Hearings*, Toronto, Ontario, 26 June 1992.

16 RCAP, *Public Hearings: Overview of the First Round*, 47.

17 Florence Boucher, *RCAP Public Hearings*, Lac La Biche, Alberta, 9 June 1992.

18 Joyce Courchene, President, Nongom Ikkwe Women's Indigenous Collective, *RCAP Public Hearings*, Winnipeg, Manitoba, 3 June 1993.

19 Voyageur, "Contemporary Indian Women," 109. See also RCAP, *Public Hearings: Overview of the First Round*, 46; RCAP, *Public Hearings: Overview of the Second Round* (Ottawa: Minister of Supply and Services Canada, 1993), 31.

20 RCAP, *Public Hearings: Overview of the First Round*, 4.

21 Freda Albert, Manitoba Indigenous Women's Collective, *RCAP Public Hearings*, Thompson, Manitoba, 31 May 1993.

22 RCAP, *Public Hearings, Toward Reconciliation: Overview of the Fourth Round* (Ottawa: Minister of Supply and Services Canada, 1994), 23. See also RCAP, *Report, Volume 4*, 72.

23 See Evelyn Webster, Indigenous Women's Collective, *RCAP Public Hearings*, Winnipeg, Manitoba, 22 April 1992; Sharon McIvor, Executive Council Member, Native Women's Association of Canada, *RCAP Public Hearings*, Toronto, Ontario, 25 June 1992; and Tobique Women's Group, *RCAP Public Hearings*, Tobique, New Brunswick, 2 November 1992.

24 RCAP, *Public Hearings: Overview of the First Round*, 47.

25 See ibid., 24; RCAP, *Public Hearings: Discussion Paper 1, Framing the Issues* (Ottawa: Royal Commission on Aboriginal Peoples, 1992), 12; RCAP, *Public Hearings: Overview of the Second Round*, 37; RCAP, *Public Hearings: Exploring the Options, Overview of the Third Round* (Ottawa: Minister of Supply and Services Canada, 1993), 4, 9-10; RCAP, *Public Hearings: Toward Reconciliation, Overview of the Fourth Round*, 24; and RCAP, *Report, Volume 4*, 62-68.

26 See RCAP, *Public Hearings: Overview of the First Round*, 25; and RCAP, *Public Hearings: Discussion Paper 1*, 32.

27 Lynn Brooks, Executive Director, Status of Women Council of the NWT, *RCAP Public Hearings*, Yellowknife, Northwest Territories, 7 December 1992.

28 RCAP, *Public Hearings: Exploring the Options, Overview of the Third Round*, ix. See also 4, 7.

29 Teressa Nahanee, "Dancing with a Gorilla: Aboriginal Women, Justice, and the Charter," in RCAP, *Aboriginal Peoples and the Justice System: Report of the National Round Table on Aboriginal Justice Issues* (Ottawa: Minister of Supply and Services Canada, 1993), 371.

30 See RCAP, *Public Hearings: Discussion Paper 1*, 13; RCAP, *Public Hearings: Overview of the Second Round*, 37; RCAP, *Public Hearings: Exploring the Options, Overview of the Third Round*, 10.

31 RCAP, *Report, Volume 4*, 149.

32 Ibid.

33 Ibid., 522.

34 Ibid., 149.

35 Ibid., 522.

36 Rosemarie Kuptana, President, Inuit Tapirisat of Canada, *RCAP Public Hearings*, Toronto, Ontario, 26 June 1992.

37 RCAP, *Report, Volume 4*, 522.

38 Dorothy McKay, *RCAP Public Hearings*, Big Trout Lake, Ontario, 3 December 1992.

39 RCAP, *Report, Volume 4*, 69.

40 Ibid., 151.

41 Jo-Anne Fiske, "The Womb Is to the Nation as the Heart Is to the Body: Ethnopolitical Discourses of the Canadian Indigenous Women's Movement," *Studies in Political Economy* 51 (1996): 69.

42 Ibid.

43 Veena Das, "Cultural Rights and the Definition of Community," in Oliver Mendelsohn and Upendra Baxi, eds., *The Rights of Subordinated Peoples* (Delhi: Oxford University Press, 1994), 123.

44 Will Kymlicka, *Multicultural Citizenship: A Liberal Theory of Minority Rights* (Oxford: Clarendon Press, 1995), 36.

45 Ibid.

46 J. Anthony Long and Katherine Beaty Chiste, "Indian Governments and the Canadian Charter of Rights and Freedoms," *American Indian Culture and Research Journal*, 18, 2 (1994): 96.

47 RCAP, *Report, Volume 2: Restructuring the Relationship—Part One* (Ottawa: Minister of Supply and Services Canada, 1996), 226.

48 Ibid., 227.

49 Ibid., 230.

50 RCAP, *Public Hearings: Overview of the First Round*, 41.

51 RCAP, *Report, Volume 2*, 230.

52 Menno Boldt, *Surviving as Indians: The Challenge of Self-Government* (Toronto: University of Toronto Press, 1993), 148.

53 RCAP, *Public Hearings: Toward Reconciliation, Overview of the Fourth Round*, 23-24.

54 On this point, see Boldt, *Surviving as Indians*, 152.

55 Ibid., 153.

56 Ibid.
57 RCAP, *Report, Volume 2*, 231.
58 Ibid., 230.
59 Ibid., 232.
60 Boldt, *Surviving as Indians*, 153. See also Jodi Cockerill and Roger Gibbins, "Reluctant Citizens? First Nations in the Canadian Federal State," in J. Rick Ponting, ed., *First Nations in Canada*, 400.
61 Cockerill and Gibbins, "Reluctant Citizens?," 391.
62 Ibid., 399.
63 Fiske provides a spirited defence of precisely this view in "The Womb Is to the Nation as the Heart Is to the Body," 65-95.
64 RCAP, *Public Hearings: Exploring the Options, Overview of the Third Round*, 10.
65 Ibid.
66 Since renamed The Congress of Aboriginal Peoples.
67 RCAP, *Public Hearings, Toward Reconciliation: Overview of the Fourth Round*, 40.
68 John Gray, "After the New Liberalism," *Social Research* 61, 3 (1994): 726.
69 Iris Marion Young, *Justice and the Politics of Difference* (Princeton: Princeton University Press, 1990), 46.
70 Bhikhu Parekh, "Discourses on National Identity," *Political Studies* 42 (1994): 504.

CHAPTER 5: ABORIGINAL BOUNDARIES AND THE DEMAND FOR EXTERNAL EQUALITY

1 Chief Harold Turner, Swampy Cree Tribal Council, *RCAP Public Hearings*, The Pas, Manitoba, 20 May 1992.
2 Chief Eli Mandamin, Shoal Lake Band, *RCAP Public Hearings*, Kenora, Ontario, 28 October 1992.
3 Windigo First Nations Council, *RCAP Public Hearings*, Sioux Lookout, Ontario, 2 December 1992.
4 Frank Palmater, New Brunswick Aboriginal Peoples Council, *RCAP Public Hearings*, Moncton, New Brunswick, 14 June 1993.
5 Royal Commission on Aboriginal Peoples (hereafter RCAP), *Public Hearings, Discussion Paper 1: Framing the Issues* (Ottawa: Royal Commission on Aboriginal Peoples, 1992), 20.
6 Windigo First Nations Council, *RCAP Public Hearings*, Sioux Lookout, Ontario, 2 December 1992.
7 Patrick Macklem, *Indigenous Difference and the Constitution of Canada* (Toronto: University of Toronto Press, 2001), 119-25.
8 This concern echoes that of James Tully, who argues that relations between Aboriginal and non-Aboriginal peoples in Canada should be built upon the principles of mutual recognition, intercultural negotiation, mutual respect, sharing, and mutual responsibility. Tully's objective is that these principles be used in the service of preserving and protecting cultural and political structures of Aboriginal difference, in particular nations. My emphasis is slightly different. I am less concerned about the preservation of Aboriginal cultural and political structures as an end in itself and more concerned about how the political principles of equality and freedom from domination can be harnessed to help promote the power of both Aboriginal individuals and communities in their wide-ranging quests to be self-defining within Canada. See James Tully, "A Just Relationship between Aboriginal and Non-Aboriginal Peoples of Canada," in Curtis Cook and Juan

D. Landau, eds., *Aboriginal Rights and Self-Government: The Canadian and Mexican Experience in North American Perspective* (Montreal: McGill-Queen's University Press, 2000), 43-44.

9 Iris Marion Young, *Justice and the Politics of Difference* (Princeton: Princeton University Press, 1990), 173.

10 Ibid., 163-74.

11 Macklem, *Indigenous Difference and the Constitution of Canada*, 119-25 (formal equality), 126-28 (substantive equality).

12 Ibid., 127.

13 On this point, see RCAP, *Public Hearings: Overview of the First Round* (Ottawa: Royal Commission on Aboriginal Peoples, 1992), 36-48.

14 Augie Fleras and Jean Leonard Elliott, *The Nations Within: Aboriginal-State Relations in Canada, the United States, and New Zealand* (Toronto: Oxford University Press, 1992), 24.

15 Ibid.

16 Patricia Monture-Angus, *Journeying Forward: Dreaming First Nations' Independence* (Halifax: Fernwood Publishing, 1999), 23, 27.

17 Tully, "A Just Relationship between Aboriginal and Non-Aboriginal Peoples of Canada," 43-53.

18 Fleras and Elliott, *The Nations Within*, 24.

19 Radha Jhappan, "The Federal-Provincial Power-Grid and Aboriginal Self-Government," in François Rocher and Miriam Smith, eds., *New Trends in Canadian Federalism* (Peterborough: Broadview Press, 1995), 156.

20 A number of examples are Gerald R. Alfred, *Heeding the Voices of Our Ancestors: Kahnawake Mohawk Politics and the Rise of Native Nationalism* (Toronto: Oxford University Press, 1995); Kelly Gallagher-Mackay, "Interpreting Self-Government: Approaches to Building Cultural Authority," *Canadian Native Law Reporter* 4 (1997): 14-20; James Youngblood Henderson, "Empowering Treaty Federalism," *Saskatchewan Law Review* 58, 2 (1994): 241-329, and "Implementing the Treaty Order," in Richard Gosse, James Youngblood Henderson, and Roger Carter, eds., *Continuing Poundmaker and Riel's Quest* (Saskatoon: Purich Publishing, 1994); Will Kymlicka, *Multicultural Citizenship: A Liberal Theory of Minority Rights* (Oxford: Clarendon Press, 1995); Samuel V. LaSelva, *The Moral Foundations of Canadian Federalism: Paradoxes, Achievements, and Tragedies of Nationhood* (Montreal: McGill-Queen's University Press, 1996), 137-54; Macklem, *Indigenous Difference and the Constitution of Canada*; David Miller, *On Nationality* (Oxford: Clarendon Press, 1995), 115-17; James Tully, *Strange Multiplicity: Constitutionalism in an Age of Diversity* (Cambridge, UK: Cambridge University Press, 1995), and "A Just Relationship between Aboriginal and Non-Aboriginal Peoples of Canada"; Jeremy Webber, *Reimagining Canada: Language, Culture, Community, and the Canadian Constitution* (Montreal: McGill-Queen's University Press, 1994), 263-68.

21 RCAP, *Report, Volume 2: Restructuring the Relationship—Part One* (Ottawa: Minister of Supply and Services Canada, 1996).

22 LaSelva, *The Moral Foundations of Canadian Federalism*, 138.

23 See, in particular, Henderson, "Empowering Treaty Federalism," 241-329; Macklem, *Indigenous Difference and the Constitution of Canada*, 132-59, 180-84; and Tully, "A Just Relationship between Aboriginal and Non-Aboriginal Peoples in Canada," 40-43.

24 On this distinction, see RCAP, *Report, Volume 2*, 374.

25 Ibid., 172. Macklem's discussion of how Aboriginal self-government might be exercised

within the constitutional rules of Canadian federalism closely parallels that of RCAP. See Macklem, *Indigenous Difference and the Constitution of Canada*, 172-80.

26 Ibid., 240.

27 Ibid.

28 Ibid., 374.

29 Cairns also notes that Indian peoples in a third order of government will have to involve themselves in shared rule relations at the provincial and territorial levels. Indeed, as Cairns observes, it is surprising that RCAP did not mention the importance of this aspect of shared rule given that, in a number of legislatures, Aboriginal representation is now considerable (e.g., Manitoba, Nunavut, Northwest Territories). See Alan C. Cairns, *Citizens Plus: Aboriginal Peoples and the Canadian State* (Vancouver: UBC Press, 2000), 146-51.

30 RCAP, *Partners in Confederation: Aboriginal Peoples, Self-Government, and the Constitution* (Ottawa: Minister of Supply and Services Canada, 1993), 38.

31 RCAP, *Report, Volume 2*, 223-24.

32 Ibid., 224.

33 Cairns, *Citizens Plus*, 129.

34 P.G. McHugh, "Aboriginal Identity and Relations in North America and Australasia," in Ken S. Coates and P.G. McHugh, eds., *Living Relationships (Kokiri ngatahi): The Treaty of Waitangi in the New Millennium* (Wellington: Victoria University Press, 1998), 121.

35 Wayne Warry, *Unfinished Dreams: Community Healing and the Reality of Aboriginal Self-Government* (Toronto: University of Toronto Press, 1998), 50.

36 See John Breuilly, *Nationalism and the State*, 2nd ed. (Chicago: University of Chicago Press, 1993), 1-9; Omar Dahbour, "The Nation-State as Political Community: A Critique of the Communitarian Argument for National Self-Determination," *Canadian Journal of Philosophy* supplementary volume 22 (1996): 322; Thomas Hylland Eriksen, *Ethnicity and Nationalism: Anthropological Perspectives* (London: Pluto Press, 1993), 99-100; Miller, *On Nationality*, 18-19; and Jeff Spinner, *The Boundaries of Citizenship: Race, Ethnicity, and Nationality in the Liberal State* (Baltimore: Johns Hopkins University Press, 1994), 140-45.

37 Alfred, *Heeding the Voices of Our Ancestors*, 9. For a similar argument, see Hurst Hannum, *Autonomy, Sovereignty, and Self-Determination: The Accommodation of Conflicting Rights*, rev. ed. (Philadelphia: University of Pennsylvania Press, 1990), 23-25.

38 Alfred, *Heeding the Voices of Our Ancestors*, 14. On this point, see also Menno Boldt, *Surviving as Indians: The Challenge of Self-Government* (Toronto: University of Toronto Press, 1993), 133; and Richard Spaulding, "Peoples as National Minorities: A Review of Will Kymlicka's Arguments for Aboriginal Rights from a Self-Determination Perspective," *University of Toronto Law Journal* 47, 1 (1997): 38.

39 Alfred, *Heeding the Voices of Our Ancestors*, 15.

40 Charles Taylor, *Reconciling the Solitudes: Essays on Canadian Federalism and Nationalism* (Montreal: McGill-Queen's University Press, 1993), 181-84; and Kymlicka, *Multicultural Citizenship*, 189-91.

41 Kymlicka, *Multicultural Citizenship*, 190.

42 Taylor, *Reconciling the Solitudes*, 163-64.

43 Taylor has written a short defence of the Nisga'a treaty in which he outlines his position on Aboriginal rights. See Charles Taylor, "On the Nisga'a Treaty," *BC Studies* 120 (1998-99): 37-40.

44 Tully, "A Just Relationship between Aboriginal and Non-Aboriginal Peoples in Canada," 43.
45 Ibid., 53, 56, 58, 64.
46 Ibid., 46.
47 Ibid., 56.
48 On a related matter, Cairns has pointed out to me that the Parti Québécois's national-ist argument for special status within or independence from Canada is seldom made in cultural terms – although preservation of the French language remains important. He says that, generally, nationalist arguments are now made in terms of identity rather than culture or value differences. This position is in stark contrast to the Quebec nationalism of fifty years ago, represented perhaps best in the Tremblay Report of the mid-1950s, which, as Cairns writes, portrayed French and English Canada as cultural polar oppo-sites. See Cairns, in Douglas E. Williams, ed., *Reconfigurations: Canadian Citizenship and Constitutional Change* (Toronto: McClelland and Stewart, 1995), 298. Cairns also sug-gests that the Quebec evolution from communal identity based on cultural difference to one based on community identification may well be paralleled by Aboriginal peoples.
49 Macklem, *Indigenous Difference and the Constitution of Canada*, 119-28.
50 Section 35(1) of the Constitution Act, 1982, reads, "The existing Aboriginal and treaty rights of the Aboriginal peoples of Canada are hereby recognized and affirmed."
51 *R. v. Sparrow* (1990), 70 D.L.R. (4th), 407.
52 RCAP, *Report, Volume 2*, 199-203.
53 Paul Tennant, as cited in Douglas Todd, "A Government Is Born," *Vancouver Sun* 4 November 2000: A20.
54 *Nisga'a Final Agreement*, Chapter 11, 159.
55 Ibid., Chapter 3, 31.
56 Ibid., Chapter 11, 165-79.
57 While the commitment to negotiate fiscal financing agreements is provided for in the treaty, the actual agreements are not intended to be treaty agreements. See ibid., Chapter 15, 212.
58 See ibid., Chapter 5, 67 (forests); Chapter 8, 107, 112-19 (fish); Chapter 9, 146-47, 148-49 (trapping, wildlife, and migratory birds); Chapter 10, 155-58 (environmental assess-ment and protection).
59 Ibid., Chapter 2, 17.
60 Douglas Sanders, "'We Intend to Live Here Forever': A Primer on the Nisga'a Treaty," *U.B.C. Law Review* 33, 1 (1999): 117.
61 *Nisga'a Final Agreement*, Chapter 2, 19.
62 The treaty was initialled on 4 August 1998, ratified first by the Nisga'a people, then the province of British Columbia, and then the Parliament of Canada, and it came into ef-fect on 11 May 2000.
63 Government of Canada, Federal Policy Guide, *Aboriginal Self-Government: The Government of Canada's Approach to Implementation of the Inherent Right and Negotiation of Aboriginal Self-Government* (Ottawa: Minister of Public Works and Government Services Canada, 1995), 17.
64 See Henderson, "Empowering Treaty Federalism"; Macklem, *Indigenous Difference and the Constitution of Canada*, 151-56, 180-84; and Tully, "A Just Relationship between Aboriginal and Non-Aboriginal Peoples of Canada," 48, 49, 51, 62.

65 On this point, see Sanders, "'We Intend to Live Here Forever,'" 105.
66 Taiaiake Alfred, *Peace, Power, Righteousness: An Indigenous Manifesto* (Don Mills: Oxford University Press, 1999), 100.
67 Claude Denis, *We Are Not You: First Nations and Canadian Modernity* (Peterborough: Broadview Press, 1997), 33.
68 Monture-Angus, *Journeying Forward,* 13.
69 Alfred, *Peace, Power, Righteousness,* 119.
70 Government of Canada, Federal Policy Guide, *Aboriginal Self-Government,* 4, 7.
71 Ibid., 11.
72 Ibid., 5.
73 Dan Russell, *A People's Dream: Aboriginal Self-Government in Canada* (Vancouver: UBC Press, 2000), 202.
74 As cited in J. Rick Ponting, "Self-Determination: Editor's Introduction to Part 4," in J. Rick Ponting, ed., *First Nations in Canada: Perspectives on Opportunity, Empowerment, and Self-Determination* (Toronto: McGraw-Hill Ryerson, 1997), 362.
75 Monture-Angus, *Journeying Forward,* 127. Alfred makes a similar point in *Peace, Power, Righteousness,* 120-21.
76 J. Rick Ponting, "An Overview of First Nations' Empowerment and Disempowerment: Editor's Introduction to Part 2," in Ponting, ed., *First Nations in Canada,* 142.
77 Ibid.
78 See Gallagher-Mackay, "Interpreting Self-Government," 14-15.
79 See Michael S. Whittington, "Aboriginal Self-Government in Canada," in Michael Whittington and Glen Williams, eds., *Canadian Politics in the 21st Century,* 5th ed. (Scarborough: Nelson, 2000), 114.
80 Government of Canada, Federal Policy Guide, *Aboriginal Self-Government,* 17.

CHAPTER 6: ABORIGINAL IDENTITY AND THE DESIRE FOR INTERNAL EQUALITY

1 Sharon McIvor, Executive Council Member, Native Women's Association of Canada, *RCAP Public Hearings,* Toronto, Ontario, 25 June 1992.
2 Royal Commission on Aboriginal Peoples (hereafter RCAP), *Report, Volume 4: Perspectives and Realities* (Ottawa: Minister of Supply and Services Canada, 1996), 151.
3 RCAP, *Public Hearings: Overview of the First Round* (Ottawa: Royal Commission on Aboriginal Peoples, 1992), 3. See also 21, 59.
4 Michele Rouleau, Quebec Native Women's Association, *RCAP Public Hearings,* Montreal, Quebec, 27 May 1993.
5 Evidence that equality is of fundamental importance to organizations representing Aboriginal women was also made clear in constitutional discussions of the 1980s and 1990s. During the 1983 first ministers' conference, for example, the Native Women's Association of Canada was instrumental in gaining an amendment to section 35 of the Constitution: "Notwithstanding any other provision of this Act, the Aboriginal and treaty rights referred to in subsection (1) are guaranteed equally to male and female persons."
6 Lillian Sanderson, La Ronge Native Women's Council, *RCAP Public Hearings,* La Ronge, Saskatchewan, 28 May 1992. The demand for equality was ubiquitous in the presentations of both individual women speaking on their own behalf and organizations mandated to represent the interests of women more generally. For examples, see Madeleine Parent, *RCAP Public Hearings,* Montreal, Quebec, 5 May 1993; Dorothy

McKay, *RCAP Public Hearings*, Big Trout Lake, Ontario, 3 December 1992; Marlene Pierre, Ontario Native Women's Association, *RCAP Public Hearings*, Thunder Bay, Ontario, 27 October 1992; Marguerite Saunderson, Northern Women's Resource Services, *RCAP Public Hearings*, Thompson, Manitoba, 1 June 1993; and Marilyn Fontaine, Aboriginal Women's Unity Coalition, *RCAP Public Hearings*, Winnipeg, Manitoba, 23 April 1992.

7 Jason Thomas, All Nations Youth Council, *RCAP Public Hearings*, Prince George, British Columbia, 31 May 1993. The general theme of youth empowerment is repeatedly emphasized in the report of the Royal Commission on Aboriginal Peoples as well. See *Report, Volume 4*, 148-49, 151, 180, 193-94.

8 RCAP, *Report, Volume 4*, 588.

9 Avigail Eisenberg makes this point more broadly with respect to all socially significant groups in *Reconstructing Political Pluralism* (Albany: State University of New York Press, 1995), 190.

10 The question concerning to what degree the 626,000 respondents regard themselves as Aboriginal is not addressed in the survey. For example, Paul Tennant has pointed out to me that some individuals may have a strong identification, regarding themselves as Aboriginal in all possible situations. Other individuals, meanwhile, may have a weaker identification, regarding themselves as Aboriginal for some purposes and Canadian for others. What Tennant suggests, in other words, is that census responses are not necessarily a very meaningful measure of Aboriginal identity.

11 RCAP, *Report, Volume 1: Looking Forward, Looking Back* (Ottawa: Minister of Supply and Services Canada, 1996), 15.

12 P.G. McHugh, "Aboriginal Identity and Relations in North America and Australasia," in Ken S. Coates and P.G. McHugh, eds., *Living Relationships (Kokiri ngatahi): The Treaty of Waitangi in the New Millennium* (Wellington: Victoria University Press, 1998), 158.

13 James Frideres suggests that, as of 2001, the potential pool of applicants for reinstatement is likely exhausted. Based on Department of Indian Affairs and Northern Development figures, the number of reinstated Indians is slightly more than 100,000, comprising 17 percent of the total registered Indian population of 622,901. See James S. Frideres and René R. Gadacz, *Aboriginal Peoples in Canada: Contemporary Conflicts*, 6th ed. (Toronto: Prentice Hall, 2001), 33-35.

14 More specifically, the criteria for obtaining legal status are as follows. Individuals who obtain status through section 6(2) and who marry non-Indians cannot pass status on to their children. If Indians under 6(2) marry Indians under 6(1), then their children will be registered under 6(1). If Indians under 6(1) marry one another, then their children will be registered under 6(1). If 6(2) Indians marry one another, then their children will be registered under 6(1). If Indians under 6(1) marry non-Indians, then their children will be registered under 6(2). As Stewart Clatworthy and Anthony Smith point out, under the rules of Bill C-31, the key to retaining Indian legal status is ongoing "in-marriage" among Indians. See Stewart Clatworthy and Anthony Smith, *Population Implications of the 1985 Amendments to the Indian Act: Final Report* (Ottawa: Assembly of First Nations, 1992), i.

15 Ibid.

16 Ibid., ii, 19.

17 Ibid., vii.

18 RCAP, *Report, Volume 2: Restructuring the Relationship—Part One* (Ottawa: Minister of Supply and Services Canada, 1996), 239.

19 RCAP, *Report, Volume 4*, 53, 60.

20 RCAP, *Report, Volume 2*, 237.

21 Ibid.

22 Ibid.

23 Ibid., 238.

24 Jeremy Webber develops a similar response to the potential problem of political abuse of power within Aboriginal communities in *Reimagining Canada: Language, Culture, Community, and the Canadian Constitution* (Montreal and Kingston: McGill-Queen's University Press, 1994), 268-69.

25 Iris Marion Young, *Justice and the Politics of Difference* (Princeton: Princeton University Press, 1990), 48.

26 Alan C. Cairns, *Reconfigurations: Canadian Citizenship and Constitutional Change*, ed. Douglas E. Williams (Toronto: McClelland and Stewart, 1995), 255.

27 John Borrows, "'Landed' Citizenship: Narratives of Aboriginal Political Participation," in Alan C. Cairns et al., eds., *Citizenship, Diversity, and Pluralism: Canadian and Comparative Perspectives* (Montreal: McGill-Queen's University Press, 1999), 75.

28 The Royal Commission explores the nature of some of these divisions in a chapter entitled "Separate Worlds." See RCAP, *Report, Volume 1*, 43-97.

29 Borrows, "'Landed' Citizenship," 75.

30 Elizabeth Frazer and Nicola Lacey, *The Politics of Community: A Feminist Critique of the Liberal-Communitarian Debate* (New York: Harvester Wheatsheaf, 1993), 198, 199.

31 See, especially, Eisenberg, *Reconstructing Political Pluralism*, 186-92; Milton Fisk, "Community and Morality," *Review of Politics* 55, 4 (1993): 615; Frazer and Lacey, *The Politics of Community*, 186; Nancy L. Rosenblum, "Pluralism and Self-Defense," in Nancy L. Rosenblum, ed., *Liberalism and the Moral Life* (Cambridge, MA: Harvard University Press, 1989), 220-26; and James Tully, *Strange Multiplicity: Constitutionalism in an Age of Diversity* (Cambridge, UK: Cambridge University Press, 1995), 207-8.

32 Eisenberg, *Reconstructing Political Pluralism*, 187.

33 Frazer and Lacey, *The Politics of Community*, 174.

34 See, for example, Menno Boldt's important discussion on this matter of leadership and the concentration of power in Aboriginal communities in *Surviving as Indians: The Challenge of Self-Government* (Toronto: University of Toronto Press, 1993), Chapter 3. See also Taiaiake Alfred, *Peace, Power, Righteousness: An Indigenous Manifesto* (Don Mills: Oxford University Press, 1999); and Strater Crowfoot, "Leadership in First Nation Communities: A Chief's Perspective on the Colonial Millstone," in J. Rick Ponting, ed., *First Nations in Canada: Perspectives on Opportunity, Empowerment, and Self-Determination* (Toronto: McGraw-Hill Ryerson, 1997), 299-325.

35 See Government of Canada, Federal Policy Guide, *Aboriginal Self-Government: The Government of Canada's Approach to the Implementation of the Inherent Right and Negotiation of Aboriginal Self-Government* (Ottawa: Minister of Public Works and Government Services Canada, 1995), 4.

36 Ibid.

37 Teressa Nahanee, "Dancing with a Gorilla: Aboriginal Women, Justice, and the Charter,"

in RCAP, *Aboriginal Peoples and the Justice System: Report of the National Round Table on Aboriginal Justice Issues* (Ottawa: Minister of Supply and Services Canada, 1993), 371.

38 On this point, see RCAP, *Public Hearings: Overview of the Second Round* (Ottawa: Minister of Supply and Services Canada, 1993), 31. See also the presentations to RCAP by the Quebec Native Women's Association and the National Action Committee on the Status of Women, both in Montreal, Quebec, 25-28 May 1993.

39 *Corbiere v. Canada* (Minister of Indian and Northern Affairs) [1999] 2 S.C.R., 203-89.

40 *Corbiere v. Canada,* as reprinted in *Canadian Native Law Reporter* 3 (1999): 20.

41 Ibid.

42 Doris Young, Indigenous Women's Collective, *RCAP Public Hearings*, Winnipeg, Manitoba, 22 April 1992.

CONCLUSION

1 Michael Walzer, *Spheres of Justice: A Defense of Pluralism and Equality* (New York: Basic Books, 1983), 319.

BIBLIOGRAPHY

BOOKS, ARTICLES, AND CASES

Abramson, Harold J. "Assimilation and Pluralism." In *The Harvard Encyclopedia of American Ethnic Groups*, ed. Stephen A. Thernstrom. Cambridge, MA: Harvard University Press, 1980.

Abu-Laban, Baha, and Donald Mottershead. "Cultural Pluralism and Varieties of Ethnic Politics." *Canadian Ethnic Studies* 8, 3 (1981): 44-63.

Addis, Adeno. "Individualism, Communitarianism, and the Rights of Ethnic Minorities." *Notre Dame Law Review* 66, 5 (1991): 1219-80.

Akzin, Benjamin. *State and Nation*. London: Hutchinson University Library, 1964.

Alfred, Gerald R. *Heeding the Voices of Our Ancestors: Kahnawake Mohawk Politics and the Rise of Native Nationalism*. Toronto: Oxford University Press, 1995.

Alfred, Taiaiake. *Peace, Power, Righteousness: An Indigenous Manifesto*. Don Mills: Oxford University Press, 1999.

Asch, Michael, and Norman Zlotkin. "Affirming Aboriginal Title: A New Basis for Comprehensive Claims Negotiations." In *Aboriginal and Treaty Rights in Canada: Essays on Law, Equality, and Respect for Difference*, ed. Michael Asch. Vancouver: UBC Press, 1997.

Barth, Fredrik, ed. *Ethnic Groups and Boundaries: The Social Organization of Cultural Difference*. Boston: Little, Brown, 1969.

Benjamin, Martin. *Splitting the Difference: Compromise and Integrity in Ethics and Politics*. Kansas: University Press of Kansas, 1990.

Bentley, Arthur. *The Process of Government: A Study of Social Pressures*. Chicago: University of Chicago Press, 1908.

Boldt, Menno. *Surviving as Indians: The Challenge of Self-Government*. Toronto: University of Toronto Press, 1993.

Boldt, Menno, and J. Anthony Long. "Tribal Traditions and European-Western Political Ideologies: The Dilemma of Canada's Native Indians." In *The Quest for Justice: Aboriginal*

Peoples and Aboriginal Rights, ed. Menno Boldt and J. Anthony Long. Toronto: University of Toronto Press, 1985.

Borrows, John. "'Landed' Citizenship: Narratives of Aboriginal Political Participation." In *Citizenship, Diversity, and Pluralism: Canadian and Comparative Perspectives*, ed. Alan C. Cairns et al. Montreal: McGill-Queen's University Press, 1999.

Brass, Paul. "Ethnic Groups and the State." In *Ethnic Groups and the State*, ed. Paul Brass. London: Croom Helm, 1985.

——. *Ethnicity and Nationalism: Theory and Comparison.* New Delhi/Newbury Park, CA: Sage Publications, 1991.

Breuilly, John. *Nationalism and the State*, 2nd ed. Chicago: University of Chicago Press, 1993.

Bruner, Edward M. "Ethnology as Narrative." In *The Anthropology of Experience*, ed. Victor W. Turner and Edward M. Bruner. Urbana: University of Illinois Press, 1986.

Bullivant, Brian M. *Pluralism: Cultural Maintenance and Evolution.* Clevedon: Multilingual Matters, 1984.

Cairns, Alan C. *Citizens Plus: Aboriginal Peoples and the Canadian State.* Vancouver: UBC Press, 2000.

——. "The End of Internal Empire: The Emerging Aboriginal Policy Agenda." In *Governance in the 21st Century: Proceedings of a Symposium Held in November 1999 under the Auspices of the Royal Society of Canada*, ed. David M. Hayne. Toronto: University of Toronto Press, 2000.

——. "Finding Our Way: Rethinking Ethnocultural Relations in Canada" [book review]. *Canadian Journal of Political Science* 32, 2 (1999): 369-71.

——. *Reconfigurations: Canadian Citizenship and Constitutional Change.* Ed. Douglas E. Williams. Toronto: McClelland and Stewart, 1995.

Chartrand, Paul L.A.H. "The Aboriginal Peoples of Canada and Renewal of the Federation." In *Rethinking Federalism: Citizens, Markets, and Governments in a Changing World*, ed. Karen Knop et al. Vancouver: UBC Press, 1995.

Chiste, Catherine Beaty. "Aboriginal Women and Self-Government: Challenging Leviathan." *American Indian Culture and Research Journal* 18, 3 (1994): 19-43.

Churchill, Ward. "The Tragedy and the Travesty: The Subversion of Indigenous Sovereignty in North America." *American Indian Culture and Research Journal* 22, 2 (1998): 1-69.

Clatworthy, Stewart. *Migration and Mobility of Canada's Aboriginal Population.* Canada: Canada Mortgage and Housing Corporation, 1996.

Clatworthy, Stewart, and Anthony Smith. *Population Implications of the 1985 Amendments to the Indian Act: Final Report.* Ottawa: Assembly of First Nations, 1992.

Cockerill, Jodi, and Roger Gibbins. "Reluctant Citizens? First Nations in the Canadian Federal State." In *First Nations in Canada: Perspectives on Opportunity, Empowerment, and Self-Determination*, ed. J. Rick Ponting. Toronto: McGraw-Hill Ryerson, 1997.

Cohen, Jean L. "Democracy, Difference, and the Right of Privacy." In *Democracy and Difference: Contesting the Boundaries of the Political*, ed. Seyla Benhabib. Princeton: Princeton University Press, 1996.

Corbiere v. Canada (Minister of Indian and Northern Affairs) [1999] 2 S.C.R.

Cornell, Stephen. "The Variable Ties that Bind: Content and Circumstance in Ethnic Processes." *Ethnic and Racial Studies* 19, 2 (1996): 265-89.

Crowfoot, Strater. "Leadership in First Nation Communities: A Chief's Perspective on the Colonial Millstone." In *First Nations in Canada: Perspectives on Opportunity,*

208 Bibliography

Empowerment, and Self-Determination, ed. J. Rick Ponting. Toronto: McGraw-Hill Ryerson, 1997.

Dahbour, Omar. "The Nation-State as Political Community: A Critique of the Communitarian Argument for National Self-Determination." *Canadian Journal of Philosophy* supplementary volume 22 (1996): 311-43.

Dahl, Robert A. *Democracy in the United States: Promise and Performance,* 2nd ed. Chicago: Rand McNally, 1972.

Daly, Markate. "Introduction." In *Communitarianism: A New Public Ethics,* ed. Markate Daly. Belmont: Wadsworth Publishing Company, 1994.

Das, Veena. "Cultural Rights and the Definition of Community." In *The Rights of Subordinated Peoples,* ed. Oliver Mendelsohn and Upendra Baxi. Delhi: Oxford University Press, 1994.

Denis, Claude. *We Are Not You: First Nations and Canadian Modernity.* Peterborough: Broadview Press, 1997.

De Vos, George. "Ethnic Pluralism: Conflict and Accommodation." In *Ethnic Identity: Cultural Continuities and Change,* ed. George De Vos and Lola Romanucci-Ross. Palo Alto: Mayfield Publishing Company, 1975.

Dickson, Brian. "Opening Statement by the Right Honourable Brian Dickson, Former Chief Justice of the Supreme Court of Canada." In *Opening Statements on the Occasion of the Launch of the Public Hearings of the Royal Commission on Aboriginal Peoples.* Ottawa: Minister of Supply and Services Canada, 1992.

Dion Stout, Madeleine (with Catherine R. Bruyere). "Stopping Family Violence: Aboriginal Communities Enspirited." In *First Nations in Canada: Perspectives on Opportunity, Empowerment, and Self-Determination,* ed. J. Rick Ponting. Toronto: McGraw-Hill Ryerson, 1997.

Driedger, Leo. "Introduction: Ethnic Identity in the Canadian Mosaic." In *The Canadian Ethnic Mosaic: A Quest for Identity,* ed. Leo Driedger. Toronto: McClelland and Stewart, 1978.

Duclos, Nitya. "Lessons of Difference: Feminist Theory on Cultural Diversity." *Buffalo Law Review* 38, 2 (1990): 325-81.

Dworkin, Ronald. *A Matter of Principle.* Cambridge, MA: Harvard University Press, 1985.

Dyck, Rand. *Canadian Politics: Critical Approaches,* 2nd ed. Scarborough: Nelson Canada, 1996.

Eisenberg, Avigail. *Reconstructing Political Pluralism.* Albany: State University of New York Press, 1995.

Emberley, Julia V. *Thresholds of Difference: Feminist Critique, Native Women's Writings, Postcolonial Theory.* Toronto: University of Toronto Press, 1993.

Enloe, Cynthia H. *Ethnic Conflict and Political Development.* Boston: Little, Brown, 1973.

Eriksen, Thomas Hylland. *Ethnicity and Nationalism: Anthropological Perspectives.* London: Pluto Press, 1993.

Fierlbeck, Katherine. "The Ambivalent Potential of Cultural Identity." *Canadian Journal of Political Science* 29 (1996): 3-22.

Fisk, Milton. "Community and Morality." *Review of Politics* 55, 4 (1993): 593-616.

Fiske, Jo-Anne. "Political Status of Native Indian Women: Contradictory Implications of Canadian State Policy." *American Indian Culture and Research Journal* 19, 2 (1995): 1-30.

——. "The Womb Is to the Nation as the Heart Is to the Body: Ethnopolitical Discourses of the Canadian Indigenous Women's Movement." *Studies in Political Economy* 51 (1996): 65-95.

Flanagan, Tom. *First Nations? Second Thoughts.* Montreal: McGill-Queen's University Press, 2000.

Fleras, Augie, and Jean Leonard Elliott. *The Nations Within: Aboriginal-State Relations in Canada, the United States, and New Zealand.* Toronto: Oxford University Press, 1992.

Frazer, Elizabeth, and Nicola Lacey. *The Politics of Community: A Feminist Critique of the Liberal-Communitarian Debate.* New York: Harvester Wheatsheaf, 1993.

Frideres, James S. "Indian Identity and Social Conflict." In *The Canadian Ethnic Mosaic: A Quest for Identity*, ed. Leo Driedger. Toronto: McClelland and Stewart, 1978.

Frideres, James S., and René R. Gadacz. *Aboriginal Peoples in Canada: Contemporary Conflicts*, 6th ed. Toronto: Prentice Hall, 2001.

Gallagher-Mackay, Kelly. "Interpreting Self-Government: Approaches to Building Cultural Authority." *Canadian Native Law Reporter* 4 (1997): 1-23.

Gould, Carol. *Rethinking Democracy: Freedom and Social Cooperation in Politics, Economy, and Society.* Cambridge, UK: Cambridge University Press, 1988.

Government of Canada. *Aboriginal Self-Government: The Government of Canada's Approach to the Implementation of the Inherent Right and the Negotiation of Aboriginal Self-Government.* Federal Policy Guide. Ottawa: Minister of Public Works and Government Services Canada, 1995.

——. *Gathering Strength: Canada's Aboriginal Action Plan.* Ottawa: Minister of Public Works and Government Services Canada, 1997.

Gray, John. "After the New Liberalism." *Social Research* 61, 3 (1994): 719-35.

——. *Post-Liberalism: Studies in Political Thought.* New York: Routledge, 1993.

Green, Joyce. "Constitutionalising the Patriarchy: Aboriginal Women and Aboriginal Government." *Constitutional Forum* 4, 4 (1993): 110-20.

Hamlet of Baker Lake v. Minister of Indian Affairs (1979) 107 D.L.R. (3d), 513.

Hannum, Hurst. *Autonomy, Sovereignty, and Self-Determination: The Accommodation of Conflicting Rights*, rev. ed. Philadelphia: University of Pennsylvania Press, 1990.

Hedican, Edward J. *Applied Anthropology in Canada: Understanding Aboriginal Issues.* Toronto: University of Toronto Press, 1995.

Henderson, James Youngblood. "Empowering Treaty Federalism." *Saskatchewan Law Review* 58, 2 (1994): 241-329.

——. "Implementing the Treaty Order." In *Continuing Poundmaker and Riel's Quest*, ed. Richard Gosse, James Youngblood Henderson, and Roger Carter. Saskatoon: Purich Publishing, 1994.

Horton, John. "Liberalism, Multiculturalism, and Toleration." In *Liberalism, Multiculturalism, and Toleration*, ed. John Horton. Basingstoke: MacMillan Press, 1983.

Isaac, Thomas, and Mary Sue Maloughney. "Dually Disadvantaged and Historically Forgotten? Aboriginal Women and the Inherent Right of Aboriginal Self-Government." *Manitoba Law Journal* 21, 3 (1992): 453-75.

Jenson, Jane. "Naming Nations: Making Nationalist Claims in Canadian Public Discourse." *Canadian Review of Sociology and Anthropology* 30, 3 (1993): 337-58.

——. "Understanding Politics: Contested Concepts in Political Science." In *Canadian Politics* 2, ed. James P. Bickerton and Alain-G. Gagnon. Peterborough: Broadview Press, 1994.

Jhappan, Radha. "The Federal-Provincial Power-Grid and Aboriginal Self-Government." In *New Trends in Canadian Federalism*, ed. François Rocher and Miriam Smith. Peterborough: Broadview Press, 1995.

——. "Inherency, Three Nations, and Collective Rights: The Evolution of Aboriginal Constitutional Discourse from 1982 to the Charlottetown Accord." *International Journal of Canadian Studies* 7-8 (1993): 225-59.

Juteau, Danielle. "Multicultural Citizenship: The Challenge of Pluralism in Canada." In *Citizenship and Exclusion*, ed. Veit Bader. Basingstoke: MacMillan Press, 1997.

King, Arden R. "A Stratification of Labyrinths: The Acquisition and Retention of Cultural Identity in Modern Culture." In *Social and Cultural Identity: Problems of Persistence and Change*, ed. Thomas K. Fitzgerald. Athens: Southern Anthropological Society, 1974.

Kleinhans, Martha-Marie, and Roderick A. Macdonald. "What Is a Critical Legal Pluralism?" *Canadian Journal of Law and Society* 12 (1997): 25-46.

Kuper, Adam, ed. *Conceptualizing Society*. London: Routledge, 1992.

Kymlicka, Will. *Liberalism, Community, and Culture*. Oxford: Clarendon Press, 1991.

——. "Liberalism, Individualism, and Minority Rights." In *Law and Community: The End of Individualism?* ed. Allan C. Hutchinson and Leslie J.M. Green. Toronto: Carswell, 1989.

——. *Multicultural Citizenship: A Liberal Theory of Minority Rights*. Oxford: Clarendon Press, 1995.

Larsen, Tord. "Negotiating Identity: The Micmac of Nova Scotia." In *The Politics of Indianness: Case Studies of Native Ethnopolitics in Canada*, ed. Adrian Tanner. St. John's: Institute of Social and Economic Research, 1983.

LaSelva, Samuel V. *The Moral Foundations of Canadian Federalism: Paradoxes, Achievements, and Tragedies of Nationhood*. Montreal: McGill-Queen's University Press, 1996.

Levin, Michael D., ed. *Ethnicity and Aboriginality: Case Studies in Ethnonationalism*. Toronto: University of Toronto Press, 1993.

Long, J. Anthony, and Katherine Beaty Chiste. "Indian Governments and the Canadian Charter of Rights and Freedoms." *American Indian Culture and Research Journal* 18, 2 (1994): 91-119.

MacIntyre, Alasdair. *After Virtue: A Study in Moral Theory*. Notre Dame: University of Notre Dame Press, 1984.

——. *Whose Justice? Which Rationality?* Notre Dame: University of Notre Dame Press, 1988.

Macklem, Patrick. "Distributing Sovereignty: Indian Nations and Equality of Peoples." *Stanford Law Review* 45 (1993): 1311-67.

——. "Ethnonationalism, Aboriginal Identities, and the Law." In *Ethnicity and Aboriginality: Case Studies in Ethnonationalism*, ed. Michael D. Levin. Toronto: University of Toronto Press, 1993.

——. *Indigenous Difference and the Constitution of Canada*. Toronto: University of Toronto Press, 2001.

——. "Normative Dimensions of an Aboriginal Right of Self-Government." *Queen's Law Journal* 21, 1 (1995): 173-219.

Margalit, Avishai, and Moshe Halbertal. "Liberalism and the Right to Culture." *Social Research* 61, 3 (1994): 491-508.

Mayberry-Lewis, David. *Indigenous Peoples, Ethnic Groups, and the State*. Boston: Allyn and Bacon, 1997.

McHugh, P.G. "Aboriginal Identity and Relations in North America and Australasia." In

Living Relationships (Kokiri ngatahi): The Treaty of Waitangi in the New Millennium, ed. Ken S. Coates and P.G. McHugh. Wellington: Victoria University Press, 1998.

McIlwraith, Thomas. "The Problem of Imported Culture: The Construction of Sto:lo Identity." *American Indian Culture and Research Journal* 20, 4 (1996): 41-70.

McLennan, Gregor. *Pluralism*. Minneapolis: University of Minnesota Press, 1995.

Mercredi, Ovide, and Mary Ellen Turpel. *In the Rapids: Navigating the Future of First Nations*. Toronto: Penguin Books, 1994.

Merry, Sally Engle. "Legal Pluralism." *Law and Society Review* 22, 5 (1988): 869-901.

Mihesuah, Devon A. "American Indian Identities: Issues of Individual Choices and Development." *American Indian Culture and Research Journal* 22, 2 (1998): 193-226.

Miller, David. *On Nationality*. Oxford: Clarendon Press, 1995.

Monture-Angus, Patricia. *Journeying Forward: Dreaming First Nations' Independence*. Halifax: Fernwood Publishing, 1999.

Moss, Wendy. "Indigenous Self-Government in Canada and Sexual Equality under the Indian Act: Resolving Conflicts between Collective and Individual Rights." *Queen's Law Journal* 15, 2 (1990): 279-305.

Mouffe, Chantal. "Democracy, Power, and the 'Political.'" In *Democracy and Difference: Contesting the Boundaries of the Political*, ed. Seyla Benhabib. Princeton: Princeton University Press, 1996.

Nahanee, Teressa. "Dancing with a Gorilla: Aboriginal Women, Justice, and the Charter." In *Aboriginal Peoples and the Justice System: Report of the National Round Table on Aboriginal Justice Issues*, ed. Royal Commission on Aboriginal Peoples. Ottawa: Minister of Supply and Services Canada, 1993.

Norris, Mary Jane. "Contemporary Demography of Aboriginal Peoples in Canada." In *Visions of the Heart: Canadian Aboriginal Issues*, ed. David Alan Long and Olive Patricia Dickason. Toronto: Harcourt Brace Canada, 1996.

Novak, Michael. "Pluralism: A Humanist Perspective." In *Harvard Encyclopedia of American Ethnic Groups*, ed. Stephen A. Thernstrom. Cambridge: Harvard University Press, 1980.

Olthuis, John, and Roger Townshend. "The Case for Native Sovereignty." In *Crosscurrents: Contemporary Political Issues*, ed. Mark Charlton and Paul Barker. Scarborough: ITP Nelson, 1998.

Parekh, Bhikhu. "Discourses on National Identity." *Political Studies* 42 (1994): 492-504.

Phillips, Anne. *Democracy and Difference*. Cambridge, UK: Polity Press, 1993.

Pocklington, Tom. "Arguing for Aboriginal Self-Government." In *Democracy, Rights, and Well-Being in Canada*, ed. Don Carmichael, Tom Pocklington, and Greg Pyrcz. Toronto: Harcourt Brace and Company, Canada, 2000.

Ponting, J. Rick. "Historical Overview and Background: Part II 1970-1996." In *First Nations in Canada: Perspectives on Opportunity, Empowerment, and Self-Determination*, ed. J. Rick Ponting. Toronto: McGraw-Hill Ryerson, 1997.

—. "An Overview of First Nations' Empowerment and Disempowerment: Editor's Introduction to Part 2." In *First Nations in Canada: Perspectives on Opportunity, Empowerment, and Self-Determination*, ed. J. Rick Ponting. Toronto: McGraw-Hill Ryerson, 1997.

—. "Self-Determination: Editor's Introduction to Part 4." In *First Nations in Canada: Perspectives on Opportunity, Empowerment, and Self-Determination*, ed. J. Rick Ponting. Toronto: McGraw-Hill Ryerson, 1997.

Poole, Ross. "National Identity, Multiculturalism, and Aboriginal Rights: An Australian Perspective." *Canadian Journal of Philosophy*, supplementary volume 22 (1996): 407-38.

Rawls, John. *A Theory of Justice*. Cambridge, MA: Harvard University Press, 1971.

Reaume, Denise G. "Justice between Cultures: Autonomy and Protection of Cultural Affiliation." *U.B.C. Law Review* 29, 1 (1995): 117-41.

R. v. Sparrow (1990), 70, D.L.R. (4th).

Rex, John. *Ethnic Minorities in the Modern Nation State: Working Papers in the Theory of Multiculturalism and Political Integration*. New York: St. Martin's Press, 1996.

Richardson, Boyce, ed. *Drum Beat: Anger and Renewal in Indian Country*. Toronto: Summerhill Press, 1990.

Rosenblum, Nancy L. "Pluralism and Self-Defense." In *Liberalism and the Moral Life*, ed. Nancy L. Rosenblum. Cambridge, MA: Harvard University Press, 1989.

Royal Commission on Aboriginal Peoples. *Aboriginal Peoples in Urban Centres: Report of the National Round Table on Aboriginal Urban Issues*. Ottawa: Minister of Supply and Services Canada, 1993.

——. *Partners in Confederation: Aboriginal Peoples, Self-Government, and the Constitution*. Ottawa: Minister of Supply and Services Canada, 1993.

——. *Public Hearings, Discussion Paper 1: Framing the Issues*. Ottawa: Royal Commission on Aboriginal Peoples, 1992.

——. *Public Hearings, Discussion Paper 2: Focusing the Dialogue*. Ottawa: Minister of Supply and Services Canada, 1993.

——. *Public Hearings, Exploring the Options: Overview of the Third Round*. Ottawa: Minister of Supply and Services Canada, 1993.

——. *Public Hearings: Overview of the First Round*. Ottawa: Royal Commission on Aboriginal Peoples, 1992.

——. *Public Hearings: Overview of the Second Round*. Ottawa: Minister of Supply and Services Canada, 1993.

——. *Public Hearings, Toward Reconciliation: Overview of the Fourth Round*. Ottawa: Minister of Supply and Services Canada, 1994.

——. *Report, Volume 1: Looking Forward, Looking Back*. Ottawa: Minister of Supply and Services Canada, 1996.

——. *Report, Volume 2: Restructuring the Relationship—Parts One and Two*. Ottawa: Minister of Supply and Services Canada, 1996.

——. *Report, Volume 3: Gathering Strength*. Ottawa: Minister of Supply and Services Canada, 1996.

——. *Report, Volume 4: Perspectives and Realities*. Ottawa: Minister of Supply and Services Canada, 1996.

——. *Report, Volume 5: Renewal: A Twenty-Year Commitment*. Ottawa: Minister of Supply and Services, 1996.

——. *Treaty Making in the Spirit of Co-Existence: An Alternative to Extinguishment*. Ottawa: Minister of Supply and Services Canada, 1995.

Russell, Dan. *A People's Dream: Aboriginal Self-Government in Canada*. Vancouver: UBC Press, 2000.

Rustin, Michael. *For a Pluralist Socialism*. London: Verso, 1985.

Salee, Daniel. "Identities in Conflict: The Aboriginal Question and the Politics of Recognition in Quebec." *Ethnic and Racial Studies* 18, 2 (1995): 277-314.

Sandel, Michael. *Liberalism and the Limits of Justice.* Cambridge, UK: Cambridge University Press, 1982.

Sanders, Douglas. "'We Intend to Live Here Forever': A Primer on the Nisga'a Treaty." *U.B.C. Law Review* 33, 1 (1999): 103-28.

Sawchuck, Joe, ed. *Readings in Aboriginal Studies, Volume 2: Identities and State Structures.* Brandon: Bearpaw Publishing, 1992.

Seymour, Michael, Jocelyne Couture, and Kai Neilson. "Introduction: Questioning the Ethnic/Civic Dichotomy." *Canadian Journal of Philosophy* supplementary volume 22 (1996): 1-61.

Smith, Anthony D. *National Identity.* Reno: University of Nevada Press, 1991.

Spaulding, Richard. "Peoples as National Minorities: A Review of Will Kymlicka's Arguments for Aboriginal Rights from a Self-Determination Perspective." *University of Toronto Law Journal* 47, 1 (1997): 35-113.

Spinner, Jeff. *The Boundaries of Citizenship: Race, Ethnicity, and Nationality in the Liberal State.* Baltimore: Johns Hopkins University Press, 1994.

Taylor, Charles. *Multiculturalism and "The Politics of Recognition."* Ed. Amy Gutmann. Princeton: Princeton University Press, 1992.

——. "On the Nisga'a Treaty." *BC Studies* 120 (1998-99): 39-40.

——. *Reconciling the Solitudes: Essays on Canadian Federalism and Nationalism.* Montreal: McGill-Queen's University Press, 1993.

——. *Sources of the Self: The Making of Modern Identity.* Cambridge, MA: Harvard University Press, 1989.

Tennant, Paul. "Aboriginal Peoples and Aboriginal Title in British Columbia Politics." In *Politics, Policy, and Government in British Columbia,* ed. R.K. Carty. Vancouver: UBC Press, 1996.

Truman, David. *The Governmental Process.* New York: Alfred A. Knopf, 1951.

Tully, James. "A Just Relationship between Aboriginal and Non-Aboriginal Peoples in Canada." In *Aboriginal Rights and Self-Government: The Canadian and Mexican Experience in North American Perspective,* ed. Curtis Cook and Juan D. Landau. Montreal: McGill-Queen's University Press, 2000.

——. *Strange Multiplicity: Constitutionalism in an Age of Diversity.* Cambridge, UK: Cambridge University Press, 1995.

Voyageur, Cora J. "Contemporary Indian Women." In *Visions of the Heart: Canadian Aboriginal Issues,* ed. David Alan Long and Olive Patricia Dickason. Toronto: Harcourt Brace and Company, Canada, 1996.

Walzer, Michael. *Spheres of Justice: A Defense of Pluralism and Equality.* New York: Basic Books, 1983.

Warry, Wayne. *Unfinished Dreams: Community Healing and the Reality of Aboriginal Self-Government.* Toronto: University of Toronto Press, 1998.

Webber, Jeremy. "Individuality, Equality, and Difference: Justifications for a Parallel System of Aboriginal Justice." In *Aboriginal Peoples and the Justice System: Report of the National Round Table on Aboriginal Justice Issues,* ed. Royal Commission on Aboriginal Peoples. Ottawa: Minister of Supply and Services Canada, 1993.

——. *Reimagining Canada: Language, Culture, Community, and the Canadian Constitution.* Montreal: McGill-Queen's University Press, 1994.

——. "Relations of Force and Relations of Justice: The Emergence of Normative

Community between Colonists and Aboriginal Peoples." *Osgoode Hall Law Journal* 33, 4 (1995): 623-60.

Whittington, Michael S. "Aboriginal Self-Government in Canada." In *Canadian Politics in the 21st Century,* 5th ed., ed. Michael Whittington and Glen Williams. Scarborough: Nelson, 2000.

Wilson, Richard A. *Human Rights, Culture, and Context: Anthropological Perspectives.* London: Pluto Press, 1997.

Young, Iris Marion. *Justice and the Politics of Difference.* Princeton: Princeton University Press, 1990.

PUBLIC HEARINGS, ROYAL COMMISSION ON ABORIGINAL PEOPLES

Albert, Freda. Manitoba Indigenous Women's Collective. Thompson, Manitoba, 31 May 1993.

Allen, Bertha. Native Women's Association of the Northwest Territories. Yellowknife, Northwest Territories, 7 December 1992.

Arey, Rita. President, Northwest Territories Status of Women. Inuvik, Northwest Territories, 6 May 1992.

Blacksmith, Jack. Waswanipi Band Councillor. Waswanipi, Quebec, 9 June 1992.

Brooks, Catherine. Executive Director of Anduhyaun. Toronto, Ontario, 25 June 1992.

Brooks, Lynn. Executive Director, Status of Women Council of NWT. Yellowknife, Northwest Territories, 7 December 1992.

Boucher, Florence. Lac La Biche, Alberta, 9 June 1992.

Cootes, Charlie. Chief of the Uchucklesaht Tribe. Port Alberni, British Columbia, 20 May 1992.

Courchene, Joyce. President, Nongom Ikkwe Women's Indigenous Collective. Winnipeg, Manitoba, 3 June 1993.

Donovan, Margaret. Vice President, Gwich'in Tribal Council. Inuvik, Northwest Territories, 5-6 May 1992.

Fontaine, Marilyn. Aboriginal Women's Unity Coalition. Winnipeg, Manitoba, 23 April 1992.

Guilbeaut, Mary. Vice President, Indigenous Women's Collective. Winnipeg, Manitoba, 21-23 April 1992.

Kuptana, Rosemarie. President, Inuit Tapirisat of Canada. Toronto, Ontario, 26 June 1992.

Labillois, Wallace. Kingsclear, New Brunswick, 19 May 1992.

LeBlanc, Dawna. Nishnaabe Language Teachers Association. Sault Ste. Marie, Ontario, 11 June 1992.

Mandamin, Eli. Chief, Shoal Lake Band. Kenora, Ontario, 28 October 1992.

McDonald, Dorothy. Chief, Fort McKay Indian Band. Fort McMurray, Alberta, 16 June 1992.

McGregor, Violet. Elder, Birch Island Reserve. Ottawa, Ontario, November 1993.

McIvor, Sharon. Executive Council Member, Native Women's Association of Canada. Toronto, Ontario, 26 June 1992.

McKay, Dorothy. Big Trout Lake, Ontario, 3 December 1992.

Mercredi, Ovide. Grand Chief of the Assembly of First Nations. Toronto, Ontario, 26 June 1992.

Nelson, Terry. Rouseau River First Nation. Rouseau River, Manitoba, 8 December 1992.

Palmater, Frank. New Brunswick Aboriginal Peoples Council. Moncton, New Brunswick, 14 June 1993.

Parent, Madeleine. Montreal, Quebec, 5 May 1993.

Pierre, Marlene. Ontario Native Women's Association. Thunder Bay, Ontario, 27 October 1992.

Rouleau, Michele. Quebec Native Women's Association. Montreal, Quebec, 27 May 1993.

Sanderson, Lillian. La Ronge Native Women's Council. La Ronge, Saskatchewan, 28 May 1992.

Saunderson, Marguerite. Northern Women's Resource Services. Thompson, Manitoba, 1 June 1993.

Smith, Dan. President, United Native Nations of B.C. Vancouver, British Columbia, 2 June 1993.

Stevens, Peter. Eskasoni, Nova Scotia, 6-7 May 1992.

Thomas, Jason. All Nations Youth Council. Prince George, British Columbia, 31 May 1993.

Tobique Women's Group. Tobique, New Brunswick, 2 November 1992.

Turner, Harold. Chief, Swampy Cree Tribal Council. The Pas, Manitoba, 19-20 May 1992.

Webster, Evelyn. Indigenous Women's Collective. Winnipeg, Manitoba, 22 April 1992.

Windigo First Nations Council. Sioux Lookout, Ontario, 2 December 1992.

INDEX

and difference approach to identity, 4, 44
on "formal" and "substantive" objectives of
    Aboriginal concern for equality, 123
on relationship of "formal equality" between
    Aboriginal nations and Canadian state, 117
on treaty federalism, 141
on use of cultural difference and historical
    nationhood, 44
Margalit, Avishai, 7
Marginalization, of women and youth in Aboriginal
    communities, 99-100, 151
Mayberry-Lewis, David, 52
McHugh, P.G., 9, 42, 43
on ancestry and Indian status, 157
on sovereigntist approach to Aboriginal self-
    government, 129
Mercredi, Ovide, 66
Métis people, xii, xiii, 77, 140
Miller, David, 82, 83
Monture-Angus, Patricia
on Aboriginal self-government as self-defining,
    124
critique of treaty process, 144
Mouffe, Chantal, 16
Multiculturalism. See Pluralism

Nation
Aboriginal, as different from ethnic group, 56-7
Aboriginal nations, ix, xiii, 72-8, 83, 176
characteristics of, 6-7
and culture, 6-7, 12, 74
definition, 6, 8
incorporation into state, 2-3
and nationalism, 8
nationhood as aspect of ethnic identity, 12, 16
and personal identity, in difference approach, 4
territory as key element, 12
National Action Committee on the Status of
    Women, 107
Nationalism
Aboriginal, in reaction to White Paper (1969), 66
definition, 8
as key theme at RCAP hearings, 66-7
state-based vs. community-based, 133
Native Council of Canada, 107
Native Women's Association of Canada (NWAC),
    93, 103
Nisga'a treaty
Aboriginal critiques of, 142-3
Aboriginal forms of government established, 138
as precedent for Aboriginal self-government
    negotiations, 137, 142-3, 180
terms, 137-40

NWAC. See Native Women's Association of Canada
    (NWAC)

Patriarchy. See Gender relations
Pluralism. See also Communitarian pluralism;
    Individualist pluralism; Relational pluralism
American pluralists, 27
assumption of group diversity in society, 37
Canada as pluralist state, x
and democracy, 16, 17
and government policy, 17
as political principle to protect group diversity, 18
as social theory, 17
as tool for understanding Aboriginal politics, 18
types, x, 18, 37
"Politics of Recognition, The" (Taylor), 20
Ponting, J. Rick, 145
Power. See also Colonialism; Discrimination, in
    Aboriginal communities; Gender relations;
    Leadership, Aboriginal
distribution within Aboriginal communities, 151
and equality in relational pluralism, 34
political
    and boundaries in relational pluralism, 34-5
    as characteristic of nations, 6, 8
Provincial governments, First Nations' refusal to
    negotiate with, 142

Quebec-Canada relations, according to communi-
    tarian pluralism, 133
Quebec Native Women's Association, 107

R. v. Sparrow (1990), 136-7
Rawls, John, 28
RCAP. See Royal Commission on Aboriginal
    Peoples (RCAP)
Relational pluralism. See also Communitarian plu-
    ralism; Individualist pluralism; Pluralism
and Aboriginal identity, x, 120-2, 157, 162-3,
    165-7, 172
and Aboriginal self-government, 37-8, 130, 133,
    140-1, 146, 147, 179-82
and equality in relationships, 113-14
and Indian status, 157
individual and collective rights, 98-100, 149-50
justice, view of, 35
on power and relationships, 30, 31-37, 155-6, 172
support for Aboriginal self-development and
    freedom of choice, 135, 173
view of Aboriginal-Canadian state relations as
    cooperative, 129
view of Charter of Rights and Freedoms in
    relation to self-government, 168-9